An Exposition on the

Genesis

And Part of the Eleventh

An unfinished commentary on the Bible, found among the author's papers after his death, in his own handwriting; and published in 1691, by Charles Doe, in a folio volume of the works of John Bunyan.

Written by

John Bunyan

Author of Pilgrim's Progress

This edition edited, with introduction and notes by

Paul Taylor

Also included - introduction and notes from the 1853 edition, edited by George Offor.

Published by J6D Publications, 2010
9 Parnell Close
Littlethorpe
Leicestershire
LE19 2JS

http://shop.justsixdays.co.uk

All rights reserved

The text of this book is in the public domain. The introduction and notes are copyright © Paul Taylor

ISBN: 978-0-9564606-2-2

Commentary on Genesis

Contents

Preface (Paul Taylor)	5
Advertisement by the Editor (George Offor)	10
Chapter 1	15
Chapter 2	46
Chapter 3	60
Chapter 4	104
Chapter 5	145
Chapter 6	161
Chapter 7	192
Chapter 8	213
Chapter 9	251
Chapter 10	282
Chapter 11	297
Mr Offor's Footnotes	302

Commentary on Genesis

Preface

By Paul Taylor

All of John Bunyan's writings are precious and beautiful. His famous *Pilgrim's Progress* is one of the masterpieces of the English language, as well as a favourite amongst Christian readers and theologians alike. But once people have read this marvellous book[i], they need to be aware that Bunyan wrote so much more. I have previously published his *The Holy War*[ii]. Other fiction includes *Pilgrim's Progress Part 2*, and *The History of Mr Badman*.

Bunyan also wrote theological volumes. It may come as a surprise to many to find that he wrote a commentary on Genesis. It would appear that his *Genesis* was actually to be a commentary on the whole Bible, but never completed. Indeed, he completed notes on chapters 1 to 10, and part of chapter 11, but there the manuscript ends.

I know of no separately available edition of this commentary. It is included as part of Bunyan's complete works. There are a couple of editions of his complete works – the best being that published by Banner of Truth. It was originally published by Charles Doe, with a whole portfolio of his works, in 1691 – three years after his death. But, as far as I know, no one has published the Genesis commentary by itself.

Now I have enjoyed reading this commentary; especially as I wrote a commentary myself on chapters 1

---

[i] Available in many editions, such as the lovely Answers in Genesis edition.

[ii] Available from *Just Six Days Publications* < http://shop.justsixdays.co.uk >

to 11[iii]. In following the commentary, however, a number of points will need to be borne in mind.

First, Bunyan was not writing about creation and evolution. That argument was not an issue, in the late 17th Century. James Hutton – who pioneered the concept of millions of years, and who so strongly influenced Charles Lyell, and therefore Charles Darwin – was not born until 1726. So Bunyan's focus was not on scientific issues. Anyone looking for early proto-creationist writing will be disappointed. Having said that - anyone hoping to find early support for old-earth positions will also be disappointed. It is clear that Bunyan believed Genesis to be true – he just didn't feel the need to spend time proving it.

Second, Bunyan was wanting to teach spiritual truths. To our minds, his comments on the early chapters may, therefore, appear to be over-spiritualising matters. For example, read what he has to say on Genesis 1:14.

> The sun is in this place a type of Christ, the Sun of Righteousness: The moon is a type of the church, in her uncertain condition in this world: The stars are types of the several saints and officers in this church. And hence it is that the sun is said not only to rule, but it, with the moon and stars, to be set for signs, and for seasons, and for days, and for years, &c. (Rev 1:20). But if we take the heaven for the church, then how is she beautified, when the Son of God is placed in the midst of her! (Rev 1:12,13). And how plainly is her condition made out, even by the changing, increasing, and diminishing of the moon! And how excellent is that congregation

---

[iii] *Just Six Days* was published by *Just Six Days Publishing* – it was later republished by Master Books under the title *The Six Days of Genesis*.

of men, that for light and glory are figured by the stars! (Matt 28:20).

From this day's work much might be observed. *First,* That forasmuch as the sun was not made before the fourth day, it is evident there was light in the world before the sun was created; for in the first day God said, Let there be light, and there was light. This may also teach us thus much, That before Christ came in person, there was spiritual light in the saints of God. And again, That as the sun was not made before the fourth day of the creation, so Christ should not be born before the fourth mystical day of the world; for it is evident, that Christ, the true light of the world, was not born till about four thousand years after the world was made. *Second,* As to the moon, there are four things attending her, which fitly may hold forth the state of the church. (1.) In that she changeth from an old to a new, we may conceive, that God by making her so, did it to show he would one day make a change of his church, from a Jewish to a Gentile congregation. (2.) In that she increaseth, she showeth the flourishing state of the church. (3.) In her diminishing, the diminishing state of the church. (4.) The moon is also sometimes made to look as red as blood, to show how dreadful and bloody the suffering of the church is at some certain times. *Third,* By the stars, we understand two things. (1.) How innumerable the saints, those spiritual stars shall be (Heb 11:12). (2.) How they shall differ each from other in glory (1 Cor 15:41).

The equation of the sun with Christ might seem to us to be reading too much into the text. In today's climate, such spiritualising might cause confusion. However, we need to remember Bunyan's purpose, in teaching spiritual truths to his readers. In this context, his words seem highly appropriate.

I have not amended any of Bunyan's text. It is better for it to stand alone. However, there are some places where I felt it needed comment. In these places, I have used small italic footnotes, which can be read at the foot of the text. I have entered my footnotes in a modern font, slightly reduced in size (Calibri), whereas I have deliberately used an older font (Bookman Old Style) for Bunyan's text, as I thought it looked more appropriate. As I am using George Offer's version, it should be observed that he also included footnotes. These are shown in the text by ordinal numbers in small square brackets. Offor's footnotes can actually be read in a section at the end of the book. I do not always agree with Offor's comments, but I have not footnoted either his introduction or his footnotes, as I thought this would needlessly complicate the text.

An Exposition on the FIRST TEN CHAPTERS OF GENESIS, And Part of the Eleventh

An unfinished commentary on the Bible, found among the author's papers after his death, in his own handwriting; and published in 1691, by Charles Doe, in a folio volume of the works of John Bunyan.

Advertisement by the Editor

By George Offor

Being in company with an enlightened society of Protestant dissenters of the Baptist denomination, I observed to a doctor of divinity, who was advancing towards his seventieth year, that my time had been delightfully engaged with John Bunyan's commentary on Genesis. "What," said the D.D., with some appearance of incredulity, "Bunyan a commentator—upon Genesis!! Impossible! Well, I never heard of that work of the good Bunyan before. Why, where is it to be found?" Yes, it is true that he has commented on that portion of sacred scripture, containing the cosmogony of creation—the fall of man—the first murder—the deluge—and other facts which have puzzled the most learned men of every age; and he has proved to be more learned than all others in his spiritual perceptions. He graduated at a higher university—a university unshackled by human laws, conventional feelings, and preconceived opinions. His intense study of the Bible, guided by the teaching of the Holy Spirit, enabled him to throw a new and beautiful light upon objects which are otherwise obscure. Oh! that young ministers, while attaining valuable book learning, may see the necessity of taking a high degree in, and of never forgetting this Bible university! Reader, is it not surprizing, that such a treatise should have remained comparatively hidden for more than one hundred and fifty years. It has been reprinted in many editions of Bunyan's works: but in all, except the first, with the omission of the scripture references; and with errors of so serious a character as if it was not intended to be read. Even in printing the text of Genesis 7:7 Noah's three sons do not enter the ark! although in 8:16 they are

Commentary on Genesis

commanded to go forth out of the ark. It is now presented to the public exactly as the author left it, with the addition of notes, which it is hoped will illustrate and not encumber the text.

This exposition is evidently the result of long and earnest study of the holy scriptures. It is the history of the creation and of the flood explained and spiritualized, and had it been originally published in that form and under a proper title, it would most probably have become a very popular work. The author's qualifications for writing this commentary were exclusively limited to his knowledge of holy writ. To book learning he makes no pretensions. He tells us that in his youth "God put it into my parents" hearts to put me to school, to learn to read and write as other poor men's children; though, to my shame, I confess, I did soon lose that little I learnt even almost utterly." In after life, his time was occupied in obtaining a livelihood by labour. When enduring severe mental conflicts, and while he maintained his family by the work of his hands, he was an acceptable pastor, and extensively useful in itinerant labours of love in the villages round Bedford. His humility, when he had used three common Latin words, prompted him to say in the margin, "The Latine I borrow." And this unlettered mechanic, when he might have improved himself in book wisdom, was shut up within the walls of a prison for nearly thirteen years, for obeying God, only solaced with his Bible and Fox's Book of Martyrs. Yet he made discoveries relative to the creation, which have been very recently again published by a learned philosopher, who surprised and puzzled the world with his vestiges of creation. Omitting the fanciful theories of the vestige philosopher, his two great facts, proved by geological discoveries, are—

I. That when the world was created and set in motion, it was upon principles by which it is impelled on to perfection—a state of irresistible progress in improvement. This is the theory of Moses: and Bunyan's exposition is, that all was finished, even to the creation of all the souls which were to animate the human race, and then God *rested* from his work.

II. The second geological discovery is that the world was far advanced towards perfection producing all that was needful for human life, before man was created. Upon this subject, Bunyan's words are—"God shews his respect to this excellent creature, in that he first provideth for him before he giveth him his being. He bringeth him not to an empty house, but to one well furnished with all kind of necessaries, having beautified the heaven and the earth with glory, and all sorts of nourishment for his pleasure and sustenance." But the most pious penetration is exhibited in the spiritualizing of the creation and of the flood—every step produces some type of that new creation, or regeneration, without which no soul can be fitted for heaven. The dim twilight before the natural sun was made, is typical of the state of those who believed before Christ, the Sun of righteousness, arose and was manifested. The fixed stars are emblems of the church, whose members all shine, but with different degrees of lustre—sometimes eclipsed, and at others mistaken for transient meteors. The whales and lions are figures of great persecutors. But the most singular idea of all is, that the moral degradation of human nature before the flood, was occasioned by hypocrisy and persecution for conscience sake, arising from governors interfering with matters of faith and worship; in fact, that a STATE CHURCH occasioned the deluge—and since that time has been the fruitful source of the miseries and wretchedness that has afflicted mankind. His prediction of the outpouring of the Spirit in the conversion of sinners, when the church shall be no longer enthralled and persecuted by the state, is remarkable. "O thou church of God in England, which art now upon the waves of affliction and temptation, when thou comest out of the furnace, if thou come out at the bidding of God, there shall come out with thee, the fowl, the beast, and abundance of creeping things. O Judah, he hath set an harvest for thee, when I returned the captivity of my people." May this prediction soon be verified, and the temporal government no longer vex and torment the church by interfering with spiritual things.

It is remarkable that of the vast number of pious and enlightened mechanics who adorn this country and feed its prosperity, so few read the extraordinary writings of John Bunyan, a brother mechanic; for with the exception of the Pilgrim's Progress and Holy War, they are comparatively little known. His simple but illustrative commentary—his book of Antichrist—his solemn and striking treatise on the resurrection and final judgment—in fact, all his works, are peculiarly calculated to inform the minds of the millions—to reform bad habits, and, under the divine blessing, to purify the soul with that heavenly wisdom which has in it the promise of the life that now is as well as of that which is to come. It is also a fact which ought to be generally known, that those preachers who have edited Bunyan's works and have drunk into his spirit, have been most eminently blessed in their ministry; Wilson, Whitefield, and Ryland, can never be forgotten. If the thousands of godly preachers who are scattered over our comparatively happy island were to take Bunyan's mode of expounding scripture as their pattern, it would increase their usefulness, and consequently their happiness, in the great work of proclaiming and enforcing the doctrines of the gospel.

GEO OFFOR.

In the first edition of this commentary, a series of numbers from 1 to 294 were placed in the margin, the use of which the editor could not discover; probably the work was written on as many scraps of paper, thus numbered to direct the printer. They are omitted, lest, among divisions and subdivisions, they should puzzle the reader.

Chapter 1

I. Of God.

God *is* a Spirit (John 4:24), eternal (Deu 33:27), infinite (Rom 1:17-20), incomprehensible (Job 11:7), perfect, and unspeakably glorious in his being, attributes, and works (Gen 17:51; Isa 6:3; Exo 33:20). "The eternal God." "Do not I fill heaven and earth? saith the Lord" (Jer 23:24). "Neither is there any creature that is not manifest in his sight" (Heb 4:13; Pro 15:11).

In his attributes of wisdom, power, justice, holiness, mercy, &c., he is also inconceivably perfect and infinite, not to be comprehended by things in earth, or things in heaven; known in the perfection of his being only to himself. The seraphims cannot behold him, but through a veil; no man can see him in his perfection and live.

His attributes, though apart laid down in the word of God, that we, being weak, might the better conceive of his eternal power and godhead; yet in him they are without division; one glorious and eternal being. Again, though sometimes this, as of wisdom, or that, as of justice and mercy, is most manifest in his works and wonders before men; yet every such work is begun and completed by the joint concurrence of all his attributes. No act of justice is without his will, power, and wisdom; no act of mercy is against his justice, holiness and purity. Besides, no man must conceive of God, as if he consisted of these attributes, as our body doth of its members, one standing here, another there, for the completing personal subsistence. For though by the word we may distinguish, yet may we not divide them, or presume to appoint them their places in the Godhead. Wisdom is in his justice, holiness is in his power, justice is in his mercy, holiness is in his love, power is in his goodness (1 John 1:9, Num 14:17,18).

Wherefore, he is in all his attributes almighty, all-wise, holy and powerful. Glory is in his wisdom, glory is in his holiness, glory is in his mercy, justice, and strength; and "God is love" (1 John 4:16).[1]

II. Of the Persons or Subsistances in the Godhead.

The Godhead is but one, yet in the Godhead there are three[i]. "There are three that can bear record in heaven" (1 John 5:7-9). These three are called "the Father, the Son [Word], and the Holy Spirit"; each of which is really, naturally and eternally God: yet there is but one God. But again, because the Father is of himself, the Son by the Father, and the Spirit from them both, therefore to each, the scripture not only applieth, and that truly, the whole nature of the Deity, but again distinguisheth the Father from the Son, and the Spirit from them both; calling the Father HE, by himself; the Son HE, by himself; the Spirit HE, by himself. Yea, the Three of themselves, in their manifesting to the church what she should believe concerning this matter, hath thus expressed the thing: "Let us make man in OUR image, after OUR likeness" (Gen 1:26). Again, "The man is become as one of US" (Gen 3:22). Again, "Let US go down, and there confound their language" (Gen 11:6,7). And

---

[i] It is important to Bunyan first to establish the nature of God, as Trinity. I concur with this approach. It is noteworthy that Bunyan sees fit to begin his comments on Genesis 1 with underlining the truth about the Trinity.

again, "Whom shall I send, and who will go for US?" (Isa 6:8). To these general expressions might be added, That Adam heard the voice of the Lord God walking in the midst of the garden: Genesis 3:8. Which voice John will have, to be one of the Three, calling that which Moses here saith is the voice, the word of God: "In the beginning," saith he, "was the word": the voice which Adam heard walking in the midst of the garden. This word, saith John, "was with God," this "word was God. The same was in the beginning with God" (John 1:1,2). Marvellous language! Once asserting the unity of essence, but twice insinuating a distinction of substances therein. "The word was with God, the word was God, the same was in the beginning with God." Then follows, "All things were made by him," the word, the second of the three.

Now the godly in former ages have called these three, thus in the Godhead, Persons or Subsistances; the which, though I condemn not, yet choose rather to abide by scripture phrase, knowing, though the other may be good and sound, yet the adversary must needs more shamelessly spurn and reject, when he doth it against the evident text.

To proceed the, *First*, There are Three. *Second*, These three are distinct.

First, By this word Three, is intimated the Father, the Word, and the Holy Ghost, and they are said to be three, 1. Because those appellations that are given them in scripture, demonstrate them so to be, to wit, Father, Son and Holy Ghost. 2. Because their acts one towards another discover them so to be.

Secondly, These three are distinct. 1. So distinct as to be more than one, only: There are three. 2. So distinct as to subsist without depending. The Father is true God, the Son is true God, the Spirit is true God. Yet the Father is one, the Son is one, the Spirit is one: The Father is one of himself, the Son is one by the Father, the Spirit is one from them both. Yet the Father is not above the Son, nor the Spirit inferior to either: The Father is God, the Son is God, the Spirit is God.

Among the three then there is not superiority. 1. Not as to time; the Father is from everlasting, so is the Son, so is the Spirit. 2. Not as to nature, the Son being of the substance of the Father, and the Spirit of the substance of them both. 3. The fulness of the Godhead is in the Father, is in the Son, and is in the Holy Ghost.

The Godhead then, though it can admit of a Trinity, yet it admitteth not of inferiority in that Trinity: if otherwise, then less or more must be there, and so either plurality of gods, or something that is not God: so then, Father, Son and Spirit are in the Godhead, yet but one God; each of these is God over all, yet no Trinity of Gods, but one God in the Trinity.

Explication.—The Godhead then is common to the three, but the three themselves abide distinct in that Godhead: Distinct, I say, as Father, and Son, and Holy Spirit. This is manifest further by these several positions.

First, Father and Son are relatives, and must needs therefore have their relation as such: A Father begetteth, a Son is begotten.

Proof.—"Who hath ascended up into heaven, or descended? Who hath gathered the wind in his fists? Who hath bound the waters in a garment? What *is* his name, and what *is* his son's name, if thou canst tell?" (Pro 30:4).

"God so loved the world, that he gave his only begotten Son," &c. (John 3:16).

"The Father sent the Son to be the Saviour of the world" (1 John 4:14).

Secondly, The Father then cannot be that Son he begat, nor the Son that Father that begat him, but must be distinct as such.

Proof.—"I am one that bear witness of myself, and the Father that sent me beareth witness of me" (John 8:17,18).

"I came forth from the Father, and am come into the world"; again, "I leave the world, and go to the Father" (John 16:28).

"The Father judgeth no man, but hath committed all judgment unto the Son: That all *men* should honour the Son, even as they honour the Father" (John 5:22,23).

Thirdly, The Father must have worship as a Father, and the Son as a Son.

Proof.—They that worship the Father must worship him "in spirit and in truth: for the Father seeketh such to worship him" (John 4:23,24).

And of the Son he saith, and "when he bringeth in the first begotten into the world, he saith, And let all the angels of God worship him" (Heb 1:6).

Fourthly, The Father and Son have really these distinct, but heavenly, relative properties, that discover them, as such, to be two as well as one.

Proof.—"The Father loveth the Son, and sheweth him all things" (John 5:20).

"Therefore doth my Father love me, because I lay down my life, that I might take it again" (John 10:17). The Father sent the Son; the Father commanded the Son; the Son prayed to the Father, and did always the things that pleased him.

The absurdities that flow from the denial of this are divers, some of which hereunder follow.

1. *Absurdity.*—It maketh void all those scriptures that do affirm the doctrine; some of which you have before.

2. *Absurdity.*—If in the Godhead there be but one, not three, then the Father, Son, or the Spirit, must needs be that one, if any one only: so then the other two are nothing. Again, If the reality of a being be neither in the Father, Son, nor Spirit, as such, but in the eternal deity, without consideration of Father, Son, and Spirit as three; then neither of the three are anything but notions in us, or manifestations of the Godhead; or nominal distinctions; so related by the word; but if so, then when the Father sent the Son, and the Father and Son the Spirit, one notion sent another, one manifestation sent another. This being granted, this unavoidably follows, there was no Father to beget a Son, no Son to be sent to save us, no Holy Ghost to be sent to comfort us, and to guide us into all the truth of the Father and Son, &c. The most amounts but to this, a notion sent a notion, a distinction sent a distinction, or one manifestation sent

another. Of this error these are the consequences, we are only to believe in notions and distinctions, when we believe in the Father and the Son; and so shall have no other heaven and glory, than notions and nominal distinctions can furnish us withal.

3. *Absurdity.*—If Father and Son, &c., be no otherwise three, than as notions, names, or nominal distinctions; then to worship these distinctly, or together, as such, is to commit most gross and horrible idolatry: For albeit we are commanded to fear that great and dreadful name, The Lord our God; yet to worship a Father, a Son, and Holy Spirit in the Godhead, as three, as really three as one, is by this doctrine to imagine falsely of God, and so to break the second commandment: but to worship God under the consideration of Father, and Son, and Holy Ghost, and to believe them as really three as one when I worship, being the sum and substance of the doctrine of the scriptures of God, there is really substantially three in the eternal Godhead.

But to help thee a little in thy study on this deep.

1. Thou must take heed when thou readest, there is in the Godhead, Father, and Son, &c., that thou do not imagine about them according to thine own carnal and foolish fancy; for no man can apprehend this doctrine but in the light of the word and Spirit of God. "No man knoweth the Son, but the Father; neither knoweth any man the Father, save the Son; and *he* to whom the Son will reveal *him*" (Matt 11:27). If therefore thou be destitute of the Spirit of God, thou canst not apprehend the truth of this mystery as it is in itself, but will either by thy darkness be driven to a denial thereof; or if thou own it, thou wilt (that thy acknowledgment notwithstanding) falsely imagine about it.

2. If thou feel thy thoughts begin to wrestle about this truth, and to struggle concerning this one against another; take heed of admitting of such a question, How can this thing be? For here is no room for reason to make it out, here is only room to believe it is a truth. You find not one of the prophets propounding an argument to prove it; but asserting it, they let it lie, for faith to take it up and embrace it.

"The grace of the Lord Jesus Christ, and the love of God, and the communion of the Holy Ghost, *be* with you all. Amen" (2 Cor 13:14).

III. Of the Creation of the World

The Apostle saith, That "to us *there is but* one God, the Father, of whom *are* all things, and we in him, and one Lord Jesus Christ, by whom *are* all things, and we by him" (1 Cor 8:6). "God that made the world" (Acts 17:24). "All things were made by him; and without him was not any thing made that was made" (John 1:3). This world therefore had a beginning, and was created by the God of heaven. Which work, because it is wonderful, and discovereth much of the greatness, of the wisdom and power of the eternal Godhead, it behoveth such poor mortals as we to behold these works of the mighty God, that thereby we may see how great he is, and be made to cry out, What is man! [2] (Psa 8:3,4)

Now in the creation of the world we may consider several things; as, What was the order of God in this work? And, whether there was a secret or mystery in this work containing the truth of some higher thing? For the first of these:

Of the Order of God in Making the World.

[THE HEAVEN.]

Although God be indeed omnipotent, and not only can, but doth do whatsoever he will; and though to do his works he needeth not length of time; yet it pleased him best, in the creation of the world (though it could, had it pleased him, have done all by one only word) to proceed by degrees from one thing to another, to the completing of six days' work in the making thereof.[ii]

And forasmuch as this work went on by degrees, now this thing, and then another, it may not be amiss, if in our discourse on this wonderful work, we begin where God began; and if we can, go wondering after him who hath thus wrought.

1. The first thing that God made was time; I say, it was time: All the plain in which he would build this beautiful world; he made nothing before, but in the beginning:

> "In the beginning God created the heaven and the earth" (Gen 1:1).

[ii] Bunyan asserts a very modern argument at this point. God did not have to use six days - but He did. Many people - particularly those who want to beolieve in evolution and millions of years - have said to me that God could have made the world in any way He chose, and they won't limit God to using six days. In one sense they are right. God can do what He pleases. But in another sense they are profoundly wrong. You see, God **could** have used any method He chose, but He has gone to the trouble of telling us exactly what He **did** do, so who are we to believe otherwise?

In the beginning of time. "For *in* six days the LORD made heaven and earth, the sea, and all that in them *is*" (Exo 20:11). Therefore the first day must first have a beginning to be. Whatsoever was before time, was eternal; but nothing but God himself is eternal, therefore no creature was before time. Time, therefore, which was indeed the beginning, was the first of the creatures of God.

2. I think, the second of creatures that the Lord created, were the holy angels of God, they being called the morning stars, as created and shining in the morning of the world; and therefore they are said to be by, when the corner-stone of the universe was laid; that is, when he "laid the foundations" of the world: Then "the morning stars sang together, and all the sons of God shouted for joy" (Job 5:4-7).

3. I think the third thing that the Lord created, was these large and copious heavens; for they are mentioned with respect to their being before the earth, or any visible creature. "In the beginning God created the heavens" (Gen 1:1), &c. Neither do I think that the heavens were made of that confused chaos that afterwards we read of. It is said, he stretched out the heavens as a curtain, and with his hand he hath spanned the heavens (Psa 104:2; Isa 40:22; 48:13).; intimating, that they were not taken out of that formless heap, but were immediately formed by his power. Besides, the Holy Ghost, treating of the creating of heaven and earth, he only saith, The earth was void, and without form; but no such thing of the heavens.

[THE EARTH.]

4. The fourth thing that God created, it was (in mine opinion) that chaos[iii], or first matter, with which he in the six days framed this earth, with its appurtenances; for the visible things that are here below, seem to me to be otherwise put into being and order, than time, the angels, and the heavens, they being created in their own simple essence by themselves: But the things that are visibly here below, whatever their essence and nature be, they were formed of that first deformed chaos. "In the beginning God created the heaven and the earth, and the earth was without form and void" (Gen 1:1,2). He saith not so of the heavens; they, as I said, were at first stretched forth as a curtain; indeed they were afterwards garnished with the beauty which we now behold; but otherwise they had, at their first instant of being, that form which now they have. This seems clear by the antithesis which the Holy Ghost put between them, God created the heaven and the earth, but "the earth was without form and void" (Gen 1:2). The earth was without form, &c., without order; things were together on a confused heap; the waters were not divided from the earth, neither did those things appear which are now upon the face of the earth; as man, and beast, fish, fowls, trees, and herbs; all these did afterwards shew themselves, as the word of God gave them being, by commanding their appearance, in what form, order, place and time he in himself had before determined; but all, I say, took their matter and substance of that first chaos, which he in the first day of the world had commanded to appear, and had given being to: And therefore 'tis said, God said, Let the earth bring forth

---

[iii] It should be noted that in Bunyan's subsequent arguments, he does not imply that the chaos was *immoral*, as some try to do today, but rather that it indicates incompleteness. Nevertheless, it may be that Bunyan is attempting to make too much of a distinction between the heavens and the earth, in support of his argument that the heavens were not in chaos.

grass, herbs, trees, &c., (v 12) and that the waters brought forth the fish, and fowl, yea, even to the mighty whales (vv 21,22). Also the earth brought forth cattle, and creeping things (v 24). And that God made man of the dust of the ground (3:19). All these things therefore were made of, or caused by his word distinctly to appear, and be after its kind, of that first matter which he had before created by his word. Observe therefore, That the matter of all earthly things was made at the same instant, but their forming, &c., was according to the day in which God gave them their being, in their own order and kind. And hence it is said, that after that first matter was created, and found without form and void, that the Spirit of God moved upon the face of the waters; that is to work, and cause those things to appear in their own essence and form, which, as to matter and substance, was before created: Wherefore it follows, And God said, Let there be light; and God divided the light from the darkness, &c. Now he set to putting in frame that which before lay in disorder and confusion: And this was a great part of the six days' work; I say, a great part, but not all; for (as I said) before that time, the angels, and the heavens were made; yea, after the beginning of the morning of the first day. I am of the belief, that other things also, that were formed after, were not made of that first chaos, as the sun, the moon, the stars, the light, the souls of men, and possibly the air, &c. The sun, and moon, and stars, are said to be made the fourth day, yet not of the body of heaven itself, much less, in my opinion, of any earthly matter: God made them, and set them in the firmament of heaven (vv 16,17). So the light that was made before, it seems to be a thing created after the heavens and the earth were created: Created, I say, as a thing that wanted a being before, any otherwise, than in the decree of God: and God said, Let there be light; Let it have a being (v 3). And so, though the body of man was made of the substance of earth, yet as to his soul, it is said, God breathed into his nostrils the breath of life, and man became a living soul (2:7).

Whether there was a secret or mystery in this work, containing the truth of some higher thing.

Though God in very deed, by his eternal power, created heaven and earth of things that do not appear, we that are Christians believe: yet in this his wonderful work, neither his will or understanding did here terminate, or make a stop; but being infinite in wisdom, he made them, that both as to matter and manner, they might present unto us, as in a mystery, some higher and more excellent thing; in this wisdom he made them all. And hence it is that other things are also called a creation: As, 1. The essential conversion of a sinner (2 Cor 5:17). 2. The recovery of the church from a degenerate state (Rev 21:5).

And therefore, as Moses begins with the creation of the world, so John begins with the gospel of salvation (Gen 1:1; John 1:1). There is also besides many excellent things in the manner and order of the creation of the world, held forth to those that have understanding: Some of which I may touch upon by way of observation. But to begin with the first:

The first appearance of this earthy part of the world, is recorded to be but a formless and void heap or chaos; and such is man before a new creation: formless, I mean, as to the order of the Testament of Christ, and void of the holy order thereof: And hence Jeremiah, when he would set forth the condition of a wicked people, he doth it under this metaphor: "I beheld [saith he] the earth, and, lo, *it was* without form and void" (Jer 4:23). Indeed, the world would make this a type of Christ; to wit, a man of no form or comeliness (Isa 53:2). But 'tis only true of themselves; they are without a New Testament impression upon them; they are void of the sovereign grace of God. So then the power of God gave the world a being, but by his word he set it in form and beauty; even as by his power he gives a being to man, but by his word he giveth him New Testament framing and glory (Eph 2:10-13). This is still followed by that which follows:

> And darkness was upon the face of the deep (v 2).

The Deep here, might be a type of the heart of man before conversion[iv]; and so Solomon seems to intimate. Now as the darkness of this world did cover the face of this first chaos; so spiritual darkness the heart of the sons of men: and hence they are said to be darkened, to be in darkness, yea, to be very darkness itself.

> "And the Spirit of God moved upon the face of the waters."

A blessed emblem of the word of God in the matter of regeneration; for as the first chaos remained without form, and void, until the Spirit of God moved to work upon it, and by working, to put this world into frame and order; so man, as he comes into the world, abides a

---

[iv] This is an example, perhaps, of Bunyan's over-spiritualisation in his interpretations, as mentioned in my Preface. In fact, in scripture, darkness is not always indicative of evil. For example, Abraham's darkness in Genesis 15:12 is derived from the same root word, *chôshek* (חֹשֶׁךְ) - Strong's number 2822. When we note Bunyan's over-spiritualisation of the text, however, this does not prevent us from appreciating the truth of the spiritual lessons that he is drawing.

confused lump, an unclean thing; a creature without New Testament order, until by the Spirit of the Lord he is transformed into the image of Jesus Christ (Gal 1:15).

"And the Spirit of God moved upon the face."

Solomon compares the heart to a man's face; because as in the face may be discerned whether there is anger or otherwise; so by the inclinations of the heart are discovered the truth of the condition of the man, as to his state either for heaven or hell. And besides, as the Spirit of God moved upon the face of the waters; so in the work of our conversion, the Spirit of God beginneth with the heart of the sons of men; because the heart is the main fort (Acts 2:37). Now if the main fort be not taken, the adversary is still capable of making continual resistance. Therefore God first conquers the heart; therefore the Spirit of God moveth upon the face of our heart, when he cometh to convert us from Satan to God.

"And God said, Let there be light."

This is the first thing with which God began the order of the creation; to wit, light, "Let there be light": From which many profitable notes may be gathered, as to the order of God in the salvation of the soul. As,

1. When the Holy Ghost worketh upon us, and in us, in order to a new creation; he first toucheth our understanding, that great peace of the heart, with his spiritual illumination (Matt 4:16). His first word, in order to our conversion, is, Let there be light: light, to see their state by nature; light, to see the fruits and effects of sin; light, to see the truth and worth of the merits of Jesus Christ; light, to see the truth and faithfulness of God, in

keeping promise and covenant with them that embrace salvation upon the blessed terms of the gospel of peace (Heb 10:32). Now that this word, Let there be light, was a semblance of the first work of the Holy Ghost upon the heart, compare it with that of Paul to the Corinthians; "For God, who commanded the light to shine out of darkness," that is, at the beginning of the world, "hath shined in our hearts to *give* the light of the knowledge of the glory of God in the face of Jesus Christ" (2 Cor 4:6).

2. "And God said, Let there be light." As here, the light of this world; so in conversion, the light of the New Testament of Christ, it comes by the word of God. No word, no light: therefore the apostle saith, He "hath brought life and immortality to light through the gospel" (2 Tim 1:10). And therefore Paul saith again, That salvation is manifest through preaching, through the expounding or opening of the word of faith.

3. "And God said, Let there be light; and there was light": He spake the word, and it was done; all that darkness that before did cover the face of the deep, could not now hinder the being of light. So neither can all the blindness and ignorance that is in the heart of man, hinder the light of the knowledge of the glory of God in the face of Jesus Christ (Rev 3:7). When it pleaseth God to reveal, it is revealed; when he openeth, none can shut: He said, Let there be light, and there was light.

And God saw that the light was good. Truly the light is good (saith Solomon) and a pleasant thing it is for the eye to behold the sun. It was good, because it was God's creature; and so in the work of grace that is wrought in our hearts, that light of the new covenant, it is good, because it is God's work, the work of his good pleasure (2 Thess 1:11); that good work which he hath not only begun, but promised to fulfil until the day of Jesus Christ (Phil 1:6).

God saw that the light was good. The darkness that before did cover the face of the waters, was not a creature of God, but a privation, or that which was caused by reason that light was not as yet in the world: so sin, that darkness that might be felt, is not the workmanship of God in the soul, but that which is the work of the devil; and that taketh occasion to be, by reason that the true light, as yet, doth not shine in the soul.

"And God divided the light from the darkness." As Paul saith, What communion hath light with darkness? they cannot agree to dwell together (2 Cor 6:14). We see the night still flies before the day, and dareth not come upon us again, but as the light diminisheth and conveyeth itself away. So it is in the new creation; before the light of the glorious gospel of Christ appears, there is night, all night, in the soul (Eph 5:8): but when that indeed doth shine in the soul, then for night there is day in the soul: "Ye were darkness [saith Paul] but now *are ye* light in the Lord" (v 9): And, "The darkness is past [saith John] and the true light now shineth" (1 John 2:8).

"And God divided the light from the darkness."

God took part with the light, and preserved it from the darkness. By these words, it seems that darkness and light began the quarrel, before that bloody bout of Cain and Abel (Gal 5:17). The light and the darkness struggled together, and nothing could divide or part them but God. Darkness is at implacable enmity with light in the creation of the world; and so it is in that rare work of regeneration, the flesh lusteth against the spirit, and the spirit against the flesh; as Peter saith, Fleshly lusts, they war against the soul. This every Christian feels, and also that which I mentioned before, namely, That before he be capable of opposing antichrist, with Abel, in the world, he findeth a struggling in his own soul between the light and the darkness that is there.

> "And God called the light Day, and the darkness he called Night."

God doth not only distinguish by separating, but also by certain characters; that things which are distinguished and separate, may to us be the better known; he did so here in the work of creating the world, and he doth so also in the great concern of man's eternal happiness. The place of felicity is called heaven: The place of torment is called hell: that which leads to hell is called sin, transgression, iniquity, and wickedness; that which leads to heaven, righteousness, holiness, goodness and uprightness: even as in these types God called the light day, of which the godly are the children (1 Thess 5:5); but the darkness he called night, of which all ungodly men are the inhabiters and children also. Thus after the Spirit of God had moved upon the face of the waters; after God had commanded the light to shine, and had divided between the light and the darkness, and had characterized them by their proper names, he concludes the first day's work, "And the evening and the morning were the first day." In which conclusion there is wrapped up a blessed gospel-mystery; for God, by concluding the first day here, doth shew us how we ought to determine that one is made indeed a Christian: Even then when the Spirit of God hath moved upon the face of the heart, when he hath commanded that light should be there, when he divideth between, or setteth the light at variance with the darkness; and when the soul doth receive the characters of both, to observe them, and carry it to each according to the mouth of God.

> "And God saith, Let there be a firmament" (v 6).

This firmament he calleth heaven (v 8). Now this firmament, or heaven, was to make a separation, or to divide between the waters and the waters (v 7); To separate, I say, the waters from the waters; the waters which were under the firmament, from the waters which were above the firmament. Now by waters is signified in the scriptures many things, as afflictions, worldly people (Psa 69:1,2), and particularly the saints (Rev 19:6); but in this place is figured forth, all the people in the world, but so as consisting of two parts, the children of God, and the children of the wicked one: They under the heaven, figure out the world, or ungodly: they above the firmament, the elect and chosen of God. And hence in scripture the one is called heaven, and the other is called earth, to signify the separation and difference that there is between the one and the other.

> "And God made the firmament, and divided the waters - from the waters."

Indeed the world think that this separation comes, or is made, through the captiousness of the preacher: But in truth it is the handy work of God; And God made the firmament, and God divided, &c. "I," saith he, "will put enmity between thee and the woman, and between thy seed and her seed" (Gen 3:15). The good seed are the children of the kingdom of God, but the bad are the children of the wicked one (Matt 13:38).

> "And God made the firmament, and divided the waters which *were* under the firmament, from the waters which *were* above the firmament: and it was so" (v 7).

Whatsoever the Lord doth, it abideth for ever (Eccl 3:14). And again, What he hath made crooked, who can make straight? (Eccl 1:15). He said it in the beginning, and behold how it hath continued! Yea, though there hath been endeavours on Satan's part, to mingle his children with the seed of men; yet it hath not been possible they should ever cleave one to another, "even as iron is not mixed with clay" (Dan 2:43). Yea, let me add further, What laws have been made, what blood hath been shed, what cruelty hath been used, and what flatteries and lies invented, and all to make these two waters and people one? And yet all hath failed, and fallen short of producing the desired effect; for the Lord hath made a firmament, even heaven itself hath divided between them.

> "And God called the firmament heaven. And the evening and the morning were the second day" (v 8).

After the waters were divided from the waters, God called the cause of dividing, heaven; and so concluded the second day's work. And indeed it was a very great work, as in the antitype we feel it to this very day. Dividing work is difficult work, and he that can, according to God, completely end and finish it, he need do no more that day of his life.

> "And God said, Let the waters under the heaven be gathered together unto one place, and let the dry *land* appear: and it was so" (v 9).

Although in the second day's work, the waters above the firmament, and those that be under, are the two peoples, or great families of the world (Pro 8:31); yet because God would shew us by things on earth, the flourishing state of those that are his (Hosea 10:12; Joel 2:21-23; Psa 91:1; Heb 6:7), therefore he here doth express his mind by another kind of representation of things (Jer 4:3,4): "And God said, Let the waters under the heaven be gathered together unto one place; and let the dry *land* appear." The waters here signifying the world; but the fruitful earth, the thrifty church of God. That the fruitful earth is a figure of the thriving church of God in this world, is evident from many scriptures, (and there was nothing but thriftiness till the curse came). And hence it is said of the church, That she should break the clods of the ground; that she should sow righteousness, and reap it; that she should not sow among thorns; that if this be done, the heart is circumcised, and spiritual fruit shall flow forth, and grow abundantly: And hence again it is that the officers and eminent ones in the church, are called vines, trees, and other fruitful plants. And hence it is said again, When the Lord reigneth, let the earth (that is, the church) rejoice. That earth which bringeth forth fruit meet for him by whom it is dressed, receiveth blessing from God. In all which places, and many more that might be named, the earth is made a figure of the church of God; and so I count it here in this place.

> "And God said, Let the waters under the heaven be gathered into one place."

Let them be together: It is not thus of all waters, but of the sea, which is still here a type of the world. Let them be so together, that the earth may appear; that the church may be rid of their rage and tumult, and then she will be fruitful, as it follows in this first book of Genesis. The church is then in a flourishing state, when the world is farthest off from her, and when the roaring of their waves are far away. Now therefore let all the wicked men be far from thence (Ezra 6:6): The Lord gather these waters, which in another place are called the doleful creatures, and birds of prey; Let these, O Lord, be gathered together to their own places, and be settled in the land of Shinar upon their own base (Zech 5:11): Then the wilderness and the solitary places shall be glad for them; that is, for that they are departed thence, the desert shall rejoice and blossom as a rose (Isa 34 and 35).

"And God called the dry *land* Earth; and the gathering together of the waters called he seas: and God saw that *it was* good" (v 10).

God saw, that to separate the waters from the earth was good: And so it is, for then have the churches rest. Then doth this earth bring forth her fruit, as in the 11th and 12th verses may here be seen.

"And God said, Let there be lights in the firmament of the heaven" (v 14).

The wisdom of God, is there to make use of figures and shadows, even where most fit things, the things under consideration, may be most fitly demonstrated. The dividing the waters from the waters, most fitly doth show the work of God in choosing and refusing; by dividing the waters from the earth, doth show how fruitful God's earth, the church is, when persecutors are made to be far from thence.

Wherefore he speaketh not of garnishing of his church until he comes to this fourth day's work: by his Spirit he hath garnished the heavens, that most fitly showing the glory of the church.

Let there be lights; to wit, the sun, the moon, and the stars.

The sun is in this place a type of Christ, the Sun of Righteousness: The moon is a type of the church, in her uncertain condition in this world: The stars are types of the several saints and officers in this church. And hence it is that the sun is said not only to rule, but it, with the moon and stars, to be set for signs, and for seasons, and for days, and for years, &c. (Rev 1:20). But if we take the heaven for the church, then how is she beautified, when the Son of God is placed in the midst of her! (Rev 1:12,13). And how plainly is her condition made out, even by the changing, increasing, and diminishing of the moon! And how excellent is that congregation of men, that for light and glory are figured by the stars! (Matt 28:20).

From this day's work much might be observed.

First, That forasmuch as the sun was not made before the fourth day, it is evident there was light in the world before the sun was created[v]; for in the first day God said,

[v] Bunyan's logic here, in determining that there was light before the creation of the Sun, is impeccable. He was not hamstrung by modern so-called "discoveries". Today, we should not be intimidated by those who start their interpretation by assuming *historical science* to be true, but

Let there be light, and there was light. This may also teach us thus much, That before Christ came in person, there was spiritual light in the saints of God. And again, That as the sun was not made before the fourth day of the creation, so Christ should not be born before the fourth mystical day of the world; for it is evident, that Christ, the true light of the world, was not born till about four thousand years after the world was made[vi]. *Second*, As to the moon, there are four things attending her, which fitly may hold forth the state of the church. (1.) In that she changeth from an old to a new, we may conceive, that God by making her so, did it to show he would one day make a change of his church, from a Jewish to a Gentile congregation. (2.) In that she increaseth, she showeth the flourishing state of the church. (3.) In her diminishing, the diminishing state of the church. (4.) The moon is also sometimes made to look as red as blood, to show how dreadful and bloody the suffering of the church is at some certain times.

Third, By the stars, we understand two things. (1.) How innumerable the saints, those spiritual stars shall be (Heb 11:12). (2.) How they shall differ each from other in glory (1 Cor 15:41).

"And God said, Let there be lights in the firmament of the heaven, to divide the day from the night."

For though before the light was divided from the darkness, yet the day and night was not so kept within

---

rather begin our work, as Bunyan did, from the truth of scripture.

[vi] Bunyan is right about the dating of Christ's birth, but for the wrong reason. There is nothing else in scripture that leads us to suppose that each day can be taken figuratively as a thousand years of history.

their bounds, as now by these lights they were: probably signifying, that nothing should be so clearly distinguished and made appear, as by the sun light of the gospel of Christ: for by that it is that "the shadows flee away" (Song 2:17). The light of the sun gathers the day to its hours, both longer and shorter, and forceth also the night to keep within his bounds.

> "And God made two great lights; the greater light to rule the day, and the lesser light to rule the night" (v 16).

Signifying, That Christ should be the light and governor of his church, which are the children of the day; but the church, a light to the children of the night, that by them they might learn the mysteries of the kingdom. Saith Christ to his own, "Ye are the light of the world": And again, "Let your light so shine, - that men may see," &c., for though they that only walk in the night, cannot see to walk by the sun, yet by the moon they may. Thus the heaven is a type of the church, the moon a type of her uncertain state in this world; the stars are types of her immovable converts; and their glory, of the differing degrees of theirs, both here, and in the other world. Much more might be said, but I pass this.

> "And God said, Let the waters bring forth abundantly the moving creature that hath life" (v 20).

The sea, as I said, is a figure of the world; wherefore the creatures that are in it, of the men of the world (Zech 13:8; Isa 60:5). This sea bringeth forth small and great beasts, even as the world doth yield both small and great persecutors, who like the fishes of prey, eat up and devour what they can of those fish that are of another condition. Now also out of the world that mystical sea, as fishers do out of the natural; both Christ and his servants catch mystical fish, even fish as of the great sea.

In the sea God created great whales, he made them to play therein.

Which whales in the sea are types of the devils in the world: Therefore as the devil is called, the prince of this world; so the whale is called, king over all the children of pride (Job 41:33,34).

"And God said, Let the earth bring forth the living creature after his kind" (v 24).

Of the beginning of this sixth day's work that may be said which is said of the fishes, and the rest of the sea; for as there is variety of fish in the one, so of beasts and cattle in the other, who also make a prey of their fellows, as the fishes do; a most apt representation of the nature and actions of bloody and deceitful men: Hence persecutors are called bulls, bears, lions, wolves, tigers, dragons, dogs, foxes, leopards, and the like.[3]

"And God said, Let us make man" (v 26).

I observe, that in the creation of the world, God goeth gradually on, from things less, to things more abundantly glorious; I mean, as to the creation of this earth; and the things that thereto appertain. First he bringeth forth a confused chaos, then he commands matter to appear distinct, then the earth bringeth forth trees, and herbs, and grass; after that beasts; and the sea, fowls; and last of all, Let us make man. Now passing by the doctrine of the trinity, because spoken to before, I come to make some observation upon this wonderful piece of the workmanship of God.

"Let us make man." Man in whom is also included the woman, was made the last of the creatures. From whence we may gather,

God's respect to this excellent creature, in that he first provideth for him, before he giveth him his being: He bringeth him not to an empty house, but to one well furnished with all kind of necessaries, having beautified the heaven and the earth with glory, and all sorts of nourishment, for his pleasure and sustenance.[4]

"Let us make man in our image, after our likeness."

An image, or the likeness of any thing, is not the thing of which it is a figure; so here, Adam is an image, or made in the likeness of God. Now as Adam is the image of God, it must either respect him, as he consisteth of the soul, as a part; or as he consists of a body and soul together: If as he is made a reasonable soul, then he is an excellent image of the eternal Godhead, the attributes of the one being shadowed out by the qualities and passions of the other; for as there is in the Godhead, power, knowledge, love, and righteousness; so a likeness of these is in the soul of man, especially of man before he had sinned: And as there is passions of pity, compassion, affections, and bowels in man; so there are these in a far more infinite way in God.

Again, If this image respect the whole man, then Adam was a figure of God, as incarnate; or of God, as he was to be made afterwards man. And hence it is, that as Adam is called the image of God (Rom 5:14); so also is Christ himself called and reckoned as the answering antitype of such an image.

But again, Though Adam be here called the image or similitude of God; yet but so as that he was the shadow of a more excellent image. Adam was a type of Christ, who only is "the express image" of his Father's person, and the likeness of his excellent glory (Heb 1:3). For those things that were in Adam, were but of a humane, but of a created substance; but those that were in Christ, of the same divine and eternal excellency with the Father.

Is Christ then the image of the Father, simply, as considered of the same divine and eternal excellency with him? Certainly, No: for an image is doubtless inferior to that of which it is a figure. Understand then, that Christ is the image of the Father's glory, as born of the Virgin Mary, yet so, as being very God also: Not that his Godhead in itself was a shadow or image, but by the acts and doing of that man, every act being infinitely perfect by virtue of his Godhead, the Father's perfections were made manifest to flesh. An image is to be looked upon, and by being looked upon, another thing is seen; so by the person and doings of the Lord Jesus, they that indeed could see him as he was, discovered the perfection and glory of the Father.—"Philip, He that hath seen me hath seen the Father; and how sayest thou *then*, Shew us the Father?" (John 14:9). Neither the Father nor the Son can by us at all be seen, as they are simply and entirely in their own essence. Therefore the person of the Father must be seen by us, through the Son, as consisting of God and man; the Godhead, by working effectually in the manhood, shewing clearly there through the infinite perfection and glory of the Father:

"The word was made flesh, and - [then] we beheld his glory, the glory as of the only begotten of the Father, [He being in his personal excellencies, infinitely and perfectly, what is recorded of his Father,] full of grace and truth" (John 1:14). So again, he "is the image of the invisible God" (Col 1:15). The Godhead is indeed invisible; how then is Christ the image of it? Not by being invisible also; for so is he as much hid as the Father; but being clothed with flesh, that the works of the Son might by us be seen, he thereby presenteth to us, as in a figure, the eternal excellency of the Father. And hence as he is called "an image," he is also called "the first-born" of every creature (Col 1:18). His being a creature, respecting his manhood, and his birth, and his rising again from the dead. Therefore a little after, he is called, "the first-born from the dead" (v 19): And in another place, "the first-begotten of the dead" (Rev 1:5): And "the first-fruits of them that slept" (1 Cor 15:20). So then, though Adam was the image of God, yet God's image but as a mere creature: But Christ though a creature as touching his manhood; yet being also God, as the Father, he shewed forth expressly, in capital characters, by all his works and doings in the world, the beauty and glory of the Father: "The light of the knowledge of the glory of God," is given "in the face of Jesus Christ" (2 Cor 4:6). Where by face, we must understand that which is visible, that being open when all else is covered, and that by which most principally we are discovered to others, and known. Now as to the case in hand, this face must signify to us the personal virtues and doings of Christ, by which the glory of the Father is exposed; the glory of his justice, by Christ's exactness of life; the glory of his love, by Christ's compassion to sinners, &c.

Ver. 26. "And God said, Let us make man in our image, after our likeness: and let them have

> dominion over the fish of the sea, and over the fowl of the air, and over the cattle, and over all the earth, and over every creeping thing that creepeth upon the earth."

As Adam was a type of Christ, as the image and glory of God; so by these words he further showeth, that he was a type of his sovereign power; for to him be dominion and power everlasting (Heb 2:8,9), "to whom be praise and dominion for ever" (1 Peter 4:11; Jude 25). Now by the fish of the sea, the beasts of the earth, the fowls of the air, and every creeping thing, we may understand all creatures, visible and invisible, whether they be men, angels, or devils; in heaven, earth, or under the earth: also all thrones, authorities and powers, whether in heaven, in earth, or hell: Christ is made head over all; He hath also a name above every name, "not only in this world, but in that which is to come" (Eph 1:25).

> Ver. 28. "And God blessed them; and God said unto them, [that is, to the man and his wife] Be fruitful, and multiply, and replenish the earth, and subdue it," &c.

This in the type doth show, in the antitype, how fruitful Christ and his church shall be; and how he at last shall, all over the earth, have a seed to replenish and subdue it by the power of the immortal seed of the word of God: how his name shall be reverenced from one end of the earth to the other: how the kingdoms of the earth shall ALL at last become the kingdoms of our Lord, and of his Christ.

"And subdue it." God did put that majesty and dread upon Adam, at his creation, that all the beasts of the field submitted themselves unto him. As God also said to Noah, "The fear of you and the dread of you shall be upon every beast of the earth, and upon every fowl of the air, upon all that moveth *upon* the earth, and upon all the fishes of the sea; into your hand are they delivered" (Gen 9:2).

> "And God said, Behold I have given you every herb bearing seed, which *is* upon the face of all the earth; and every tree, in the which *is* the fruit of a tree yielding seed; to you it shall be for meat" (Gen 1:29).

These herbs and trees are types of the wholesome word of the gospel, on which both Christ, his church, and unconverted sinners, ought to feed and be refreshed; and without which thee is no subsisting either of one or the other: "He causeth the grass to grow for the cattle, and herb for the service of man: that he may bring forth food out of the earth; and wine *that* maketh glad the heart of man, *and* oil to make *his* face to shine, and bread *which* strengtheneth man's heart" (Psa 104:14,15).

> "And God saw every thing that he had made, and, behold, *it was* very good" (v 31).

All things have their natural goodness by creation. Things are not good, because they have a being only, but because God gave them such a being. Neither did God make them, because he saw they would attract a goodness to themselves; but he made them in such kind, as to bring forth that goodness he before determined they should. "And the evening and the morning were the sixth day."

Chapter II.

> Ver. 3. "And God blessed the seventh day, and sanctified it: because that in it he had rested from all his work which God created and made."

The seventh day did signify two things:

First, Christ Jesus, who is as well the rest of the justice of God, as a rest for sinful man.

Secondly, It was also a type of that glorious rest that saints shall have when the six days of this world are fully ended.

For the first, the apostle makes the sabbath a shadow of Jesus Christ, "a shadow of things to come; but the body [or substance] *is* of Christ" (Col 2:17). And hence it is that he is so often said to be "a rest" to the Gentiles, a glorious rest, and that he promiseth rest to such as cast their burthen upon him (Matt 11:29).

The second also the apostle asserteth in that fourth chapter to the Hebrews, "There remaineth therefore a rest," or the keeping of a sabbath, "to the people of God" (v 9 read also vv 4-11). Which sabbath, as I conceive, will be the seventh thousand of years, which are to follow immediately after the world hath stood six thousand first: for as God was six days in the works of creation, and rested the seventh; so in six thousand years he will perfect his works and providences that concern this world. As also he will finish the toil and travel of his saints, with the burthen of the beasts, and the curse of the ground; and bring all into rest for a thousand years. A day with the Lord, is as a thousand years: wherefore this blessed and desirable time is also called "a day," "a great day," "that great and notable day of the Lord" (Acts 2:20), which shall end in the eternal judgment of the world. God hath held forth this by several other shadows, as the sabbath of weeks, the sabbath of years, and the great jubilee, which is to be the year after forty-nine years are expired (Lev 25:1-13). Of all which, more in their place, if God permit.

> Ver. 4. "These *are* the generations of the heavens and of the earth when they were created, in the day that the LORD God made the earth and the heavens."

Moses seems by these words, "In the day," to insist principally upon them in their first and primitive state, before there was sin or curse in the world; for in the day that they were created, there was a far more glorious lustre and beauty than now can be seen; the heaven, for sin, is, as it were, turned into brass; and the rain into powder and dust, in comparison of what it was as it came from the fingers of God. The earth hath also from that time a curse upon it; yea, the whole creation, by sin, is even "made subject to vanity," is in travail, and groans under the burthen that sin hath brought upon it (Rom 8:19-23).

> Ver. 5. "And every plant of the field before it was in the earth, and every herb of the field before it grew."

Thus it was in the first creation; they therefore became neither herbs nor trees, by the course of nature, but by the creation of God. And even so it is in the new creation, men spring not up by nature to be saints: No, not in the church of God, but first they are created in Christ Jesus, and made meet to be partakers of the benefit, and then planted in the church of God; "planted," I say, as plants before prepared. Indeed hypocrites, and formal professors, may spring up in the church, by virtue of her forms, and outward services, as thorns and thistles spring up in the earth, by virtue of her moisture and heartiness. But these are but the fruits of the curse, and are determined to be burned at last in the fire: "Every plant [saith Christ] which my heavenly Father hath not planted, shall be rooted up" (Matt 15:13; Heb 6:8).[5]

"For the Lord God had not caused it to rain upon the earth." This is the reason that they came not up by nature first, but were first created, then planted, then made to grow. So the reason why men by nature grow not in the church, is, because the Lord doth not cause it to rain upon them, they still abiding and doing according to the course of this world; but he plants them in his house by the mighty power of his word and Spirit, by which they are created saints, and then they afterwards grow in grace, and in the knowledge of our Lord and Saviour Jesus Christ. "And *there was* not a man to till the ground." It seems by this there was a kind of necessity why God should make man, yea, a multitude of men; for otherwise he had made what before he made in vain; that is, his end in making so glorious a creature as this world, which was to shew forth his glory by, had been void, and without effect; for although it was glorious, as it came out of the hand of God; yet it was not of power so to preserve itself, but would, without men to look after and dress it, be turned into a wilderness.

Thus it is with the world of men, if there was not the second Adam to plough them and sow them, they could none of them become saints; No, not the elect themselves; because the means are determined, as well as the end.

By this we may likewise see what a woeful condition that people is in, that have no ministers of the word of the gospel: "My people perish, [are destroyed] for lack of knowledge" (Hosea 4:6): And again, "Where *there is* no vision, the people perish" (Pro 29:18). Pray therefore to the Lord of the harvest, that he would send out his ploughers to plough, and his labourers into his harvest.

Ver. 6. "But there went up a mist from the earth, and watered the whole face of the ground."

Although as yet there was no ploughman nor rain, yet a mist arose from the earth; so where there is not the word of the gospel, there is yet sufficiency of light, to teach men how to govern themselves in civil and natural society. But this is only "a mist," men cannot gospelly grow by this; therefore, as in the next verse, of necessity man must be formed.

But again, I have sometimes thought by this mist, might be held forth that nourishment men had by the doctrine of faith, before the gospel was divulged by Moses, the prophets, or Christ, &c. for before these, that nourishment the church received, was but slender and short, even as short as the nourishing of the mist is to sober and moderate showers of rain; to which both the law and the gospel is compared.

Again, I have also sometimes thought, that by this mist might be typified those excellent proverbs and holy sayings of the men of old, before there was a written word; for it cannot be but the godly did contain in proverbs, and certain sayings, the doctrine of salvation hereafter, and of good living here [see Romans 2:14]; of which we have a touch in Genesis, but more at large by that blessed book of Job; which book, in my opinion, is a holy collection of those proverbs and sayings of the ancients, occasioned by the temptation of that good man. But whatever this mist did signify (in other men's judgment) certain it is, it was for present necessity, till a man should be made to till the ground, and the fruits thereof watered with "the bottles of heaven": Which, so far as I see yet, most aptly presents us with some of all these.

Ver. 7. "And the Lord God formed man *of* the dust of the ground," &c. In the creation of man, God began with his outside; but in the work of regeneration, he first begins within, at the heart. He made him; that is, his body, of the dust of the ground; but he abides a lifeless lump, till the Lord puts forth a second act. "And [he] breathed into his nostrils the breath of life; and man became a living soul." Now he lives, now he acts: so it is in the kingdom of Christ, no man can be a living soul in that kingdom by his first creation, he must have life "breathed" into him, life and spirit from Jesus Christ (John 20:22).

Now therefore is Adam a type, yet but an earthly one, of things more high and heavenly; "And as we have borne the image of the earthy, we shall also bear the image of the heavenly" (1 Cor 15:49).

> Ver. 8. "And the Lord God planted a garden eastward in Eden, and there he put the man whom he had formed."

"And the Lord God planted a garden." Thus the Holy Ghost speaks clearer and clearer; for now he presents the church to us under the similitude of a garden, which is taken out of the wide and open field, and inclosed; "A garden inclosed *is* my sister, *my* spouse"; a garden inclosed, "a spring shut up, a fountain sealed" (Cant 4:12); and there he put the man whom he had formed. An excellent type of the presence of Christ with his church (Rev 1:12,13).

Ver. 9. "And out of the ground made the Lord God to grow every tree that is pleasant to the sight," &c.

These trees, and their pleasurableness, do shew us the beauty of the truly godly, whom the Lord hath beautified with salvation. And hence it is said, the glory of Lebanon, of Sharon, and of Carmel, is given to the church: that is, she is more beautified with gifts and graces than can by types and shadows be expressed. "The tree of life also in the midst of the garden, and the tree of knowledge of good and evil."

This "tree of life," was another type of Christ, as the bread and healing medicine of the church, that stands "in the midst of the paradise of God" (Rev 2:7; 22:2).

The tree of the knowledge of good and evil, was a type of the law, or covenant of works, as the sequel of the story clearly manifesteth; for had not Adam eaten thereof, he had enjoyed for ever his first blessedness. As Moses saith, "It shall be our righteousness, if we observe to do all these commandments before the Lord our God, as he hath commanded us" (Deu 6:25). But both Adam and we have touched, that is, broken the boughs and fruit of this tree, and therefore now for ever, by the law, no man can stand just before God (Gal 2:16).

> Ver. 10. "And a river went out of Eden to water the garden; and from thence it was parted, and became into four heads."

This river while it abided in Eden, in the garden, it was the river of God; that is, serviceable to the trees and fruit of the garden, and was herein a type of those watering ministers that water the plants of the Lord. But observe, when it had passed the garden, had gotten without the bound of the garden, from thence it was parted, and became into four heads; from thence it was transformed, or turned into another manner of thing: it now became into four heads; a type of the four great monarchies of the world, of which Babylon, though the first in order of being, yet the last in a gospel or mysterious sense. The fourth is the river Euphrates, that which was the face of the kingdom of Babel of old. Hence note, That how eminent and serviceable soever men are while they abide in the garden of Eden, THE CHURCH; yet when they come out from thence, they evilly seek the great things of the world: one is for compassing the whole land of Havilah, where is gold; another is for compassing this, a third that, and a fourth another thing, according as you see these four heads did. Observe again, That while men abide in the church of God, there is not by them a seeking after the monarchies of this world; but when they depart from thence, then they seek and strive to be heads; as that cursed monster the pope, forsaking the garden of God, became in a manner the prince of all the earth: Of whom Tyrus mentioned by Ezekiel, was a very lively type, "Thou hast been in Eden, the garden of God; every precious-stone, [that is, doctrine,] *was* thy covering; as the sardius, topaz, diamond," &c., "till iniquity was found in thee" (Eze 28:13-18)[vii]; till thou

---

[vii] Since the time of Thomas Chalmers, there have been those who have

leftest thy station, and place appointed of God, and then thou wast cast as profane out of the mountain of God, yea, though a covering cherub. See it again in Cain, who while he continued in the church, he was a busy sacrificer, as busy as Abel his brother; but when he left off to fear the Lord, and had bloodily butchered his holy brother, then he seeks to be a head, or monarch; then he goeth and buildeth a city to preserve his name and posterity for ever (Gen 4:17).

Ver. 15. "And the Lord God took the man, and put him into the garden of Eden, to dress it and to keep it."

In this also Adam was a figure of our Lord Jesus Christ, as pastor and chief bishop of his church. "I the Lord, [saith Christ,] do keep it; I will water it every moment, I will keep it night and day" (Isa 27:3).

"And the Lord God took the man." No man taketh this honour upon him, but he that is called of God, as was Aaron. Blessed is he also that can say as the prophet Amos; "And the Lord took me [said he] as I followed the flock, and the Lord said unto me, Go, prophesy unto my people Israel" (Amos 7:15).

"To dress it and to keep it." He that is not dressed, is not kept: That is a sad judgment, That which dieth, let it die; That which is diseased, let it not be dressed, let it die of that disease. By dressing therefore I understand, pruning, manuring and the like, which the dresser of the vineyard was commanded to do, without which all is

---

suggested that the Eden mentioned in Ezekiel is not the same as the Eden of Genesis, but rather that it precedes the other. Bunyan suggests that the two referemces to Eden refer to the same Garden. Bunyan would, therefore, have found the concept of the Gap Theory to be mistaken - as do we.

overrun with briers and nettles, and is fit for nothing but cursing, and to be burned (Luke 13:6-9; Pro 24:30-34; Heb 6:7,8).

> "And the Lord commanded the man, saying, Of every tree of the garden thou mayest freely eat" (v 16).

It is God's word that giveth us power to eat, to drink, and do other our works, and without the word we may do nothing. The command gave Adam leave: "Every creature of God *is* good, and nothing to be refused, if it be received with thanksgiving; for it is sanctified by the word of God [by the command of the word, and by receiving of it according to the limits thereof,] and prayer" (1 Tim 4:4,5).

> Ver. 17. "But of the tree of the knowledge of good and evil, thou shalt not eat of it."

I said before, What God's word prohibits, we must take care to shun.

This "tree of knowledge," as I said before, was a type of the covenant of works, the which had not Adam touched, (for by touching it he broke that covenant,) he then had lived ever, but touching it he dies (Gen 3:3).

Adam going into the garden under these conditions and penalties, was therein a type of the humiliation of Christ; who at his coming into the world, was made under the law, under its command and penalty, even as other men, but without sin (Gal 4:4,5).

> "For in the day that thou eatest thereof thou shalt surely die."

"For in the day." Adam lived to God no longer than while he kept himself from eating forbidden fruit; in that very day he died; first a spiritual death in his soul; his body also was then made capable of mortality[viii], and all diseases, which two great impediments in time brought him down to dust again.

> Ver. 18. "And the Lord God said, *It is* not good that man should be alone; I will make him an help meet for him."

By these words, Adam's state, even in innocency, seems to crave for help; wherefore it is manifest that that state is short of that we attain by the resurrection from the dead; yea, for as much as his need required earthly help, it is apparent his condition was not heavenly; "The first man *is* of the earth, earthy: the second man *is* the Lord from heaven" (1 Cor 15:47). Adam in his first estate was not spiritual: "That *was* not first which is spiritual, but that which is natural; and afterwards that which is spiritual" (v 46). Wherefore those that think it enough to attain to the state of Adam in innocency, think it sufficient to be mere naturalists; think themselves well, without being made spiritual: yea, let me add, they think it safe standing by a covenant of works; they think themselves happy, though not concerned in a covenant of grace; they think they know enough, though ignorant of a mediator, and count they have no need of the intercession of Christ.[6]

[viii] Note that Bunyan concurs with modern creationists, that the verse in question does not imply that Adam would die instantly, but that death would now be inevitable, where before it was impossible.

Adam stood by a covenant of works: Adam's kingdom was an earthly paradise; Adam's excellency was, that he had not need of a Saviour; and Adam's knowledge was ignorance of Jesus Christ: Adam in his greatest glory, wanted earthly comforts; Adam in his innocency, was a mere natural man.

> Ver. 19. "And out of the ground the Lord God formed every beast of the field, and every fowl of the air."

This proveth further what I said at first, That in the first chaos was contained all that was made upon the earth.

> "And brought *them* unto Adam, to see what he would call them: and whatsoever Adam called every living creature, that *was* the name thereof."

In this Adam was a lively type of the Lord Christ's sovereign and glorious power over all flesh: "Thou hast given him power over all flesh, that he should give eternal life to as many as thou hast given him" (John 17:2).

> "And brought *them* unto Adam to see what he would call them."

So Christ nameth the world; whom he will he calleth saints; and whom he will he calleth the world, "ungodly," "serpents," "vipers," and the like. "I pray for them, I pray not for the world" (John 17:9).

"And whatsoever Adam called every living creature, that *was* the name thereof." Even as Christ passes sentence, so shall their judgment be.

> Ver. 20. "And Adam gave names to all cattle, and to the fowl of the air, and to every beast of the field."

So Christ judgeth of angels, devils, and men.

> "But for Adam, there was not found an help meet for him."

All the glory of this world, had not Adam had a wife, could not have completed this man's blessedness; he would yet have been wanting: so all the glory of heaven, considering Christ as mediator, could not, without his church, have made him up complete. The church, I say, "which is his body, the fulness of him that filleth all in all."

> Ver. 21, 22. "And the Lord God caused a deep sleep to fall upon Adam, and he slept: and he took one of his ribs, and closed up the flesh instead thereof; and the rib which the Lord God had taken from man, made he a woman, and brought her unto the man."

In these words we find an help provided for Adam; also whence it came. The help was a wife; she came out of his side; she was taken thence while Adam slept. A blessed figure of a further mystery. Adam's wife was a type of the church of Christ; for that she was taken out of his side, it signifies we are flesh of Christ's flesh, and bone of Christ's bone (Eph 5:30). And in that she was taken thence while Adam slept, it signifies, the church is

Christ's, by virtue of his death and blood: "Feed the church of God, which he hath purchased with is own blood" (Acts 20:28).

"And he brought her to the man." That is, And God brought her to the man. By which he clearly intimates, That as the church is the workmanship of God, and the purchase of the blood of Christ; so yet she cannot come to Christ, unless brought to him of God: "No man can come to me [saith Christ] except the Father which hath sent me, draw him" (John 6:44).

> Ver. 23. "And Adam said, This *is* now bone of my bones, and flesh of my flesh: she shall be called Woman, because she was taken out of Man."

In that Adam doth thus acknowledge his wife to be bone and flesh of his substance, it shews us, that Christ will acknowledge those that are his: "He is not ashamed to call them brethren, saying, I will declare thy name unto my brethren, in the midst of the church will I sing praise unto thee" (Heb 2:11,12).

And observe it, He said, "She is bone of my bone," &c. before that God, that brought her to him; intimating, that Christ both owns us now at his Father's right hand, and will not be ashamed of us, even in the day of judgment (Matt 10:33; Luke 12:8).

> Ver. 24. "Therefore shall a man leave his father and his mother, and shall cleave unto his wife: and they shall be one flesh."

This ought to be truly performed in our married estate in this world. But here endeth not the mystery.

"Therefore shall a man leave his father." Thus did Christ when he came into the world to save sinners: He came forth from the Father; "I came forth from the Father, and am come into the world" (John 16:28).

"Therefore shall a man leave his father and his mother." The Jewish church may, in a mystical sense, be called the mother of Christ; for she was indeed God's wife, and of her came his Son Jesus Christ: yet his mother he left and forsook, to be joined to his Gentile spouse, which is now his only wife.[ix]

Ver. 25. "And they were both naked, the man and his wife, and were not ashamed."

No sin, no shame: Let men stand where God hath set them, and there is no cause of shame, though they be exposed in outward appearance to never so much contempt.

"And they were both naked." Apparel is the fruits of sin; wherefore let such as pride themselves therein, remember, that they cover one shame with another. But let them that are truly godly have their apparel modest and sober, and with shamefacedness put them on, remembering always the first cause of our covering our nakedness, was the sin and shame of our first parents (1 Peter 3:3).

[ix] Some of Bunyan's analogies are helpful. This is not one of them. It is his conjecture that the Jews can be likened to the mother of Christ. I think there is little evidence for this. Had Bunyan lived long enough to comment on the Abrahamic Covenant, he might have realised the insolubility of God's Covenant with the Jewish people.

Chapter III.

> Ver. 1. "Now the serpent was more subtil than any beast of the field which the Lord God had made. And he said unto the woman, Yea, hath God said, Ye shall not eat of every tree of the garden?"

In these words we have an entrance of the first great spiritual conflict that was fought between the devil and flesh; and it is worth the observing, how the enemy attempted, engaged, and overcame the world (2 Cor 11:3).

1. He tempts by means; he appeareth not in his own shape and hue, but assumeth the body of one of the creatures, the body of the serpent, and so begins the combat. And from hence it is, that in after ages he is spoken of under the name of that creature, "the dragon, that old serpent which is the devil, and Satan" (Rev 20:2); because, as the Holy Ghost would have us beware of the devil, so of the means and engines which he useth; for where one is overcome by his own fearful appearance, ten thousand are overcome by the means and engines that he useth.

2. "The serpent was more subtil." The devil, in his attempts after our destruction, maketh use of the most suitable means. The serpent was more subtil, therefore the cunning of the devil was least of all discerned. Had he made use of some of the most foolish of the creatures, Adam had luckily started back, for he knew the nature of all the creatures, and gave them names accordingly; wherefore the serpent, Adam knew, was subtil, therefore Satan useth him, thereby to catch this goodly creature.

Hereby the devil least appeared; and least appearing, the temptation soonest took the tinder.[7]

"Now the serpent was more subtil." More subtil. Hence the devil is called, "the serpent with heads," [with great cunning;] "the crooked serpent," [with knotty objections;] "the piercing serpent," [for he often wounds;] and his ways are called "devices," "temptations," "delusions," "wiles," "power," and "the gates of hell"; because of their mighty prevalency. This is he that undertook our first parents.

But how did he undertake them?

He labours to make them question the simplicity of the word of God, bearing Adam's wife in hand, that there must needs be some meaning that palliates the text; Hath God said ye shall not eat of the tree? Which interrogatory suggested them with a strong doubt that this word would not appear a truth, if you compare it with the 4th verse.

Hence learn, that so long as we retain the simplicity of the word, we have Satan at the end of the staff; for unless we give way to a doubt about that, about the truth and simplicity of it, he gets no ground upon us. And hence the apostle says, He feared lest by some means, as the serpent beguiled Eve through his subtilty, so our minds should be corrupted from the simplicity that is in Christ (2 Cor 11:3); that is, lest our minds should be drawn off from the simplicity of the word of the gospel by some devilish and delusive arguments; For mark, Satan doth not first of all deny, but makes a doubt upon the word, whether it is to be taken in this or another sense; and so first corrupting the mind with a doubt about the simplicity of the true sense, he after brings them to a denial thereof; "Hath God said, Ye shall not eat of every tree of the garden?"

> Ver. 2. "And the woman said unto the serpent, We may eat of the fruit of the trees of the garden."

"And the woman said." Indeed, the question was put to her, but the command was not so immediately delivered to her: "The Lord God commanded the man" (2:16). This therefore I reckon a great fault in the woman, an usurpation, to undertake so mighty an adversary, when she was not the principal that was concerned therein; nay, when her husband who was more able than she, was at hand, to whom also the law was given as chief. But for this act, I think it is, that they are now commanded silence, and also commanded to learn of their husbands (1 Cor 14:34,35): A command that is necessary enough for that simple and weak sex:[8] Though they see it was by them that sin came into the world, yet how hardly are some of them to this day dissuaded from attempting unwarrantably to meddle with potent enemies, about the great and weighty matters that concern eternity (1 Tim 2:11-15).

Hence note, That often they who are least able, will first adventure to put in their head to defend that, from whence they return with shame.

> "And the woman said unto the serpent, We may eat of the fruit of the trees of the garden."

This was her prologue to her defence, but that also for which she had no warrant. In time of temptation, it is our wisdom and duty to keep close to the word, that prohibits and forbids the sin; and not to reason with

Satan, of how far our outward and worldly privileges go, especially of those privileges that border upon the temptation, as she here did: We may eat of all but one. By this she goeth to the outside of her liberty, and sets herself upon the brink of the danger. Christ might have told the tempter, when he assaulted him, That he could have made stones bread; and that he could have descended from the pinnacle of the temple, as afterwards he did (Matt 4:3-7; Luke 4); but that would have admitted of other questions. Wherefore he chooseth to lay aside such needless and unwarrantable reasonings, and resisteth him with a direct word of God, most pertinent to quash the tempter, and also to preserve himself in the way. To go to the outside of privileges, especially when tempted of the devil, is often, if not always very dangerous and hazardous.

By these words therefore, in mine opinion, she spoke at this time too much in favour of the flesh; and made way for what after came upon her, We may eat of all but one.

Ver. 3. "But of the fruit of the tree which *is* in the midst of the garden, God hath said, Ye shall not eat of it, neither shall ye touch it, lest ye die."

Now, too late, she urgeth that which should have been her only stay and weapon; to wit, the express word of God; That she should, if she would have disputed with the tempter, have urged at the first that only, and have thought of nothing else. Thus did the Lord himself: but she looking first into those worthy privileges which God had given her, and dilating delightfully of them before the devil, she lost the dread of the command from off her heart, and retained now but the notion of it: which Satan perceiving, and taking heart therefrom to make his best advantage, he now adds to his former forged doubt, a plain and flat denial, "Ye shall not surely die."

> Ver. 4. "And the serpent said unto the woman, Ye shall not surely die."

When people dally with the devil, and sit too near their outward advantages; when they are tempted to break the command of God, it is usual for them, even by setting their hearts upon things that in themselves are honest and lawful, to fall into temptation: To see a piece of ground, to prove a yoke of oxen, to marry a wife, are doubtless lawful things; but upon the borders of these privileges lay the temptation of the devil; therefore by the love of these, which yet were lawful in themselves, the devil hardened the heart, and so at last made way for, and perfectly produced in them, flatly to deny, as then, to embrace the words of God's salvation (Matt 22:5; Luke 14:16-20). The like befel our first mother; wherefore though at last she freely objected the word; yet because before she had so much reasoned to the pleasing of the flesh, she lost the dread and savour of the command, and having nought but notion left, she found not wherewith to rebuke so plain a lie of the devil, but hearkened to his further reasoning.

"Ye shall not surely die." Not surely; in the word there is some slight meaning, of which you need not be so afraid. And besides,

> Ver. 5. "God doth know that in the day ye eat thereof, then your eyes shall be opened, and ye shall be as gods, knowing good and evil."

In these words two privileges are asserted: one, That their eyes should be opened; the other, That they should be as gods, knowing good and evil. The first is very desirable, and was not at all abridged by them; the second, as to their knowing good and evil, was absolutely forbidden; because they could not attain to the knowledge of that which was evil, but by transgressing, or by eating of that forbidden tree.

Hence observe, That it is usual with the devil, in his tempting of poor creatures, to put a good and bad together, that by shew of the good, the tempted might be drawn to do that which in truth is evil. Thus he served Saul; he spared the best of the herd and flock, under pretence of sacrificing to God, and so transgressed the plain command (1 Sam 15:20-22). But this the apostle saw was dangerous, and therefore censureth such, as in a state of condemnation (Rom 3:8). Thus he served Adam; he put the desirableness of sight, and a plain transgression of God's law together, that by the loveliness of the one, they might the easier be brought to do the other. O poor Eve! Do we wonder at thy folly! Doubtless we had done as bad with half the argument of thy temptation.

"Ye shall be as gods." In these words he attempts to beget in them a desire to be greater than God had made them (1 Tim 3:6). He knew this was a likely way, for by this means he fell himself; for being puffed up with pride, they left their own estate, or habitation, and so became devils, and were tumbled down to hell, where they are "reserved in everlasting chains, under darkness, unto the judgment of the great day" (Jude 6).

"Ye shall be as gods." When souls have begun to hearken to the tempter, that hearkening hath made way for, and given way to so much darkness of mind, and hardness of heart, that now they can listen to anything: as to hear God charged with folly, "Ye shall not surely die"; as to hear him made the author of ignorance, and that he delights to have it so, by seeking by a command to prohibit them from knowing what they could; for God doth know, that in the day ye eat thereof, then your eyes shall be opened; and therefore he forbids to touch it.

"Ye shall be as gods." Here is also a pretence of holiness, which he knew they were prone unto; "Ye shall be as gods," as knowing and perfect as God. Oh! Thousands are, even to this day, by such temptations overcome! Thus he wraps his temptations up in such kind of words and suggestions as will carry it either way. But mark his holiness, or the way that he prescribes for holiness; it is, if not point blank against, yet without and besides the word, not by doing what God commands, and abhorring what he forbids, but by following the delusion of the devil, and their own roving fancies; as Eve here does.

Ver. 6. "And when the woman saw that the tree *was* good for food, and that it *was* pleasant to the eyes, and a tree to be desired to make *one* wise, she took of the fruit thereof," &c.

This verse presents us with the use that Eve made of the reasonings of the serpent; and that was, to take them into consideration; not by the word of God, but as her flesh and blood did sense them: A way very dangerous and devouring to the soul, from which Paul fled, as from the devil himself: "Immediately I conferred not with flesh and blood" (Gal 1:16). Wherefore, pausing upon them, they entangled her as with a threefold cord. 1. "The lust of the flesh"; she saw it was good for food. 2. "The lust of the eye"; she saw it was pleasant to the eye. 3. "The pride of life"; a tree to be desired, to make one wise (1 John 2:16). Being taken, I say, with these three snares of the adversary, which are not of the Father, but of the world, and the devil the prince thereof, forthwith she falls before him: "And when the woman saw" this, "she took of the fruit thereof, and did eat."

"And when the woman saw." This seeing, as I said, is to be understood of her considering what Satan presented to her, and of her sensing or tasting of his doctrine; not by the word, which ought to be the touch stone of all, but by and according to her own natural reason without it. Now this makes her forget that very command that but now she had urged against the tempter: This makes her also to consent to that very reason, as an inducement to transgress; which, because it was the nature of the tree, was by God suggested as a reason why they should forbear; it was the tree of the knowledge of good and evil, therefore they should not touch it; it was the tree, that would by touching it, make them know good and evil; therefore she toucheth, and also eateth thereof. See therefore what specious pretences the devil, and those that are under the power of temptation, will have to transgress the command of God. That which God makes a reason of the prohibition, even that the devil will make a reason of their transgression.

God commands to self-denial, but the world makes that a reason of their standing off from the very grace of God in the gospel. God also commands, That we be sober, chaste, humble, just, and the like; but the devil, and carnal hearts, make these very things the argument that keeps sinners from the word of salvation. Or rather take it thus; God forbids wickedness, because it is delightful to the flesh, and draws the heart from God, but therefore carnal men love wickedness and sin: Therefore they go on in sin, and "therefore they say unto God, Depart from us, for we desire not the knowledge of thy ways" (Job 21:14; 22:15-17).

She "did eat, and gave also unto her husband with her, and he did eat."

The great design of the devil, as he supposed, was now accomplished; for he had both in the snare, both the man and his wife, and in them, the whole world that should be after. And indeed the chief design of Satan was at the head at first, only he made the weakest the conveyance for his mischief. Hence note again, That Satan by tempting one, may chiefly intend the destruction of another. By tempting the wife, he may aim at the destruction of the husband; by tempting the father, he may design the destruction of the children; and by tempting the king, he may design the ruin of the subjects. Even as in the case of David: "Satan stood up against Israel, and provoked David to number the people." He had a mind to destroy seventy thousand, therefore he tempted David to sin (1 Chron 21:1).

She gave also to her husband, and he did eat. Sin seldom or never terminates in one person; but the pernicious example of one, doth animate and embolden another; or thus, the beholding of evil in another, doth often allure a stander-by. Adam was the looker-on, he was not in the action as from the serpent: "Adam was not deceived," that is, by having to do with the devil, "but the woman, the woman being deceived, was in the transgression" (1 Tim 2:14). This should exhort all men that they take heed of so much as beholding evil done by others, lest also they should be allured. When Israel went into Canaan, God did command them not so much as to ask, How those nations served their gods? lest by so doing, Satan should get an advantage of their minds, to incline them to do the like (Deu 12:30). Evil acts, as well as evil words, will eat as doth a canker. This then is the reason of that evil-favouredness that you see attending some men's lives and professions; they have been corrupted, as Adam was, either by evil words or bad examples, even till the very face of their lives and professions are disfigured as with the pox or canker (2 Tim 2:17).

Thus have we led you through that woeful tragedy that was acted between the woman and the serpent; and have also shewed, how it happened that the serpent went away as victor.

1. The woman admitted of a doubt about the truth of the word that forbad her to eat; for unbelief was the first sin that entered the world.

2. She preferred the privileges of the flesh, before the argument to self-denial; by which means her heart became hardened, and grew senseless of the dread and terror of the words of God.

3. She took Satan's arguments into consideration, and sensed,[9] or tasted them; not by the word of God, but her own natural, or rather sore-deluded fancy.

4. She had a mind to gratify the lusts of the flesh, the lusts of the eyes, and the pride of life.

Now to speak of the evil consequences that followed this sinful act: That is not in the wisdom of mortal man to do; partly, because we know but in part even the evil and destructive nature of sin; and partly, because much of the evil that will follow this action, is yet to be committed by persons unborn. Yet enough might be said to astonish the heavens, and to make them horribly afraid (Jer 2:12). 1. By this act of these two, the whole world became guilty of condemnation and eternal judgment (Rom 5). 2. By this came all the blindness, atheism, ignorance of God, enmity and malice against him, pride, covetousness, adultery, idolatry, and implacableness, &c., that is found in all the world. By this, I say, came all the wars, blood, treachery, tyranny, persecution, with all manner of rapine and outrage that is found among the sons of men. 3. Besides, all the plagues, judgments, and evils that befal us in this world, with those everlasting burnings that will swallow up millions for ever and ever; all and every whit of these came into the world as the portion of mankind, for that first transgression of our first parents.

Ver. 7. "And the eyes of them both were opened, and they knew that they *were* naked; and they sewed fig-leaves together, and made themselves aprons."

That their eyes might be opened, was one branch of the temptation, and one of the reasons that prevailed with the woman to forsake the word of God: But she little thought of seeing after this manner, or such things as now she was made to behold. She expected some sweet and pleasant sight, that might tickle and delight her deluded fancy; but behold, sin and the wrath of God appears, to the shaking of their hearts! And thus, even to this very day, doth the devil delude the world: His temptations are gilded with some sweet and fine pretences; either they shall be wiser, richer, more in favour, live merrier, fare better, or something; and that they shall see it, if they will but obey the devil: Which the fools easily are, by these and such like things, allured to do. But behold, when their eyes are opened, instead of seeing what the devil falsely told them, they see themselves involved in sin, made guilty of the breach of God's command, and subject to the wrath of God.[10]

"And they knew that they *were* naked." Not only naked of outward clothing, but even destitute of righteousness; they had lost their innocency, their uprightness, and sinless vail, and had made themselves polluted creatures, both in their hearts and in their flesh; this is nakedness indeed; such a kind of nakedness as Aaron made Israel naked with, when he set up his idol calf for them to worship: "For Aaron had made them naked unto *their* shame" (Exo 32:25). Naked before the justice of the law.

"And they knew that they *were* naked." And they knew it: Why, did they not know it before? The text says, They were naked, and were not ashamed. O! they stood not naked before God! they stood not without righteousness, or uprightness before him, and therefore were not ashamed, but now they knew they were naked as to that.

"And they sewed fig-leaves together, and made themselves aprons." A fit resemblance of what is the inclination of awakened men, who are yet but natural! They neither think of Christ, or of the mercy of God in him for pardon, but presently they betake themselves to their own fig-leaves, to their own inventions, or to the righteousness of the law, and look for healing from means which God did never provide for cure. "When Ephraim saw his sickness, and Judah *saw* his wound, then went Ephraim to the Assyrian" (Hosea 5:13). Not to God, and sent to King Jarib, not to Christ, yet could they not heal him, nor cure him of his wound.

"And made themselves aprons." Not coats, as God did afterwards. A carnal man thinks himself sufficiently clothed with righteousness, if the nakedness which he sees, can be but covered from his own sight: As if God also did see that and only that which they have a sight of by the light of nature; and as if because fig-leaves would hide their nakedness from their sight, that therefore they would hide it from the sight of God. But alas! No man, without the help of another, can bring all his nakedness to the sight of his own eye; much is undiscovered to him, that may yet lie open and bare to a stander-by: So it is with the men that stand without Christ before God, at best they see but some of their nakedness, to wit, their most gross and worst faults, and therefore they seek to cover them; which when they have hid from their own sight, they think them hid also from the sight of God. Thus did Adam, he saw his own most shameful parts, and therefore them he covered: They made themselves aprons, or things to gird about them, not to cover them all over withal. No man by all his own doings can hide all his own nakedness from the sight of the justice of God, and yet, but in vain, as busy as Adam to do it.

"And they sewed fig-leaves together, and made themselves aprons." Fig-leaves! A poor apron, but it was the best they could get. But was that a sufficient shelter against either thorn or thistle? Or was it possible but that after a while these fig-leaves should have become rotten, and turned to dung? So will it be with all man's own righteousness which is of the law; Paul saw it so, and therefore counted it but loss and dung, that he might win Christ, and be found in him (Phil 3:7,8).

> Ver. 8. "And they heard the voice of the Lord God walking in the garden in the cool of the day: and Adam and his wife hid themselves from the

presence of the Lord God, among the trees of the garden."

"And they heard the voice of the Lord God." This voice was not to be understood according, as if it was the effect of a word; as when we speak, the sound remains with a noise for some time after; but by voice here, we are to understand the Lord Christ himself; wherefore this voice is said to walk, not to sound only: "They heard the voice of the Lord God walking." This voice John calls the word, the word that was with the Father before he made the world, and that at this very time was heard to walk in the garden of Adam: Therefore John also saith, this voice was in the beginning; that is, in the garden with Adam, at the beginning of his conversion, as well as of the beginning of the world (John 1:1).

"And they heard the voice of the Lord God walking in the garden in the cool of the day." The gospel of it is, in the season of grace; for by the cool of the day, he here means, in the patience, gentleness, goodness and mercy of the gospel; and it is opposed to the heat, fire, and severity of the law.

"And Adam and his wife hid themselves." Hence observe, That a man's own righteousness will not fortify his conscience from fear and terror, when God begins to come near to him to judgment. Why did Adam hide himself, but because, as he said, he was naked? But how could he be naked, when before he had made himself an apron? O! the approach of God consumed and burnt off his apron! Though his apron would keep him from the sight of a bird, yet it would not from the eye of the incorruptible God.

Let therefore all self-righteous men beware, for however they at present please themselves with the worthiness of their glorious fig-leaves; yet when God shall come to deal with them for sin, assuredly they will find themselves naked.[11]

"And they hid themselves." A man in a natural state, cannot abide the presence of God; yea, though a righteous man. Adam, though adorned with his fig-leaves, flies.

Observe again, That a self-righteous man, a man of the law, takes grace and mercy for his greatest enemy. This is apparent from the carriage of the Pharisees to Jesus Christ, who because they were wedded to the works of their own righteousness, therefore they hated, persecuted, condemned, and crucified the Saviour of the world. As here in the text, though the voice of the Lord God walked in the garden in the cool of the day, in the time of grace and love, yet how Adam with his fig-leaves flies before him.

"And Adam and his wife hid themselves from the presence of the Lord God." These latter words are spoken, not to persuade us that men can hide themselves from God, but that Adam, and those that are his by nature, will seek to do it, because they do not know him aright. These words therefore further shew us what a bitter thing sin is to the soul; it is only for hiding work, sometimes under its fig-leaves, sometimes among the trees of the garden. O what a shaking, starting, timorous evil conscience, is a sinful and guilty conscience! especially when 'tis but a little awakened, it could run its head into every hole, first by one fancy, then by another; for the power and goodness of a man's own righteousness, cannot withstand or answer the demands of the justice of God, and his holy law.

"And Adam and his wife hid themselves from the presence of the Lord God, among the trees of the garden." If you take the trees in a mystical sense as sometimes they may be taken (Eze 31:8-11); then take them here to signify, or to be a type of the saints of God, and then the gospel of it is, That carnal men, when they are indeed awakened, and roused out of their foolish fig-leaf righteousness; then they would be glad of some shelter with them that are saved and justified freely by grace, as they in the Gospel of Matthew; "Give us of your oil; for our lamps are gone out" (Matt 25:8). And again, The man without the wedding garment had crowded himself among the wedding guests: Had hid themselves among the trees of the garden (Matt 22:11).

Ver. 9. "And the Lord God called unto Adam, and said unto him, Where *art* thou?"

Adam having eaten of the forbidden tree, doth now fleet his station, is gone to another than where God left him. Wherefore, if God will find Adam, he must now look him where he had hid himself. And indeed so he does with "Adam, where art thou?"

"And the Lord God called," &c. Here begins the conversion of Adam, from his sinful state, to God again. But mark, it begins not at Adam's calling upon God, but at God calling upon him: "And the Lord God called unto Adam." Wherefore, by these words, we are to understand the beginning of Adam's conversion. And indeed, grace hath gone the same way with the elect, from that time to this day. Thus he dealt with Abraham, Isaac and Jacob; he called them from their native country, the country of their kindred. And hence it is, that, especially in the New Testament, the saints are said to be the Called; "Called of God," and "Called of Jesus Christ." And hence again it is that Calling is by Paul made the first demonstration of election, and that saints are admonished to prove their election by their calling; for as Adam was in a lost, miserable and perishing condition, until God called him out of those holes into which sin had driven him: so we do lie where sin and the devil hath laid us, until by the word of God we are called to the fellowship of his Son Jesus Christ.

By these words therefore we have the beginning of the discovery of effectual calling or conversion; "And the Lord God called": In which call observe three things,

1. God called so that Adam heard him. And so it is in the conversion of the New Testament saints, as Paul says, "If ye have heard him, and have been taught by him, as the truth is in Jesus" (Eph 4:21). That therefore is one discovery of effectual calling, the sinner is made to HEAR him, even to hear him distinctly, singling out the very person, calling, "Adam, Where art thou?" "Saul, Saul, why persecutest thou me?" I have called thee by thy name, thou art mine. As he also said to Moses, "I know thee by name, and thou hast also found grace in my sight" (Exo 33:12).

2. God called so, as to fasten sin upon his conscience, and as to force a confession from him of his naked and shameful state.

3. God called so, as to make him tremble under, and be afraid of the judgment of God.

"And the Lord God called unto Adam, and said unto him, Where *art* thou?" Indeed, Where art thou must of necessity be forcibly urged to every man on whose soul God doth work effectual conversion; for until the person is awakened, as to the state and condition he is in, he will not desire, nay, will not endure to be turned to God; but when in truth they are made to see what condition sin hath brought them to, namely, that it hath laid them under the power of sin, the tyranny of the devil, the strength of death, and the curse of God by his holy law; then is mercy sweet.

"Where art thou?" God knew where he was, but foolish Adam thought otherwise; he thought to hide himself from the presence of the Lord, but the Lord found him out. Indeed, deluded sinners think that they can hide themselves and sins from God. "How doth God know," say they, "Can he judge through the thick cloud?" (Job 22:13). But such shall know he sees them; they shall know it, either to their correction, or to their condemnation. "Though they dig into hell," saith God, "thence shall mine hand take them; though they climb up to heaven, thence will I bring them down: And though they hide themselves in the top of Carmel, I will search and take them out thence," &c. (Amos 9:2,3).[12] "Can any hide himself in secret places that I shall not see him, saith the Lord? Do not I fill heaven and earth? saith the Lord" (Jer 23:24).

Ver. 10. "And he said, I heard thy voice in the garden, and I was afraid, because I *was* naked; and I hid myself."

This then was the cause of his flying, he heard the voice of God: A wicked and evil conscience saith, every thing is to it as the messenger of death and destruction; for, as was said before, "the voice of the Lord walked in the garden in the cool of the day," in the time of grace and mercy. But it mattereth not whether he came with grace or vengeance; guilt was in Adam's heart, therefore he could not endure the presence of God: He "that doeth evil hateth the light" (John 3:20). And again, "The wicked flee when no man pursueth" (Pro 28:1). Cain thought all that met him, would seek his blood and life.

"I heard thy voice." Something by the word of God was spoken, that shook the heart of this poor creature; something of justice and holiness, even before they fell into this communication: for observe it, Adam went forthwith from the tree of knowledge of good and evil a convinced man, first to his fig-leaves, but they would not do; therefore he seeks to be hid among the trees. And observe again, That the insufficiency of fig-leaves were discovered by this voice of the Lord God, that at this time walked in the garden: "I heard thy voice in the garden, and I was afraid, because I *was* naked; and I hid myself." So then, there was a first and second voice which Adam heard; the first he ran away from, "I heard thy voice, and hid myself." The second was this, wherein they commune each with other. The first therefore was the word of justice, severity, and of the vengeance of God; like that in the 19th of Exodus, from the pronouncing of which, a trembling, and almost death, did seize six hundred thousand persons.

"I heard thy voice in the garden." It is a word from without that doth it. While Adam listened to his own heart, he thought fig-leaves a sufficient remedy, but the voice that walked in the garden shook him out of all such fancies: "I heard thy voice in the garden, and I was afraid, because I *was* naked; and I hid myself."

> Ver. 11. "And he said, Who told thee that thou *wast* naked? Hast thou eaten of the tree, whereof I commanded thee that thou shouldest not eat?"

"Who told thee?" This, as I said before, supposeth a third person, a preacher, and that was the Son of God; the voice of the Lord God that walked in the garden.

"Hast thou eaten of the tree?" That is, If thou hast been shewed thy nakedness, thou hast indeed sinned; for the voice of the Lord God will not charge guilt, but where and when a law hath been transgressed. God therefore, by these words, driveth Adam to the point, either to confess or deny the truth of the case. If he confess, then he concludes himself under judgment; if he deny, then he addeth to his sin: Therefore he neither denieth nor confesseth, but so as he may lessen and extenuate his sin.

> Ver. 12. "And the man said, The woman whom thou gavest *to be* with me, she gave me of the tree, and I did eat."

He had endeavoured with fig-leaves to hide his transgressions before, but that being found too scanty and short, he now trieth what he can do with arguments. Indeed he acknowledgeth that he did eat of the tree of which he was forbidden; but mark where he layeth the reason: Not in any infection which was centred in him by reason of his listening to the discourse which was between the woman and the serpent; but because God had given him a woman to be with him: "The woman whom thou gavest *to be* with me, she gave me of the tree." The woman was given for an help, not an hindrance; but

Satan often maketh that to become our snare, which God hath given us as a blessing. Adam therefore here mixeth truth with falsehood. It is true, he was beguiled by the woman; but she was not intended of God, as he would insinuate, to the end she might be a trap unto him. Here therefore Adam sought to lessen and palliate his offence, as man by nature is prone to do; for if God will needs charge them with the guilt of sin for the breach of the law, they will lay the fault upon anything, even upon God's ordinance, as Adam here doth, rather than they will honestly fall under the guilt, and so the judgment of the law for guilt. It is a rare thing, and it argueth great knowledge of God, and also hope in his mercy, when men shall heartily acknowledge their iniquities, as is evident in the case of David: "Wash me thoroughly from mine iniquity, and cleanse me from my sin. For I acknowledge my transgressions: and my sin *is* ever before me" (Psa 51:2,3). But his knowledge is not at first in young converts; therefore when God begins to awaken, they begin, as sleepy men, to creep further under their carnal covering; which yet is too short to hide them, and too narrow to cover their shame (Isa 28:20).

"The woman whom thou gavest *to be* with me, she gave me of the tree." Although, as I said, this sinner seeks to hide, or at least to lessen his sin, by laying the cause upon the woman, the gift of God; yet it argueth that his heart was now filled with shame and confusion of face, for that he had broken God's command; for indeed it is the nature of guilt, however men may in appearance ruffle under it, and set the best leg before, for their vindication; yet inwardly to make them blush and fail before their accuser. Indeed their inward shame is the cause of their excuse; even as Aaron, when he had made the golden calf, could not for shame of heart confess in plainness of speech the truth of the fact to his brother

Moses, but faulteringly: They gave me their gold, saith he, and "I cast it into the fire, and there came out this calf" (Exo 32:24). "And there came out this calf"; a pitiful fumbling speech: The Holy Ghost saith, Aaron had made them naked; "had made them naked unto *their* shame," for he, as also Adam, should, being chief and lord in their place, have stoutly resisted the folly and sin which was to them propounded; and not as persons of a womanish spirit, have listened to wicked proposals.[13]

Ver. 13. "And the Lord God said unto the woman, What *is* this *that* thou hast done?" &c.,

---

Forasmuch as Adam did acknowledge his sin, though with much weakness and infirmity, God accepts thereof; and now applieth himself to the woman, whom Satan had used as his engine to undo the world.

Hence observe, That when God sets to search out sin, he will follow it from the seduced to the seducer, even till he comes to the rise and first author thereof, as in the following words may more clearly appear. Not that he excuseth or acquitteth the seduced, because the seducer was the first cause, as some do vainly imagine; but to lay all under guilt who are concerned therein: the woman was concerned as a principal, therefore he taketh her to examination.

"And the Lord God said unto the woman, What *is* this *that* thou hast done?" What is this? God seems to speak as if he were astonished at the inundation of evil which the woman by her sin had overflowed the world withal: "What *is* this *that* thou hast done!" Thou hast undone thyself, thou hast undone thy husband, thou hast undone all the world; yea, thou hast brought a curse upon the whole creation, with an overplus of evils, plagues, and distresses.

"What *is* this *that* thou hast done!" Thou hast defiled thy body and soul, thou hast disabled the whole world from serving God; yea, moreover, thou hast let in the devil at the door of thy heart, and hast also made him the prince of the world. "What *is* this *that* thou hast done!" Ah! little, little do sinners know what they have done, when they have transgressed the law of the Lord. I say, they little know what death, what plagues, what curse, yea, what hell they, by so doing, have prepared for themselves.

"What *is* this *that* thou hast done!" God therefore, by these words, would fasten upon the woman's heart a deep sense of the evil of her doings. And indeed, for the soul to be brought into a deep sense of its sin, to cry out before God, Ah! what have I done! it is with them the first step towards conversion: "Acknowledge thy iniquity [saith God] that thou hast transgressed against me" (Jer 3:13). And again, "If we confess our sins, he is faithful and just to forgive us *our* sins, and to cleanse us from all unrighteousness" (1 John 1:9). The want of this is the cause of that obdurate and lasting hardness that continueth to possess so many thousands of sinners, they cry not out before God, What have I done? but foolishly they rush into, and continue in sin, "till their iniquity be found to be hateful," yea, their persons, because of their sin.

"What *is* this *that* thou hast done?" By this interrogatory the Lord also implieth an admonition to the woman, to plead for herself, as he also did to her husband. He also makes way for the working of his bowels towards her, which (as will be shewn anon) he flatly denies to the serpent, the devil: I say he made way for the woman to plead for, or bemoan herself; an evident token that he was unwilling to cast her away for her sin: "I have surely heard Ephraim bemoaning himself; - I will surely have mercy upon him, saith the Lord" (Jer 31:18-20). Again, by these words, he made way for the working or yearning of his own bowels over her; for when we begin to cry out of our miscarriages, and to bewail and bemoan our condition because of sin, forthwith the bowels of God begin to sound, and to move towards his distressed creature, as by the place before alleged appears. "I have surely heard Ephraim bemoaning himself;—therefore my bowels are troubled for him: I will surely have mercy upon him, saith the Lord." See also the 11th and 14th chapters of Hosea.

"And the woman said, the serpent beguiled me and I did eat." A poor excuse, but an heart affecting one; for many times want of wit and cunning to defend ourselves, doth affect and turn the heart of a stander-by to pity us. And thus, as I think, it was with the woman; she had to do with one that was too cunning for her, with one that snapt her by his subtilty or wiles; which also the woman most simply confesses, even to the provoking of God to take vengeance for her.

Ver. 14. "And the Lord God said unto the serpent, Because thou hast done this, thou *art* cursed above all cattle, and above every beast of the field."

The serpent was the author of the evil; therefore the thunder rolls till it comes over him, the hot burning thunder-bolt falls upon him.

The Lord, you see, doth not with the serpent as with the man and his wife; to wit, minister occasion to commune with him, but directly pronounceth him cursed above all, "above every beast of the field." This sheweth us, that as concerning the angels that fell, with them God is at eternal enmity, reserving them in everlasting chains under darkness. Cursed art thou: By these words, I say, they are prevented of a plea for ever, and also excluded a share in the fruits of the Messiah which should afterwards be born into the world (Heb 2:2).

"Because thou hast done this, cursed art thou." "Because thou hast done this": Not as though he was blessed before; for had he not before been wicked, he had not attempted so wicked a design. The meaning then is, That either by this deed the devil did aggravate his misery, and make himself the faster to hang in the everlasting chains under darkness; or else by this he is manifested to us to be indeed a cursed creature.

Further, "Because thou hast done this," may also signify how great complacency and content God took in Adam and his wife while they continued without transgression; But how much against his mind and workmanship this wicked work was. 1. Against his mind; for sin so sets itself against the nature of God, that, if possible, it would annihilate and turn him into nothing, it being in its nature point blank against him. 2. It is against his workmanship; for had not the power of the Messias stept in, all had again been brought to confusion, and worse than nothing: as Christ himself expresses it: "The earth, and all the inhabitants thereof, are dissolved: I bear up the pillars of it" (Psa 75:3). And again, "He upholdeth all things by the word of his power" (Heb 1:3).

Besides, this being done, man, notwithstanding the grace of God, and the merits of Jesus Christ, doth yet live a miserable life in this world; for albeit that Christ hath most certainly secured the elect and chosen of God from perishing by what Satan hath done; yet the very elect themselves are, by reason of the first transgression, so infested and annoyed with inward filth, and so assaulted still by the devil, and his vassals the proper children of hell, that they groan unutterably under their burthen; yea, all creatures, "the whole creation groaneth and travaileth in pain together until now" (Rom 8:22). And that most principally upon the very account of this first sin of Adam; it must needs be therefore, this being so high an affront to the divine majesty, and so directly destructive to the work of his hands; and the aim of the devil most principally also at the most excellent of his creation (for man was created in God's own image) that he should hereat be so highly offended, had they not sinned at all before, to bind them over for this very fact to the pains of the eternal judgment of God.

Ver. 15. "And I will put enmity between thee and the woman, and between thy seed and her seed; it shall bruise thy head, and thou shalt bruise his heel."

The woman may, in this place, be taken either really or figuratively; if really and naturally, then the threatening is also true, as to the very natures of the creatures here under consideration, to wit, the serpent and the woman, and so all that come of human race; for we find that so great an antipathy is between all such deadly beasts, as serpents and human creatures, that they abiding in their own natures, it is not possible they should ever be reconciled: "I will put enmity": I will put it. This enmity then was not infused in creation, but afterwards; and that as a punishment for the abuse of the subtlety of the serpent; for before the fall, and before the serpent was assumed by the fallen angels, they were, being God's creatures, "good," as the rest in their kind; neither was there any jarring or violence put between them; but after the serpent was become the devil's vizor, then was an enmity begot between them.

"I will put enmity between thee and the serpent." If by woman, we here understand the church, (but then we must understand the devil, not the natural serpent simply,) then also the threatening is most true; for between the church of God, and the devil, from the beginning of the world, hath been maintained most mighty wars and conflicts, to which there is not a like in all the blood shed on the earth. Yea, here there cannot be a reconciliation, (the enmity is still maintained by God): The reason is, because their natural dispositions and inclinations, together with their ends and purposes, are most repugnant each to other, even full as much as good and evil, righteousness and sin, God's glory, and an endeavour after his utter extirpation.

Indeed, Satan hath tried many ways to be at amity with the church; not because he loves her holiness, but because he hates her welfare, (wherefore such amity must only be dissembled,) and that he might bring about his enterprise, he sometimes hath allured with the dainty delicates of this world, the lusts of the flesh, of the eyes, and the pride of life: This being fruitless, he hath attempted to entangle and bewitch her with his glorious appearance, as an angel of light; and to that end hath made his ministers as the ministers of righteousness, preaching up righteousness, and contending for a divine and holy worship (2 Cor 11:12-15): but this failing also, he hath taken in hand at length to fright her into friendship with him, by stirring up the hellish rage of tyrants to threaten and molest her; by finding out strange inventions to torment and afflict her children; by making many bloody examples of her own bowels, before her eyes, if by that means he might at last obtain his purpose: But behold! all hath been in vain, there can be no reconciliation. And why, but because God himself maintains the enmity?

And this is the reason why the endeavours of all the princes and potentates of the earth, that have through ignorance or malice managed his design against the church, have fallen to the ground, and been of none effect.

God hath maintained the enmity: doubtless the mighty wonder, that their laws cannot be obeyed;[14] I mean their laws and statutes, which by the suggestion of the prince of this world they have made against the church: But if they understood but this one sentence, they might a little perceive the reason. God hath put enmity between the devil and the woman; between that old serpent called, The Devil and Satan, and the holy, and beloved, and espoused wife of Christ.

"I will put enmity between thee and the woman, and between thy seed and her seed." The seeds here are the children of both, but that of the woman, especially Christ (Gal 3:16). "God sent forth his Son made of a woman" (Gal 4:4). Whether you take it literally or figuratively; for in a mystery the church is the mother of Jesus Christ, though naturally, or according to His flesh, He was born of the virgin Mary, and proceeded from her womb: But take it either way, the enmity hath been maintained, and most mightily did shew itself against the whole kingdom of the devil, and death, and hell; by the undertaking, engaging, and war which the Son of God did maintain against them, from his conception, to his death and exaltation to the right hand of the Father, as is prophesied of, and promised in the text, "It shall bruise thy head."

"It shall bruise thy head." By head, we are to understand the whole power, subtilty, and destroying nature of the devil; for as in the head of the serpent lieth his power, subtilty, and poisonous nature; so in sin, death, hell, and the wisdom of the flesh, lieth the very strength of the devil himself. Take away sin then, and death is not hurtful: "The sting of death is sin": And take away the condemning power of the law, and sin doth cease to be charged, or to have any more hurt in it, so as to destroy the soul: "The strength of sin is the law" (1 Cor 15:56). Wherefore, the seed, Jesus Christ, in his bruising the head of the serpent, must take away sin, abolish death, and conquer the power of the grave. But how must this be done? Why, he must remove the curse, which makes sin intolerable, and death destructive. But how must he take away the curse? Why, by taking upon Him "flesh," as we (John 1:14); by being made "under the law," as we (Gal 4:4); by being made "to be sin for us" (2 Cor 5:21), and by being "made a curse for us" (Gal 3:10-13). He standing therefore in our room, under the law and the justice of God, did both bear, and overcome the curse, and so did bruise the power of the devil.

"It shall bruise thy head." To bruise is more than to break; he shall quash thy head to death; so he also quashed the heel of Christ; which would, had not his eternal power and Godhead sustained, have caused that he had perished for ever.

"And thou shalt bruise his heel." By these words, a necessity was laid upon Jesus Christ to assume our flesh, to engage the devil therein; and also because of the curse that was due to us for sin, that he might indeed deliver us therefore; even for awhile to fall before this curse, and to die that death that the curse inflicteth: "Christ hath redeemed us from the curse of the law, being made a curse for us." Thus therefore did Satan, that is, by the fruits and effects of sin, bruise, or kill, the flesh of Christ: But he being God, as the Father, it was not possible he should be overcome. Therefore his head remaineth untouched. A man's life lieth not in his heel, but in his head and heart; but the Godhead being the head and heart of the manhood, it was not possible Satan should meddle with that; he only could bruise his heel; which yet by the power of the Godhead of this eternal Son of the Father, was raised up again from the dead: "He was delivered for our offences, and was raised again for our justification" (Rom 4:25).

In these words therefore the Lord God gave Adam a promise, That notwithstanding Satan had so far brought his design to pass, as to cause them by falling from the command, to lay themselves open to the justice and wrath of God; yet his enterprise by grace, should be made of none effect. As if the Lord had said, "Adam, thou seest how the devil hath overcome thee; how he, by thy consenting to his temptation, hath made thee a subject of death and hell: but though he hath by this means made thee a spectacle of misery, even an heir of death and damnation: yet I am God, and thy sins have been against me. Now because I have grace and mercy, I will therefore design thy recovery. But how shall I bring it to pass? Why I will give my Son out of my bosom, who shall in your room, and in your nature encounter this adversary, and overcome him. But how? Why, by fulfilling my law, and by answering the penalties thereof. He shall bring in a righteousness which shall be "everlasting," by which I will justify you from sin, and the curse of God due thereto: But this work will make him smart, he must be made "a man of sorrows," for upon him will I lay your iniquities (Isa 53:6); Satan shall bruise his heel."

> Ver. 16. "Unto the woman he said, I will greatly multiply thy sorrow and thy conception; in sorrow[15] shalt thou bring forth children; and thy desire *shall be* to thy husband, and he shall rule over thee."

"I will greatly multiply thy sorrow," &c. This is true, whether you respect the woman according to the letter of the text, or as she was a figure of the church; for in both senses their sorrows for sin are great, and multiplied upon them: The whole heap of the female sex know the first,[16] the church only knows the second.

"In sorrow shalt thou bring forth children." The more fruitful, the more afflicted is the church in this world; because the rage of hell, and the enmity of the world, are by her righteousness set on fire so much the more.

But again: Forasmuch as the promise is made before this judgment of God for sin is threatened, we must count these afflictions not as coming from the hand of God in a way of vengeance, for want of satisfaction for the breach of the law; but to shew and keep us in mind of his holiness, that henceforth we should not, as at first through ignorance, so now from notions of grace and mercy, presume to continue in sin.

I might add, That by these words it is manifest, that a promise of mercy and forgiveness of sin, and great afflictions and rebukes for the same, may and shall attend the same soul: "I will greatly multiply thy sorrow," comes after the promise of grace.

"And thy desire shall be to thy husband, and he shall rule over thee." Doubtless the woman was, in her first creation, made in subordination to her husband, and ought to have been under obedience to him: Wherefore, still that had remained a duty, had they never transgressed the commandment of God; but observe, the duty is here again not only enjoined, and imposed, but that as the fruit of the woman's sin; wherefore, that duty that before she might do as her natural right by creation, she must now do as the fruits of her disobedience to God. Women therefore, whenever they would perk it and lord it over their husbands, ought to remember, that both by creation and transgression they are made to be in subjection to their own husbands. This conclusion makes Paul himself: "Let [saith he] the woman learn in silence with all subjection. But I suffer not a woman to teach, nor to usurp authority over the man, but to be in silence; for Adam was first formed, then Eve; and Adam was not deceived, but the woman being deceived, was in the transgression" (1 Tim 2:11-14).

> Ver. 17. "And unto Adam he said, Because thou hast hearkened unto the voice of thy wife, and hast eaten of the tree of which I commanded thee, saying, Thou shalt not eat of it: cursed *is* the ground for thy sake, in sorrow shalt thou eat *of* it all the days of thy life."

God having laid his censure upon the woman, he now proceedeth and cometh to her husband, and also layeth his judgment on him: The judgment is, "Cursed *is* the ground for thy sake," and in sorrow thou shalt eat thereof. The causes of this judgment are, First, For that "he hearkened to his wife": And also, "For that he had eaten of the tree."

"Because thou hast hearkened to thy wife." Why? Because therein he left his station and headship, the condition which God had appointed him, and gave way to his wife to assume it, contrary to the order of creation, of her relation, and of her sex; for God had made Adam lord and chief, who ought to have taught his wife, and not to have become her scholar.

Hence note, That the man that suffereth his wife to take his place, hath already transgressed the order of God.[17]

"Because thou hast hearkened to the voice," &c. Wicked women, such as Eve was now, if hearkened unto, are "the snares of death" to their husbands; for, because they are weaker built, and because the devil doth easier fasten with them than with men, therefore they are more prone to vanity and all mis-orders in the matters of God, than they; [the men] and so, if hearkened unto, more dangerous upon many accounts: "Did not Solomon king of Israel sin by these things? yet among many nations was there no king like him, who was beloved of his God, nevertheless even him did outlandish [wicked] women cause to sin" (Neh 13:26). "But there was none like unto Ahab, which did sell himself to work wickedness in the sight of the Lord, whom Jezebel his wife stirred up" (1 Kings 21:25).

Hence note further, That if it be thus dangerous for a man to hearken to a wicked wife, how dangerous is it for any to hearken unto wicked whores, who will seldom yield up themselves to the lusts of beastly men, but on condition they will answer their ungodly purposes! What mischief by these things hath come upon souls, countries and kingdoms, will here be too tedious to relate.

"Because thou hast hearkened to the voice of thy wife, and hast eaten of the tree." That is, From the hand of thy wife; for it was she that gave him to eat: "Therefore," &c. Although the scripture doth lay a great blot upon women, and cautioneth man to beware of these fantastical and unstable spirits, yet it limiteth man in his censure: She is only then to be rejected and rebuked, when she doth things unworthy her place and calling. Such a thing may happen, as that the woman, not the man, may be in the right, (I mean, when both are godly,) but ordinarily it is otherwise (Gen 21:12). Therefore the conclusion is, Let God's word judge between the man and his wife, as it ought to have done between Adam and his, and neither of both will do amiss; but contrariwise, they will walk in all the commandments of God without fault (Luke 1:6).

"Therefore cursed *be* the ground for thy sake." Behold what arguments are thrust into every corner, thereby to make man remember his sin; for all the toil of man, all the barrenness of the ground, and all the fruitlessness after all; What is it but the fruits of sin? Let not us then find fault with the weed, with the hotness, coldness, or barrenness of the soil; but by seeing these things, remember our sin, Cursed be the ground "for thy sake"; for this God makes our "heaven as iron," and our "earth as brass" (Exo 26:19). "The Lord shall make the rain of thy land powder and dust; from heaven shall it come down upon thee, until thou be destroyed" (Deu 28:20-24).

"In sorrow shalt thou eat *of* it all the days of thy life." He then is much deceived, who thinks to fill his body with the delicates of this world, and not therewith to drink the cruel venom of asps: Yea, "He shall suck the poison of asps, the viper's tongue shall slay him" (Job 20:16). The reason is, because he that shall give up himself to the lusts and pleasures of this life, he contracts guilt, because he hath sinned; which guilt will curdle all his pleasures, and make the sweetest of them deadly as poison.

"In sorrow shalt thou eat." Even thou that hast received the promise of forgiveness: How then can they do it with pleasure, who eat, and forget the Lord? (Pro 30:9; 31:5).

Again, Let not the sorrows, crosses, and afflictions, that attend the godly in the things of this life, weaken their faith in the promise of grace, and forgiveness of sins; for such things may befal the dearest Christian.

Ver. 18. "Thorns also and thistles shall it bring forth to thee; and thou shalt eat the herb of the field."

This shews us (as I also hinted before), That the thorns and thistles of the ground, are but as the excrements thereof; and the fruits of sin, and the curse for sin. This world, as it dropt from the fingers of God, was far more glorious than it is now: Now it is loaden with a burden of corruption, thorns, thistles, and other annoyances, which Adam knew none of in the days of his innocency. None therefore ever saw this world, as it was in its first creation, but only Adam and his wife; neither shall any ever see it, until the manifestation of the children of God: that is, until the redemption or resurrection of the saints: but then it shall be delivered from the bondage of corruption, into the glorious liberty of the children of God.

"And thou shalt eat the herb of the field." These words are for his comfort, under all the sorrow sin should bring upon him; "Thou shalt eat the herb": The herb was a type of the gospel-comforts which the destroying angels were forbidden to smite (Rev 7:3). Of these medicinal and healing herbs therefore Adam and his seed are admitted to eat, that their soul may be replenished in the midst of their sorrow.

> Ver. 19. "In the sweat of thy face shalt thou eat bread, till thou return unto the ground; for out of it wast thou taken: for dust thou *art*, and unto dust shalt thou return."

"In the sweat of thy face." This is true, whether literally or allegorically understood: For as touching the things that pertain to this life, as they become not ours without toil and labour; so the spiritual comforts of the kingdom of heaven are not obtained without travail and sweat: "Labour [saith Christ] for the bread and meat which endureth to everlasting life" (John 6:27).

"In the sweat of thy face." Those that make conscience of walking in the commandments of God, they shall be blessed with the bread of life, when others shall be hunger-bit. That may also be mystically applied, "*On* all hills that shall be digged with the mattock, there shall not come thither the fear of briars and thorns; but it shall be for the sending forth of oxen, and for the treading of lesser cattle" (Isa 7:25). The meaning is, Where people are diligent according to the word of God, especially in spiritual and heavenly things, they shall be fat and flourishing, though sorrow be mixed therewith: "When *men* are cast down: then thou shalt say, *there is lifting up*; and he shall save the humble person" (Job 22:29).

"Till thou return to the ground." A Christian should not leave off sweating labour so long as he is above the ground; even until he returneth thither, he ought to be diligent in the way and worship of God. Jacob, when sick, would worship God, though so weak as not able to do it, without leaning upon the top of his staff: A blessed example for the diligent, and reproof for those that are slothful (Heb 11:21).

"For out of it wast thou taken." That is, out of the ground. Behold how the Lord doth mix his doctrine! Now he tells him of his sin, then he promiseth to give him a Saviour, then again he shews him the fruits of his sin, and immediately after the comforts of the promise; yet again, he would have him remember that he is but a mortal creature, not to live here for ever; neither made of silver nor gold, but even of a clod of dust: "For dust thou art." Observe therefore, that in the midst of all our enjoyments, God would have us consider our frame, that we may know how frail we are.

"For out of it was thou taken." It is hard for us to believe it, though we daily see it is the way even of all the earth, to return thither again: "For dust thou *art*, and to dust shalt thou return."

Whether this was spoken to Adam, as a judgment, or a mercy, or both, is not hard to determine, (this first premised, that Adam had received the promise;) for as it was the fruit of sin, so a judgment and a token of God's displeasure; "for the wages of sin is death" (Rom 6:23).

But as it is made by the wisdom of God, a prevention of further wickedness, and a conveyance through faith in Christ, to a more perfect enjoyment of God in the heavens; so it is a mercy and blessing of God (Isa 57:1,2); For thus "to die is gain." Wherefore thus we may praise the dead, that are already dead, more than the living, which are yet alive (Eccl 4:2). This made Paul desire to depart; for he knew that through death was the way to have more perfect sight of, and more close and higher communion with the Father, and the Son, and the Spirit in the heavens (2 Cor 5:6). I have a desire to depart, and be with Christ, which is far better (Phil 1:21-23). Thus therefore those things that in their own nature are the proper fruits and wages of sin, may yet through the wisdom of God be turned about for our good (Jer 24:5); but let not this embolden to sin, but rather minister occasion to us to magnify the wisdom of God (Rom 8:28).

Ver. 20. "And Adam called his wife's name Eve; because she was the mother of all living."

By this act Adam returneth to his first station and authority in which God had placed him, from which he fell when he became a scholar to his wife; for to name the creatures, was in Adam a note of sovereignty and power: This he attained to, as an effect of his receiving the promise; for before the promise is received, man cannot serve God in his station, because as he wanteth the power of will, so also a good understanding; but when he hath received the promise, he hath also received the Holy Ghost, which giveth to the godly to know and do his duty in his station: "The spiritual" man discerneth, and so "judgeth all things"; but he is not discerned nor judged of any (1 Cor 2:15).

And he called his wife's name Eve, or Hevah: Because she gave life to, or was the first mother of all mankind. This then admits of two positions. First, That the world was created when Adam was created. And, Secondly, That there were none of the sons of men in the world before Adam, as some have not only vainly, but irreligiously and blasphemously suggested. "Eve is the mother of all living": Not a man therefore that is the son of man, but had his being since the woman was made.

> Ver. 21. "Unto Adam also and to his wife did the Lord God make coats of skins, and clothed them."

By this action the Lord God did preach to Adam, and to his wife, the meaning of that promise that you read of in verse 15. Namely, That by the means of Jesus Christ, God himself would provide a sufficient clothing for those that accept of his grace by the gospel: The coats here, being a type of that blessed and durable righteousness.

"The Lord God made the coats." Not Adam now, because now he is received into a covenant of grace with God: Indeed before he entered into this covenant, he made his own clothing, such as it was, but that could not cover his nakedness; but now the Lord will make them: And "unto Adam also and to his wife did the Lord God make coats": "Their righteousness *is* of me, saith the Lord" (Isa 54:17). Of me, that is, of my providing, of my performing. And this is the name whereby he shall be called, THE LORD OUR RIGHTEOUSNESS" (Jer 23:6).

"He made them coats, and clothed them." As the righteousness by which a sinner stands just in the sight of God from the curse, is a righteousness of God's providing; so also it is of his putting on. No man can put on the righteousness of Christ, otherwise than by God's imputation: if God reckon it ours then it is ours indeed; but if he refuseth to shew that mercy, who can impute that righteousness to me? Blessed are they to whom the Lord imputeth righteousness (Rom 4). Cursed then must they needs be to whom God hath not imputed the righteousness of his Son. "The Lord clothed them," according to that of Paul, "Christ is made unto us of God wisdom and righteousness," &c. (1 Cor 1:30). And of that God who hath made him thus to us, even of him are we in Christ Jesus.

Did the Lord God make coats of skins. The coats were made of the skins of beasts, of the skins of the slain, which were slain either for food only, or for sacrifice also: This being so, the effects of that promise mentioned before were by this action the more clearly expounded unto Adam; to wit, That Christ, "in the fulness of time," should be born of a woman clothed with flesh; and as so considered, should be made a curse, and so die that cursed death which by sin we had brought upon ourselves; the effects and fruits of which should to us be durable clothing; that is, "Everlasting righteousness" (Dan 9:24). Ver. 22, 23. "And the Lord God said, Behold, the man is become as one of us, to know good and evil: and now, [therefore] lest he put forth his hand, and take also of the tree of life, and eat, and live for ever: therefore the Lord God sent him forth from the garden of Eden, to till the ground from whence he was taken."

"Behold the man is become as one of us." These words respect the temptation of the devil; the argument that prevailed with Adam; and the fruits of their consenting: And therefore I understand them as spoken ironically, or in derision to Adam. As if God had said, "Now Adam, you see what a god you are become: The serpent told you "you should be as gods," as one that was infinite in wisdom. But behold, your godhead is horrible wickedness, even pollution of body and soul by sin. A thing you little thought of when you pleased yourself with the thought of that high attainment; and now if you be not prevented, you will proceed from evil to evil; for notwithstanding I have made promise of sending a Saviour, you will, through the pollution of your mind, forget and set at nought my promise; and seek life and salvation by that tree of life which was never intended for the justification of sinners; therefore I will turn you out of the garden, "to till the ground whence thou wast taken.""

1. Hence observe, That it often falls out, after the promised blessing is come, that God yet maketh us to possess our former sins, not that the guilt thereof might be charged to condemnation, but that remembering of them, we might blush before God, and be the more effectually driven to a continual embracing of the mercy promised.

2. Observe again, That as God would have us to remember our former sins, so he would not that we should feed upon ought but the very mercy promised. We must not rest in shadowish sacraments, as the typical tree of life, but must remember it is our duty to live by faith in the promised seed.

3. Observe also, That even our outward and temporal employments, if they be lawful and honest, are so ordered of God, as that we may gather some heavenly mystery from them: "To till the ground from whence he was taken": Mysteriously intimating two things to Adam. (1.) That seeing he was of the earth, he stood in as much need to be ordered and dressed by God, in order to his future happiness, as the ground, in order to its thrift and

fruitfulness. (2.) Again, Seeing he was taken from the ground, he is neither God, nor angel, but a poor earthen vessel, such as God can easily knock in pieces, and cause to return to the ground again. These things therefore Adam was to learn from his calling, that he might neither think too highly of himself, nor forget to live by faith, and depending on the Lord God, to be blessed of him.

> Ver. 24. "So he drove out the man; and he placed at the east of the garden of Eden Cherubims, and a flaming sword which turned every way, to keep the way of the tree of life."

"So he drove out the man." Adam was loth to forsake this garden of Eden, because there was the tree of life. The promise will hardly satisfy, where faith is weak and low. Had this man with great faith received and retained the gospel preached before, he would not have so hankered after a shadow; but the conscience being awakened, and faith low and weak there, because faith wants the flower or bloom of assurance, the ceremonial or moral law doth with ease engender bondage.

"And he placed at the east of the garden of Eden Cherubims, and a flaming sword." This shows the truth of what I said before; to wit, That Adam was loth to forsake the garden, loth to forsake his doing of something; but God sets a shaking sword against him, a sword to keep that way, or to prevent that Adam should have life by eating of the tree of life.

Observe, This tree of life, though lawful for Adam to feed on before he had transgressed, yet now is wholly forbidden him; intimating, that that which would have nourished him before he brake the law, will now avail him nothing as to life before the justice of God: the tree of life might have maintained his life before he sinned; but having done that, he hath no ways now but to live by faith in the promise; which that he might effectually do, God takes from him the use of all other things, he driveth him out of the garden, and sets to keep him from the tree of life, "Cherubims, and a flaming sword."

"And he placed at the east of the garden Cherubims, and a flaming sword." These cherubims are one sort of the angels of God, at this time made ministers of justice, shaking the flaming sword of God's severity against Adam for sin, threatening to cut him off thereby, if he ever return by the way that he went.

We read also, that the law was delivered to Israel from Sinai, by the hand and disposition of angels (Acts 7); the gospel, only by the Son himself (Heb 1:2).

To keep the way. Hence the apostle implicitly concludes it a way, that is, to death and damnation; by opposing another against it, even the new and living one; a new, not this the old; a living one, not this the dead one (Heb 10). For, for that the cherubims are here placed with a flaming, shaking sword, to keep the tree of life, it is evident that death is threatened to him that shall at any time attempt to come at, or that seeks for life that way.

"A flaming sword, turning every way to keep," &c. This still shews us, that man, though he hath already received the promise, is yet exceeding prone to seek life by another way than free grace by Jesus Christ; to wit, either by the law he hath broken, or by the law and Christ together; and so though not directly, yet "as it were by the works of the law" (Rom 9:32). But all is to no purpose, they are every way prevented. For, forsake the simplicity of the promise in the gospel, and thou shalt meet with the stroke of the justice of God; for that flaming sword of his vengeance, it turneth every way, and therefore will in every way lay wrath upon thee, if thou seek life by ought but Christ.

Chapter IV.

> Ver. 1. "And Adam knew Eve his wife; and she conceived, and bare Cain, and said, I have gotten a man from the Lord."

Now we are come to the generation of mankind. "Adam knew his wife": A modest expression; and it should teach us, in all such matters where things are discoursed of, that are either the fruits of sin, or the proper effects of man's natural infirmities, there to endeavour the use of such expressions, as neither to provide to lust, nor infect us with evil and uncivil communication. "Adam knew his wife"; Jacob, Samson, David, and others, are said to go in unto them. So as to our natural infirmities of the stool, the scripture expression is, "When thou goest abroad to ease thyself, thou shalt turn again and cover that which cometh from thee": Modest and bashful expressions, and such as become the godly, being those that are furthest off of occasioning evil, and nearest to an intimation, that such infirmities bespeak us infirm and imperfect creatures.

"And she conceived and bare Cain." The first sprout of a disobedient couple, a man in shape, but a devil in conditions. This is he that is called elsewhere, The child "of that wicked one" (1 John 3:12).

"And she said, I have gotten a man from the Lord." If Eve by these words did only ascribe the blessing of children to be the gift of God, then she spake like a godly woman; but if she supposed that this man Cain was indeed the seed promised, then it shows, that she in this was also deceived[x], and was therein a figure of all such as make false and strange delusions, signs of the mercy of God towards them: The man she thought she had got from the Lord as a mercy, and to be a Saviour, he proved a man of the devil, a curse, and to be a destroyer.

Ver. 2. "And she again bare his brother Abel, And Abel was a keeper of sheep, but Cain was a tiller of the ground."

Observe here, That the good child is not the first-born, but Abel, [a breath] (1 Cor 1:27,28). God often doth as Jacob did, even cross hands, in bestowing blessings, giving that which is best to him that is least esteemed: For Cain was the man in Eve's esteem; she thought, when she had him, she had got an inheritance; but as for Abel, he was little worth; by his name they showed how little they set by him. It is so with the sincere to this day; they bear not the name of glory with the world: Cain with them is the profitable son; Abel is of no credit with them, neither see they form or comeliness in him; he is the melancholy, or lowering child, whose countenance spoileth the mirth of the world: "The heart of the wise *is* in the house of mournings; but the heart of fools *is* in the house of mirth" (Eccl 7:4).

"And Abel was a keeper of sheep, but Cain was a tiller of the ground." By this it seems yet further, that Cain was the man in favour, even him that should, by his Father's intentions, have been heir, and have enjoyed the

---

[x] Is Bunyan a little harsh here? I am sure that what he says about Eve here is correct. But maybe also we can say that Eve's reaction at least showed that she **believed** in the seed to come - even though she was deceived into thinking that Cain might be that seed.

inheritance: He was nurtured up in his father's employment, but Abel was set in the lower rank.

It was also thus with Isaac and Jacob, Ishmael and Esau, being the eldest, and those that by intention were to be heirs.

Now in the inheritance lay, of old, a great blessing: so that Esau in losing his father's inheritance, lost also the blessing of grace, and moreover the kingdom of heaven (Heb 12:16,17). Wherefore Cain had by this the better of Abel, even as the Jews by their privileges had the better of the Gentiles (Rom 3:1,2). But mark it, the blessing of grace is not led by outward order, but by electing love: Where the person then is under the blessing of election, be he the first or the second son, the highest or lowest in the family, or whether he be more or less loved of his friends, 'tis he that with Abel hath the everlasting blessing.

Ver. 3. "And, in process of time, it came to pass that Cain brought of the fruit of the ground an offering unto the Lord."

Mark here, That the devil can suffer his children, in outward forms of worship, to be godly and righteous men: Cain, a limb of the devil, and yet the first in order that presents himself and his service to God.

Cain brought of the fruit of the ground, as of wheat, oil, honey, or the like; which things were also clean and good. Hence it is intimated, that his offering was excellent; and I conceive, not at all, as to the matter itself, inferior to that of Abel's; for in that it is said that Abel's was more excellent, it is not with respect to the excellency of the matter or things with which they sacrificed, but with respect to Abel's faith, which gave glory and acceptableness to his offering with God, "By faith he offered unto God a more excellent sacrifice than Cain" (Heb 11:4).

> "And Abel, he also brought of the firstlings of his flock and of the fat thereof" &c.

Abel, last in appearance, but in truth the first in grace; as it also is at this day: Who do so flutter it out as our ruffling formal worshippers? Alas! the good, the sincere and humble, they seem to be least and last; but the conclusion of the tragedy will make manifest that the first is last, and the last first; for the many are but called, the few are chosen.

> "And the Lord had respect unto Abel, and to his offering."

Herein are the true footsteps of grace discovered; to wit, the person must be the first in favour with God, the person first, the performance afterwards.

"And the Lord had respect to Abel." But how can God respect a man, before he respect his offering? A man's gift (saith Solomon) makes way for him: It should seem therefore that there lies no such stress in the order of words, but that it might as well be read, "The Lord had respect to Abel, because he respected his offering."

Answ. Not so: For though it be true among men, that the gift makes way for the acceptance of the person, yet in the order of grace it is after another manner; for if the person be not first accepted, the offering must be abominable; for it is not a good work that makes a good man, but a good man makes a good work. The fruit doth not make a good tree, but "a good tree bringeth forth good fruit." Make (saith Christ) the tree good, and his fruit good; or the tree evil, and his fruit evil: Do men gather grapes of thorns, or figs of thistles? Had Abel been a thorn, he had not brought forth grapes; had he been a thistle, he had not brought forth figs. So then, Abel's person must be first accepted, and after that his works.

Object. But God accepteth no man while he remains a sinner, but all men are sinners before they do good works, how then could the person of Abel be accepted first?

Answ. Abel was JUST before he did offer sacrifice. Just, I say, in the sight of God. This God witnessed by testifying of his gift: "By faith Abel offered unto God a more excellent sacrifice than Cain, by which he obtained witness that he was righteous": That is, God by accepting of the gift of Abel, did testify that Abel was a righteous man; for we know God "heareth not sinners": "The prayers of the wicked are an abomination unto God." But Abel was accepted, therefore he was righteous first.

Hence observe, That a man must be righteous before he can do any good work.

Quest. Righteous! "With what righteousness?"

Answ. With the righteousness of faith. And therefore it is said, that Abel had faith before he offered sacrifice. "By faith he offered" (Heb 11:4). Where faith is made to precede or go before the work which by faith he offered unto God.

Quest. But are not good works the righteousness of faith?

Answ. They are the fruits of faith: As here in the case of Abel; his faith produced an offering; but before he gave his offering, his faith had made him righteous; for faith respects a promise of grace, not a work of mine: Now the promise of grace, being this, that the seed of the woman, which is Christ, should destroy the power of the devil; by this Abel saw that it was Christ that should abolish sin and death by himself, and bring in "everlasting righteousness" for sinners. Thus believing, he had accepted of Christ for righteousness, which because he had done, God in truth proclaims him righteous, by accepting of his person and performances when offered.

Abel then presented his person and offering, as shrouding both, by faith, under the righteousness of Christ, which lay wrapped up in the promise; but Cain stands upon his own legs, and so presents his offering. Abel therefore is accepted, both his person and his offering, while Cain remains accursed.

> Ver. 5. "But unto Cain, and to his offering, he [the Lord] had not respect. And Cain was very wroth, and his countenance fell."

Mark: As first Abel's person is accepted, and then his offering; so first Cain's person is rejected, and afterwards his offering: For God seeth not sin in his own institutions, unless they be defiled by them that worship him; and that they needs must, when persons by[18] themselves offer sacrifice to God, because then they want the righteousness of faith.

This then made the difference betwixt Abel and his brother; Abel had faith, but Cain had none. Abel's faith covered him with Jesus Christ, therefore he stood righteous in his person before God: This being so, his offering was accepted, because it was the offering of one that was righteous.

"But unto Cain, and to his offering, the Lord had not respect." Hence note, That a Christless man is a wicked man, let him be never so full of actions that be righteous; for righteous actions make not a righteous man, the man himself must first be righteous.[19]

Wherefore, though Cain was the eldest, and first in the worship; yet Abel was the wisest, and the most acceptable therein.

"And Cain was very wroth, and his countenance fell." From these words it may be gathered, that Cain had some evident token from the observation of God's carriage towards both himself and brother; that his brother was smiled upon, but he rejected: He was wroth: wroth with God, and wroth with his brother. And indeed, before the world hate us, they must needs hate Jesus Christ: "It hated me [saith he] before *it hated* you" (John 15:18). He was wroth: and why? Wroth because his sacrifice was not accepted of God: And yet the fault was not in the Lord, but Cain: He came not before the Lord, as already made righteous with the righteousness of Christ, which indeed had been doing well, but as a cursed wicked wretch, he thought that by his own good works he must be just before the Lord.

The difference therefore that was between these worshippers, it lay not in that they worshipped divers gods, but in that they worshipped the same God after a diverse manner: The one in faith, the other without; the one as righteous, the other as wicked.

And even thus it is between us and our adversaries: We worship not divers gods, but the same God in a diverse manner: We according to faith; and they according to their OWN INVENTIONS.[20]

"And Cain was wroth." This further shows us the force of the law, and the end of those that would be just by the same; namely, That in conclusion they will quarrel with God; for when the soul in its best performances, and acts of righteousness, shall yet be rejected and cast off by God, it will fret and wrangle, and in its spirit let fly against God. For thus it judgeth, That God is austere and exacting; it hath done what it could to please him, and he is not pleased therewith. This again offendeth God, and makes his justice curse and condemn the soul. Condemn it, I say, for imagining that the righteousness of a poor, sinful, wretched creature, should be sufficient to appease eternal justice for sin. Thus the law worketh wrath, because it always bindeth our transgression to us, and still reckoneth us sinners, and accursed, when we have done our utmost to answer and fulfil it (Rom 4:15).

"And his countenance fell." However, an hypocrite, while God forbeareth to smite him, may triumph and joy in his goodness; yet when God shall pronounce his judgment according as he approve of his act, he needs must lower and fall in his countenance; for his person and gift are rejected, and he still counted a sinner.

Ver. 6. "And the Lord said unto Cain, Why art thou wroth? and why is thy countenance fallen?"

These words are applied to Cain, for a further conviction of his state to be miserable. "Why art thou wroth?" Is it because I have not accepted thy offering? This is without ground, thy person is yet an abomination to me: Must I be made by thy gift, which is polluted, for and by thy person, to justify thee as righteous? Thou hast not yet done well. Wherefore, Cain had no cause to be wroth; For God rejected only that which was sinful, as was both his person, and gift for the sake thereof: Neither had he grounds to lift up his looks on high, when he came to offer his sacrifice; because he came not as a man in a justify'd state. But "*there is* a generation *that are* pure in their own eyes, and *yet* is not washed from their filthiness. *There is* a generation, - O how lofty are their eyes! and their eyelids are lifted up" (Pro 30:12,13). Such an one, or the father of these, was Cain; he counted himself clean, and yet was not washed; he lifted up his looks on high, before he was changed from his iniquity.

> Ver. 7. "If thou doest well, shalt thou not be accepted? and if thou doest not well, sin lieth at the door. And unto thee *shall be* his desire, and thou shalt rule over him."

"If thou do well." Why, is not worshipping of God, well-doing? It may, and may not, even as the person that worships is found. If he be found righteous at his coming to worship, and if he worship according to rule, then he does well, then he is accepted of God; but if he be not found righteous before, be you sure he cannot do well, let the matter with which he worshippeth be wrong or right. "Who can bring a clean *thing* out of an unclean?" (John 14:4). Let Cain be clean, and his offering will be clean, because brought to God in a vessel that is clean; but if Cain be unclean, all the holy things he toucheth, or layeth up in his skirt, it is made unclean by the uncleanness of his person: "And so is this nation before me, saith the Lord; and so *is* every work of their hands, and that which they offer there *is* unclean" (Haggai 2:11-14).[21]

Men therefore ought to distinguish between doing and well-doing, even in the worship of God. All that worship do not do well, though the matter of worship be good in itself. Cain's offering you find not blamed, as if it had been of a superstitious complexion; but he came not aright to worship. Why? he came not as one made righteous before. Wherefore, as I have already touched, the difference that lay between the gifts of Abel and Cain, was not in the gifts themselves, but the qualifications of the persons. Abel's faith, and Cain's works, made God approve and reject the offering: "by faith Abel offered to God a more excellent sacrifice than Cain": For, as I said, Faith in Christ, as promised to come, made him righteous, because thereby he obtained "the righteousness of God"; for so was Christ in himself, and so to be to him that by faith received and accepted of him: This, I say, Abel did; wherefore now he is righteous or just before God. This being so, his offering is found to be an offering of Abel the just, and is here said to obtain witness even of God, that he was righteous, because he accepted his gift.

Wherefore, he that does well must first be good: "He that doeth righteousness is [must first be] righteous" (1 John 3:7). He is righteous first; he is righteous even as Christ is righteous, because Christ himself is the righteousness of such a person. And so on the contrary; the reason why some men's good deeds are accursed of God, it is because in truth, and according to the law, the Lord finds sin in them; which sins he cannot pardon, because he finds them not in Christ. Thus they being evil for want of the righteousness of the Son of God, they worship God as sinners, according to that of the apostle, Because they are not good, therefore they do not good, no, not one of them (Rom 3:10-12).

The way therefore to do well, it is first to receive the mercy of God in Christ; which act of thine will be more pleasing to the Divine Majesty, than all whole burnt-offerings and sacrifices: "I will have mercy [saith God] I will have mercy, and not sacrifice" (Matt 9:13; 12:7). This Cain did not understand, therefore he goes to God in his sins, and without faith in the mercy of God through Christ, he offereth his sacrifice. Wherefore because his sacrifice could not take away his sin, therefore it still abode upon him.

But "if thou doest not well, sin lieth at the door." This reasoning therefore was much to Cain's condition; he would be wroth, because God did not accept his offering, and yet he did not well: Now, if he had done well, God, by receiving of his brother's sacrifice, shows, he would have accepted him; for this is evident, they were both alike by nature; their offerings also were in themselves one as holy as the other: How then comes it to pass that both were not accepted, they both offered to God? Why, Abel only sacrificed well, because he first by faith in Christ was righteous: This because Cain wanted, "sin abideth at his door."

"And to thee *shall be* his desire, and thou shalt rule over him." That is if sin abideth at thy door still, to thee shall be his desire; he shall love, pity, pray for thee, and endeavour thy conversions; but thou shalt be lord over him, and shalt put thy yoke upon his neck. This was Jacob's portion also; for after Esau had got head, he broke Jacob's yoke from off his neck, and reigned by nineteen or twenty dukes and princes, before there was any king in Israel (Gen 27:40).

It is the lot of Cain's brood, to be lords and rulers first, while Abel and his generation have their necks under persecution; yet while they lord it, and thus tyrannically afflict and persecute, our very desire is towards them, wishing their salvation: While they curse, we bless; and while they persecute, we pray.

> Ver. 8. "And Cain talked with Abel his brother: and it came to pass, when they were in the field, that Cain rose up against Abel his brother, and slew him."

When Cain saw that by God's judgment Abel was the better worshipper, and that himself must by no means be admitted for well-doing, his heart began to be more obdurate and hard, and to grow into that height of desperateness, as to endeavour the extirpating of all true religion out of the world; which it seems he did, by killing his brother, mightily accomplish, until the days of Enos; for "then began men [again] to call upon the name of the Lord" (v 26).

Hence see the spite of the children of hell against God: They have slain thy prophets, and digged down thine altars (1 Kings 19:10). If they may have their wills, God must be content with their religion, or none; other they will not endure should have show within their reach, but with Cain, will rather kill their brother; or with the Pharisees, kill their Lord; and with the evil kings of old, will rather kill their sons and subjects. That the truth, I say, may fall to the ground, and their own inventions stand for acceptable sacrifices, they will not only envy, but endeavour to invalidate all the true worship and worshippers of God in the world; the which if they cannot without blood accomplish, they will slay and kill till their cruelty hath destroyed many ten thousands, even as Cain, who slew his brother Abel.[22]

And Cain talked with his brother. He had not a law whereby to arraign him, but malice enough, and a tongue to set all on fire, of which no doubt, by the goodly replies of his brother, was easily blown up into choler and madness, the end of which was the blood of his brother.

"And Cain talked with Abel," &c. To wit, about the goodness and truth of his religion. For that the New Testament seems to import, he slew him "because his works were righteous" (1 John 3:12); which Abel, no doubt, had justified before his brother, even then when he most set himself to oppose him. Besides this, the connection of the relation importeth, he talked with him, he slew him; he talked with him and slew him, purely upon a religious account, because his works were righteous.

Hence note, That when wicked men have the head in the world, professors had need be resolved to hazard the worst, before they do enter debate with ungodly men about the things that pertain to the kingdom of God. For behold here, words did not end in words, but from words came blows, and from blows blood. The counsel therefore is, "That you sit down first, and count up the cost," before ye talk with Cain of religion (Luke 14:27-33). "They make a man an offender for a word, and lay a snare for him that reproveth in the gate, and turn aside the just for a thing of nought" (Isa 29:21).

"And Cain talked with Abel his brother." With Abel his only brother, who also was a third part of the world. But tyrants matter nothing, neither nearness of kin, nor how much they destroy: "The brother shall betray the brother to death," &c.

"And it came to pass, when they were in the field, that Cain rose up against Abel his brother, and slew him." When they were in the field, from home, out of the sight, and far from the help of his father: Subtle persecutors love not to bite, till they can make their teeth to meet; for which they observe their time and place. Joseph was also hated of his brethren, but they durst not meddle till they found him in the field (Gen 37:15). Here it is also that the holy virgin falleth: He found her in the field,—and there was none to save her (Deut 22:27).

Hence observe again, That be the danger never so imminent, and the advantage of the adversary never so great, the sincere professor of the truth stands his ground against wind and weather. Bloody Cain daunted not holy Abel; no, though now he have his advantage of him (Dan 3:16-18). He rose up against Abel his brother, and slew him. "And wherefore slew he him? Because his own works were evil," &c. (1 John 3:12). It is therefore hence to be observed, That it is a sign of an evil way, be it covered with the name of the worship of God, when it cannot stand without the shedding of innocent blood. "Wherefore slew he him? Because his own works were evil." Had his works been good, they had been accepted of God: He had also had the joy thereof in his conscience, as doubtless Abel had; which joy and peace would have produced love and pity to his brother, as it was with his brother towards him; but his works being evil, they minister to him no heavenly joy, neither do they beget in him love to his brother; but contrariwise, his heart fill his eye with evil also; which again provoketh (while it beholdeth the godly carriage of Abel) the heart to more desperate resolutions, even to set upon him with all his might, and to cut him off from the earth. Thus the goodness of God's people provoketh to envy the wicked heart of the hypocrite. As it was betwixt Saul and David; for after Saul had seen that God had rejected him for his wickedness, the more he hated the goodness of David: "And Saul saw and knew that the Lord was with David" (1 Sam 18:8-15). "And Saul was yet the more afraid of David; and Saul became David's enemy continually" (v 29).

Ver. 9. "And the Lord said unto Cain, Where *is* Abel thy brother? And he said, I know not: *Am* I my brother's keeper?"

Cain thought it had been no more but to kill his brother, and his intentions and desires must needs be accomplished, and that himself should then be the only man. "Come, let us kill him, and the inheritance shall be ours" (Mark 12:7). But stay, Abel was beloved of his God, who had also justified his offering, and accepted it as a service more excellent than his brother's. So then, because the quarrel arose between them upon this very account, therefore Abel's God doth reckon himself as engaged (seeing he is not) to take up his servant's cause himself.

"And the Lord said unto Cain, Where *is* Abel thy brother?" A question not grounded on uncertainty, but proposed as a beginning of further reasoning; and also to make way to this wicked wretch, to discover the desperate wickedness of his bloody heart the more. For questions that stand at first afar off, do draw out more of the heart of another: and also do minister more occasion for matter, than if they had been placed more near to the matter.

"Where is Abel?" God missed the acceptable sacrifices of Abel; Abel was dead, and his sacrifices ceased, which had wont to be savoury in the nostrils of God; Cain could not supply them; his sacrifices were deficient, they were not of faith. Hence note, that if tyrants should have their will, even to the destroying of all the remnant of God, their sacrifices and worship would be yet before God as abominable as they were before.

"And the Lord said unto Cain, Where is Abel?" O dreadful question! The beginning of Cain's hell, for now God entereth into judgment with him. Wherefore, however this wretch endeavoured at first to stifle and choke his conscience, yet this was to him the arrow of death: Abel crieth, but his brother would not hear him while alive, and now being dead God hears the cry of his blood. "When he maketh inquisition for blood, he remembereth them: he forgetteth not the cry of the humble" (Psa 9:12). Blood that is shed for the sake of God's word, shall not be forgotten or disregarded of God: "Precious in his sight *is* the death of his saints" (Psa 116:15). "And precious shall their blood be in his sight" (Psa 72:14).

"Where *is* Abel thy brother?" This word, thy brother, must not be left out, because it doth greatly aggravate his wickedness. He slew "his brother"; which horrid act the very law and bond of nature forbiddeth. But when a man is given up of God, it is neither this nor another relation that will bind his hands, or make him keep within the bound of any law. Judas will seek his master's, and Absalom his father's blood. "Where is Abel thy brother?"

"And he said, I know not." He knew full well what he had done, and that by his hands his brother's blood was fallen to the ground, but now being called into question for the same, he endeavoureth to plead ignorance before God. "I know not." When men have once begun to sin, they know not where they shall end; he slew his brother, and endeavours to cover his fact with a lie. David also little thought his act of adultery would have led him to have spilt the blood of Uriah, and afterwards to have covered all with dissembling lips and a lying tongue (2 Sam 11).

"I know not: *am* I my brother's keeper?"

This is the way of all ungodly men, they will not abide that guilt should be fastened. Sin they love, and the lusts and delights thereof, but to count for it they cannot abide; they will put it off with excuses, or denials: Even like Saul, who though he had spared the cattle and Agag contrary to the command of God, yet would needs bear Samuel down, that he had kept, yea "performed the commandment of the Lord" (1 Sam 15:13,20). But they are denials to no boot, and excuses that will not profit, that are made to hide the sin of the soul from the sight and judgment of God. Lies and falsehood will here do nothing.

> Ver. 10. "And he said, What hast thou done? the voice of thy brother's blood crieth unto me from the ground."

Poor Cain, thy feeble shifts help thee nothing, thy excuses are drowned by the cries of the blood which thou hast shed.

"What hast thou done?" the blood of thy brother cries. Beware persecutors, you think that when you have slain the godly, you are then rid of them; but you are far wide, their blood which you have shed, cries in the ears of God against you. O the cries of blood are strong cries, they are cries that reach to heaven; yea they are cries that have a continual voice, and that never cease to make a noise, until they have procured vengeance form the hands of the Lord of sabbath (Job 16:18): And therefore this is the word of the Lord against all those that are for the practice of Cain: "*As* I live, saith the Lord God, I will prepare thee unto blood and blood shall pursue thee: sith thou hast not hated blood, [that is, hated to shed it,] even blood shall pursue thee" (Eze 35:6).

"The voice of thy brother's blood crieth unto me." The apostle makes this voice of the blood of Abel, a type of the voice of the justice of the law, and so extends it further than merely to the act of murder; intimating that he sheds blood, that breaks any of the commands of God, (and indeed so he doth, "he layeth wait of his *own* blood, and privily lurketh for his *own* life" (Prov 1:18). Wherefore the apostle compareth the blood of Abel and the blood of Christ together; but so as by the rule of contraries, making betwixt them a contrary voice, even as there is between a broken command and a promise of grace, the one calling for vengeance and damnation; the other calling for forgiveness and salvation; "the blood of sprinkling it speaketh better things than the blood of Abel" (Heb 12:24); that is, it calls to God to forgive the sinner; but Abel's blood, of the breach of the law, that cries damn them, damn them. Christ also sets his own blood in opposition to the blood of all that was shed before him; concluding that the proper voice of all the blood of the godly, is to call for vengeance on the persecutors, even from the blood of Abel to the blood of

Zecharias, that was slain between the altar and the temple (Matt 23:35). And let me here take leave to propound my private thoughts: namely, that the Zecharias that here is mentioned, might not be he that we find in the book of Chronicles (2 Chron 24:21); but one of that name that lived in the days of Christ, possibly John Baptist's father, or some other holy man. My reasons for this conjecture, are, 1. Because the murderers are convict by Christ himself: Zecharias, whom ye slew between the altar and the temple. 2. Because Christ makes a stop at the blood of Zecharias, not at the blood of John the Baptist: wherefore, if the person here mentioned were not murdered after, but before John the Baptist, then Christ seems to excuse them for killing his servant John; for the judgment stops at the including of the guilt of the blood of Zecharias. 3. I think such a thing, because the voice of all holy blood that hath been shed before the law by the adversary, excepting only the blood of Jesus, must needs be included here; the proper voice of his, only being to plead for mercy to the murderers. However, the voice of blood is a very killing voice, and will one day speak with such thunder and terror in the consciences of all the brood of Cain, that their pain and burthen will be for ever insupportable.

Ver. 11. "And now *art* thou cursed from the earth, which hath opened her mouth to receive thy brother's blood from thy hand."

Here begins the sentence of God against this bloody man; a sentence fearful and terrible, for it containeth a removing of him from all the privileges of grace and mercy, and a binding of him over to the punishment and pains of the damned.

"And now *art* thou cursed from the earth." Peace on earth, is one branch of those blessed tidings that were brought into the world, at the coming of the Messias (Luke 2:14). Again, before Christ was come in the flesh, it is said, He rejoiced "in the habitable part of his earth" (Pro 8:30). Wherefore, by the earth in this place, I understand the state that the men are in, to whom, by the mind of God, the gospel and grace of God is to be tendered. Now, whether it respect that state of man by nature, or the state of those that are saints, from both these privileges Cain is separate, as are all whom the Lord hath utterly rejected. Not but that yet they may live long in the world, but God hath cut them off from the earth, and all the gospel privileges therein, and set them in the condition of devils; so that as to grace and mercy they are separate therefrom, and stand as men, though alive, bound over to eternal judgment. And as to their lives, it matters not how long they live, there is "no sacrifice for their sins, but a certain fearful looking for of judgment and fiery indignation, which shall devour the adversaries" (Heb 10:26,27). So that I say, as the devils be bound in hell, so such lie bound in earth; bound I say in the chains of darkness, and their own obstinate heart, over to the day of wrath and revelation of the righteous judgment of God. Cain therefore by these words is denied the blessing of future means of grace, and stands bound over to answer for his brother's blood, which the ground had received form his cruel hand.

Ver. 12. "When thou tillest the ground, it shall not henceforth yield to thee her strength; a fugitive and a vagabond shalt thou be in the earth."

This is a branch, or the fruits of this wilful murder. Indeed, sins carry in them not only a curse with respect to eternity, but are also the cause of all the miseries of this life. "God turneth - a fruitful land into barrenness, for the wickedness of them that dwell therein" (Psa 107:34).

"When thou tillest the ground." Sin committed doth not always exclude the sinner from an enjoyment of God's mercies, but yet if unrepented of, bringeth a curse upon them. "I will curse, [saith God,] your blessings: yea, I have cursed them already, because ye do not lay *it* to heart" (Mal 2:2). This also is the reason that the table of some is made their snare, their trap, a stumbling-block and a recompence unto them (Rom 11:9); men ought not therefore to judge of the goodness of their state, by their enjoyment of God's creatures, but rather should tremble while they enjoy them, lest for sin they should become accursed to them, as were the enjoyments of this wicked man.

"A fugitive and a vagabond shalt thou be in the earth." The meaning is, thou shalt not have rest in the world, but shalt be continually possessed with a guilty conscience, which shall make thy condition restless, and void of comfort. For the man that indeed is linked in the chains of guilt and damnation, as Cain here was; he cannot rest, but (as we say) fudge up and down from place to place, because his burthen is insupportable. As David said, "Let their eyes be darkened that they see not, and make their loins continually to shake" (Psa 69:23). A continual shaking and restlessness doth therefore possess such persons as are given up of God, and swallowed up of guilt.

"A fugitive and vagabond shalt thou be in the earth." Some men certainly know, even while they are in this world, their state to be most miserable, and damnable, as Cain, Saul and Judas did; which knowledge, as I have hinted, puts them besides the very course of other carnal men; who while they behold them at quiet under their enjoyments, these cannot but wonder, fear, and be amazed with the deep cogitations which will abide upon them, of their certain misery and everlasting perdition.

Ver. 13. "And Cain said unto the Lord, My punishment *is* greater than I can bear."

Or as the margin hath it, "Mine iniquity is greater than that it may be forgiven." And both readings are true: for however some men please themselves in lessening sin, and the punishment thereof, yet a burdened conscience judgeth otherwise. And if Cain failed in either, it was in that he counted his sin (if he did so) beyond the reach of God's mercy. But again, when men persecute the worship and people of God, as Cain did his blessed and religious brother, even of spite, and because he envied the goodness of his brother's work; I question whether it be lawful for a minister to urge to such the promise of grace and forgiveness; and also whether it be the mind of God such persons should hope therein. He that sins the sin unto death, is not to be prayed for (1 John 5:16), but contrariwise he is to be taken from God's altar that he may die (Exo 21:14). This was Cain's case, and now he knew it; therefore as one excluded of God from his mercy and all the means thereof, he breaks out with roaring under the intolerable burden of the judgment of God upon him, concluding his punishment at present "greater than he could bear," and that yet his sin should remain unpardonable for ever: As saith our Lord Jesus Christ, He hath neither forgiveness here nor in the world to come (Matt 12:32).

Ver. 14. "Behold, thou hast driven me out this day from the face of the earth; and from thy face shall I be hid; And I shall be a fugitive and a vagabond in the earth, and it shall come to pass, *that* every one that findeth me shall slay me."

By these words is confirmed what was said before, to wit, to be cursed from the earth, was to be separate from the privileges of the gospel. For Cain was not now to die, neither was he driven into any den or cave; yet driven out from the face of the earth, that is, as I have said, he was excluded from a share in those special mercies that by the gospel were still offered by grace to the others that inhabited the world: The mercies, I say, that are offered by the gospel, as namely, The mercy of eternal life: For as to the blessings of this world, he had yet a notable share thereof. Besides, he groaneth under this judgment, as an insupportable curse: "Thou hast driven me out this day from the face of the earth." And indeed, if we take it according as I have laid it down, it is a curse that would break the whole world to pieces; for he that is denied a share in the grace that is now offered, must needs be denied a portion in God's kingdom. And this Cain saw; wherefore he adds in the process of his complaint, "And from thy face shall I be hid": "I shall never come into thy kingdom, I shall never see thy face in heaven." This is therefore the highest of all complaints; namely, for a man from a certain conviction that his condition must without fail be damnable, to condole and bemoan his forlorn condition.

"Thou hast driven me out." O! when God shall bind one over for his sin, to eternal judgment, who then can release him? This was Cain's state, God had bound him over. The blood of his brother was to rest upon him and not to be purged with sacrifice for ever.

"Thou hast driven me out THIS DAY." He knew by the sentence that fell from heaven upon him, even from that very day that he was made a companion of, and an associate with devils. This day, or for this day's work, I am made an inhabitant of the pit with the devil and his angels. Hence note, That God doth sometimes smite the reprobate so apparently, that himself from that day may make a certain judgment of the certainty of his damnation. Thus did Balaam: "I shall see him, but not now: I shall behold him, but not nigh" (Num 24:17). Where by now, he respects the time of grace; and by nigh, the time or day of judgment: As who should say, "I, for my sorceries, and wicked divinations, am excluded a portion in the day of grace, and therefore shall not see the Saviour NOW: I am also rejected, as to a portion in the blessed world to come: and therefore when he judgeth, I shall not see him NIGH: Nigh, as a friend, as a saviour to my soul." I doubt this is the condition of many now alive, who for their perfidiousness and treachery to Christ, and his church, have already received, even "in themselves, that recompence of their error which was meet" (Rom 1:27).

Ishmael also, in the day he laughed at Isaac (Gen 21:9), and Esau in the day he sold his birthright (Gen 27; 28), might have gathered, the one from God's concurring with the judgment of Sarah, the other, from his father's adhering to his brother; his adhering, I say, in a prophetic spirit (Gal 4:29); that from thenceforth they both were excluded grace and glory, as the apostle by the Holy Ghost afterwards doth (Heb 12:16,17).

"And from thy face shall I be hid." By face here, we are to understand God's favour, and blessed presence, which is enjoyed by the saints both here, and in the world to come (Psa 4:6,7; 16:11). Both which this wicked man, for the murdering of his brother, and his envy to the truth, now knew himself excluded from.

"From thy face shall I be HID." The pit of hell, to which the damned go, besides the torment that they meet with there, is such a region of darkness, and at such a distance from the heavens, and the glorious comfortable presence of God, that those that shall be found the proper subjects of it, shall for ever be estranged from one glimpse of him: besides, sin shall bind all their faces in secret, and so confound them with horror, shame, and guilt that they shall not be able from thenceforth for ever, so much as once to think of God with comfort.

"From thy FACE." As it were all the glory of heaven, it lieth in beholding the face of God: A thing the ungodly little think of; yet the men that have received in themselves already the sentence of eternal damnation, they know it after a wonderful rate; and the thoughts of the loss of his face and presence, doth, do what they can, as much torment them, as the thoughts of all the misery they are like to meet withal besides.

"And a fugitive and a vagabond shall I be on the earth." Even from the present frame of his spirit, Now, having received the sentence, he knew, the judgment past being unrevokable, how it would be with him all his life long; that he should spend his days in trouble and guilt, rolling under the justice of God, being always a terror and burthen to himself, to the day he was to be cut off from the earth, that he might go to the place appointed for him.

"And it shall come to pass, *that* every one that findeth me shall slay me." Guilt is a strange thing, it makes a man think that every one that sees him, hath knowledge of his iniquity. It also bringeth such a faintness into the heart (Lev 26:36), that the sound of a shaken leaf doth chase such persons: and above all things, the cries of blood are most fearful in the conscience; the cries of the blood of the poor innocents, which the seed of Cain hath shed on the face of the earth (Jer 2:34; 19:4). Thus far of Cain's complaint.

> Ver. 15. "And the Lord said unto him, Therefore whosoever slayeth Cain, vengeance shall be taken on him seven-fold. And the Lord set a mark upon Cain, lest any finding him should kill him."

By these words, the judgment is confirmed, which Cain, in the verse before, so mournfully pronounced against his own soul. As if the Lord had said, "Cain, thy judgment is as thou hast said, I have driven thee out this day from a share in my special favour; and when thy life is ended, thou shalt be hid from my face, and a blessed presence for ever; and seeing it is thus, therefore I will not suffer that thou die before thy time: Alas, thy glass will be quickly run! Besides, thy days, while thou art here, will sufficiently be filled with vexation and distress; for thou shalt always carry in thy conscience the cries of innocent blood, and the fear of the wrath of God: I have said it, and will perform it: I am not a man, that I should repent: So that thus shall thy judgment be: Therefore he that killeth Cain, I will take vengeance on him."

Hence note, That none need to add to the sorrows of the persecutors. They above all men are prepared unto wrath. Let them alone (saith Christ) they will quickly fall into the ditch. Besides, God hath taken the revengement of the blood of his servants into his own hand, and will execute his wrath himself. Therefore he saith to his saints (as in this case), "Dearly beloved, avenge not yourselves, but *rather* give place unto wrath: for it is written, Vengeance *is* mine, I will repay, saith the Lord" (Rom 12:19). And the reason is, because the quarrel is in special between the prosecutor and God himself. For we are not hated because we are men, nor because we are men of evil and debauched lives; but because we are religious; because we stand to maintain the truth of God. Therefore no man must here intercept, but must leave the enemy in the hand of that God he hath slighted and condemned. This made Moses that he meddled not with Corah and his company, but left them to that new thing which the Lord himself would do unto them, because they had condemned the ordinance of God (Num 16:25-35). This made David also that he meddled not with Saul, but left him to the vengeance of God, though he had opportunity to have destroyed him (1 Sam 24 and 26:10-12). Let us learn therefore to be quiet and patient under the hand of wicked and blood-thirsty men. Let us fall before them like holy Abel; it is and will be grief enough to them, that when we are dead, our blood will cry from the ground against them.[23]

"Therefore he that killeth Cain, vengeance shall be taken," &c. He now that shall, after this admonition, plead for religious blood with the sword, vengeance shall be taken on him, because he giveth not place to the wrath of God, but intercepts with his own, which "worketh not the righteousness of God" (James 1:19,20). Say therefore with David, when you are vexed with the persecutor, Mine hand shall not be upon him; but "*as* the Lord liveth, the Lord shall smite him; or, his day shall come to die; or, he shall descend in battle, and perish."

"Vengeance shall be taken on him seven fold." It would not be hard to shew how little they have prevailed, who have taken upon them to take vengeance for the blood of saints, on them that have been the spillers of it. But my business here is brevity, therefore I shall not launch into that deep, only shall say to such as shall attempt it hereafter, "Put up thy sword into his place; for all they that take the sword shall perish with the sword"! (Matt 26:52). And "here is the patience and faith of the saints" (Rev 13:10). Let Cain and God alone, and do you mind faith and patience; suffer with Abel, until your righteous blood be spilt: even the work of persecutors, is, for the present, punishment enough; the fruits thereof being the provoking God to jealousy, a denying of them the knowledge of the way of life, and a binding of them over to the pains and punishment of hell.

"And the Lord set a mark upon Cain." What the opinion of others is about this mark, I know not; to me it seems like those in Timothy, who had "their conscience seared with a hot iron" (1 Tim 4:2). Which words are an allusion to the way of the magistrates in their dealing with rogues and felons; who that they may be known to all, are either in the hand, shoulder, or cheek branded with a hot iron. So Cain was marked of God for a reprobate, for one that had murdered a righteous man, even of envy to the goodness of his work: But the mark (as it was on those in Timothy) was not on any outward or visible part of his body, but (as there the apostle expresseth it) even upon his very conscience; his conscience then had received the fire-mark of the wrath and displeasure of God, which, as a burning iron doth to the flesh, had left such deep impression therein, that it abode as a scar or brand upon him, in token that good would for ever after hold him for a fugitive rogue or vagabond.

"And the Lord set a mark upon Cain, lest any finding him should kill him." For though the mark was branded with burning upon his conscience, and so inward and invisible; yet the effects of this hot iron might be visible, and seen of all: the effects, I say, which were, or might be, his restlessness in every place, his dejectedness, the sudden and fearful pangs and agonies of his mind, which might break out into dolorous and amazing complaints; besides, his timorous carriage before all he met, lest they should kill him; gave all to understand, that God had with a vengeance branded him. And indeed this was such a mark as was amazing to all that beheld him, and did ten times more make them afraid of spilling blood, than if any visible mark had been set upon him; of for by his trouble and distress of mind, they saw, what was the guilt of blood: and by his continual fear and trembling under the judgment of God, what it was to be in fear of, nay, to have the first fruits of everlasting damnation. Thus therefore God reserved Cain to the judgment which he had appointed for him.

> Ver. 16. "And Cain went out from the presence of the Lord, and dwelt in the land of Nod, on the east of Eden."

The right carriage of a reprobate, and the infallible fruits of final desperation. For a man that hath received in his mind the stroke of the judgment of God, and that is denied all means of saving and sanctifying grace, (as the great transgressors are,) the presence of God is to such most dreadful; whether we understand the knowledge of him as he is in himself, or as he discovereth himself in his church; for the thought of his being, and eternal majesty, keeps the wound open, and makes terror and guilt revive. To such it would be the best of news, to hear that the Godhead doth cease to be, or that themselves were high above him. But that they are in the hand of the living God, this is the dreadful and fearful thought.

"And Cain went out from the presence of the Lord." These words may be taken many ways.

1. That he separated himself from the church (the place of God's presence) (2 Cor 6:16) which then consisted of his father and mother, and of those other children they had. And this appears by the text, "He went out from the presence of the Lord, and dwelt in the land of Nod."

2. A man goes out from the presence of God, when he withdraws his thoughts from holy meditations, and employeth the strength of his mind about the things of this life (Job 21:14-18). And thus he also did; he went into the land of Nod, and there fell to building a city, and to recreate himself with the pleasures of the flesh what he might.

3. A man goes out from the presence of God, when he throweth up the worship and way of God; and this he did in departing from the church (2 Chron 19:1-3).

4. Besides, his going out from the presence of the Lord, implieth, that he hardened his heart against him, that he set his spirit against him; that he said to God, Depart from me (Heb 3:12); that he grew an implacable enemy to him, and to every appearance of good in the world (Job 15:12,13).

"And Cain went out from the presence of the Lord." These words may also respect his being thrust out from

God, as one anathematized, accursed, or cut off, in effect the same with excommunication. But be it so, the act was extraordinary, being administered by God himself; even as he served Corah and his company, though in kind there was a difference, the one, even Cain, being yet permitted to live for a while in the world; the other being sent down quick into hell; but both, for their villany against the worship and people of God, stand bound over to answer it at the eternal judgment.

Ver. 17. "And Cain knew his wife; and she conceived, and bare Enoch: and he builded a city, and called the name of the city, after the name of his son, Enoch."

Cain's wife was his sister, or near kinswoman; for she sprang of the same loins with himself; because his mother was "the mother of all living" (Gen 3:20).[xi]

This wife bare him a son; for whose sake, as it seems, he built the city. Hence note, That men who are shut out of heaven, will yet use some means to be honourable on earth. Cain being accursed of God, yet builds him a city; the renown of which act, that it might not be forgotten, he calleth it after the name of his son. Much like this was that carnal act of blasted Absalom; because he had no child, he would erect a pillar, which must forsooth be called Absalom's place, after the name of Absalom, to keep his name in remembrance upon earth (2 Sam 18:18).

[xi] Once again, note the impeccable logic with which Bunyan works out that Cain's wife was his sister. The only people who have problems with this fact are those who come to the scriptures with a presupposition that the scriptures must be wrong.

"And he builded a city," &c. Note, That it is the design of Satan, and the deceitful heart of man, to labour to quiet a guilty conscience, not by faith in the blood of Christ, but by over much business in the things of this world.

"And called the name of the city, after the name of his son, Enoch." Although Cain had a mind to keep up his name with fame in the world, yet he would not venture to dedicate the city to his own name; that would have been too gross; and perhaps others would have called it, The CITY OF THE MURDERER; but he calleth it after the name of his son, his son Enoch; whom he pretended was a man both taught, and dedicate, as it seems his name imports. Hence note again, That men who themselves are accursed of God, will yet put as fair glosses on their actions, as their hypocritical hearts can invent. Who must this city be dedicated to, but to him whom Cain had dedicated and taught. I will not say that in truth he gave him to God, for that his reprobate heart would not suffer; but being given up of God, yet retaining, with Saul, considerations of honour: therefore, as is the custom of ungodly hypocrites, he would put the best show on his ungodly actions.

Thus Saul, when he had received the sentence of the Lord against him; yet, Turn again with me (saith he to Samuel) "*yet* honour me now before - the people, and before Israel" (1 Sam 15:30). So the money wherewith the high priests and scribes had bought the life, and obtained the death of Christ; with that they make some shew of godliness, in buying with it a piece of ground to bury strangers in (Matt 27:3-7).

> Ver. 18. "And unto Enoch was born Irad: and Irad begat Mehujael: and Mehujael begat Methusael: and Methusael begat Lamech."

These are the offspring of Cain; the English of whose names, if the nature and disposition of the persons were according, they might well be called, with abhorrence, the brood of wicked Cain, even the generation whom the Lord had cursed, notwithstanding Enoch was their father. Enoch begat Irad, a wild ass; Irad begat Mehujael, one presumptuous above measure, his name signifies, one teaching God. But "who hath directed the Spirit of the Lord?" (Isa 40:13). Or "Shall *any* teach God knowledge?" (Job 21:22). The son of this man was Methusael, asking death, the true fruit of all such presumptuous ones, "his confidence shall be rooted out of his tabernacle, and it shall bring him to the king of terrors" (Job 18:14). His son was Lamech, one poor or smitten: The first, that, as we read, did break the order of God in the matter of marriage.

> Ver. 19. "And Lamech took unto him two wives: the name of the one *was* Adah, and the name of the other Zillah."

This man was the first that brake the first institution of God concerning marriage. "He took unto him two wives." The New Testament says, Let every man have his own wife. And so said the law in its first institution: therefore plurality of wives first came into practice by the seed of cursed Cain, and for a time was suffered in the world through the hardness of man's heart.

> Ver. 20, 21. "And Adah bare Jabal: he was the father of such as dwell in tents, and *of such as*

have cattle. And his brother's name *was* Jubal: he was the father of all such as handle the harp and organ."

Jabal signifies bringing, or budding; Jubal, bringing or fading. So then in these two sons might be shewed unto us the world, as it is in its utmost glory: that is, it brings buds, it brings fading: today in the field, tomorrow in the oven: "All flesh *is* grass, and all the goodliness thereof, *is* as the flower of the field. The grass withereth, the flower fadeth: because the Spirit of the Lord bloweth upon it: surely the people *is* grass" (Isa 40:6-8).

And observe in these, the last was the musical one. Indeed, the spirit of the world, after things have budded, is so far off from remembering that they again must fade; that then it begins its Requiem; then it saith to itself, Eat, drink, and be merry; then it is for handling the harp and organ (Luke 12:16-20).

> Ver. 22. "And Zillah, she also bare Tubal-Cain, an instructor of every artificer in brass and iron: and the sister of Tubal-Cain *was* Naamah."

Tubal-Cain, a worldly possession; and Naamah, one that by her name should be beautiful. Lamech his fruit then was, a budding, fading, worldly possession, with a little deceitful, vain beauty, for "favour *is* deceitful, and beauty *is* vain: *but* a woman *that* feareth the Lord, she shall be praised" (Pro 31:30).

> Ver. 23. "And Lamech said unto his wives, Adah and Zillah, hear my voice; ye wives of Lamech, hearken unto my speech: for I have slain a man to my wounding, and a young man to my hurt."

He that sticks not to exceed in one point, will not fear to transgress in another. He had hardened his heart, by breaking the modest and orderly bounds of marriage, and so fitted himself to shed blood, or do any other wickedness.

"Hearken to me, ye wives." Lustful men break their minds to their fleshly companions, sometimes, sooner than to wiser counsellors. Even as Ahab, in the business of the vineyard of Naboth, breaks his mind to that ungodly Jezebel his wife.

"I have slain a man to my wounding." Who, or what man this murdered person was, therein the word is silent: yet this Lamech being the son of a bloody murderer, it is possible he was some godly man, one of Adam's other children, or of his grandchildren, the son of Seth: for these sons of Cain, and namely this in special, as it seems, took not heed to the mark wherewith God branded Cain; but like Belshazzar, he hardened his heart, though he knew it, and would turn murderer also (Dan 5:18-22).

"I have slain a man to my wounding." The guilt of blood who can bear? or who can help himself thereby? It is a wounding thing, it is a hurtful thing, he that sheds man's blood wrongfully, cannot establish himself thereby (Matt 22:6,7). The Jews thought to have preserved themselves and country by killing Jesus Christ; but this so provoked the justice of God, that for this thing's sake he sent the Gentiles upon them to burn up their city; who when they were come, if stories be true, slew of them eleven hundred thousand; and those of them that were taken alive, were sold to who would buy them, Thirty a penny. "Ye shed blood [says God] and shall ye possess the land? Ye stand upon your sword, ye work abomination, and ye defile every one his neighbour's wife: and shall ye possess the land?" (Eze 33:25,26).

Ver. 24. "If Cain shall be avenged sevenfold, truly Lamech seventy and sevenfold."

Though wicked men may be willingly ignorant of that part of the judgments of God, that are to premonish them, that they do not that wicked thing for which the judgment was executed; yet if there be anything like favour mixed with the judgment, of that they will take notice, to encourage themselves to evil: even as this ungodly person, he would not be stopped from blood by the judgment of God upon Cain; but rather, as it seems, because the judgment was not speedily executed, his heart was fully set in him to do evil (Eccl 8:11). Much like that of the Jews, who because Jehoiakim had slain Uriah the prophet, and yet God spared the land; therefore make that an argument to prevail with Zedekiah to kill Jeremiah also (Jer 26:20-23).

"If Cain shall be avenged sevenfold, truly Lamech seventy and sevenfold." Give wicked men leave to judge of themselves, and they will pass a sentence favourable enough. Though Lamech had not pity when he spilt blood; yea, though the judgment of God upon Cain could not hold his murderous hands: yet now he is guilty, let him but make a law in the case, and woe be to him that killeth Lamech: Vengeance shall be taken of him seventyfold and seven. Joab could with pitiless hands spill the blood of men more righteous than himself, not regarding what became of their souls: but when his blood was by vengeance required for the same, then he would take sanctuary at the horns of the altar (1 Kings 2:28). But judgment is not wholly left to me, the Lord is judge himself; before whom both Cain and Lamech, and all their successors, shall be arraigned, and receive just doom, and that never to be reversed.

> Ver. 25. "And Adam knew his wife again; and she bare a son, and called his name Seth: for God, *said she*, hath appointed me another seed instead of Abel, whom Cain slew."

Now we have done, for a while, with Cain, and are come again to the church of God. Cain had slain Abel, and by that means, for a while, had greatly suppressed the flourishing of religion; in which time his own brood began to be mighty upon earth; so increasing, as if religion was put to an end for ever. But behold their disappointment! "Adam knew his wife again," (for Adam's family was then the true church of God;) or take Adam for a type of Christ, and his wife for a type of the church, and then this observation followeth; namely, That so long as Christ and the church hath to do with one another, it is in vain for Cain to think of suppressing religion.

"Adam knew his wife again." If Eve had now been barren, or Adam had died without farther issue, then Cain might have carried the day; but behold another seed! a seed to stand in Abel's place: therefore she called his name Seth; that is, Set or Put, as namely, in the room of Abel, to stand up for, and to defend the truth against all the army and power of Cain. As Paul also saith of himself, "I am set, [or put,] for the defence of the gospel" (Phil 1:17). This man therefore, so far as can be gathered, was the first that put check to the outrage of Cain and his company. But mark some observations about him.

1. He was set in the stead or place of Abel; not an inch behind him, but even at the place where his blood was spilt. So that he that will revive lost religion, must avow it as God's Abels have done before him: every talker cannot do this. The blood that was shed before his face, must not put check to his godly stomach; yea, he must say to religion, as Ruth said once to her mother, "Where thou diest, I will die, and there will I be buried" (Ruth 1:17). This is the way to revive and to maintain the ways of God, in despite of bloody Cain.[24]

2. This Seth that was set to put check to Cain, did not do it of his own brain, but the hand of God was principal in the work. "God," said she, "hath appointed me another seed to be set in the place of Abel." And indeed it is otherwise in vain, when religion is once suppressed, to think it should ever revive again. Alas! where is the man, if he want God's Spirit, that will care for the flourishing state of religion? and that in truth will make the Lord his delight: "This *is* Zion, whom no man seeketh [for, or seeketh] after" (Jer 30:17). All men here say, "See to thine own house, David" (1 Kings 12:16). But when Seth comes, then the ground is made good again; then a living saint is found to stand and maintain that truth which but now his brother bled for. When James was killed, Peter stands up, &c. (Acts 12:1-3). And therefore Seth is said to be another seed, a man of another spirit: One who was principled with a spirit beyond and above the spirit of the world. "Another seed," one that was spirited for God's word, and God's worship, and that would maintain his brother's cause.

3. Observe, That when Seth maintains his brother's lot, you hear no more of the brood of Cain. And indeed, the way to weary out God's enemies, it is to maintain and make good the front against them: "Resist the devil, and

he will fly" (James 4:7). Now if the Captain, their king Apollion, be made to yield, how can his followers stand their ground? "The dragon, - the devil, Satan, - he was cast out into the earth, and his angels were cast out with him" (Rev 12:9). But how? It was by fighting: "Michael and his angels fought against the dragon; - and overcame him by the blood of the Lamb, and by the word of their testimony, and by not loving of their lives unto the death" (Rev 12:7,8,12).

4. Let this, in the last place, serve for persecutors, That when you have cast down many ten thousands, and also the truth to the ground; there is yet a Seth, another seed behind, that God hath appointed to stand in the stead of his brethren, by whom you will certainly be put to flight, and made to cease from oppressing the truth.

> Ver. 26. "And to Seth, to him also there was born a son; and he called his name Enos: Then began men to call upon the name of the Lord."

The Holy Ghost, in recording the birth of Enos, goeth out of his ordinary style, in that he doubleth the mentioning of his father, with respect to the birth of this son. And indeed it is worth the observing; for it staggereth the faith of some, to think that the man that makes good the ground of a murdered brother, should not leave issue behind him: But "to Seth, to him was born a son." Our faithfulness to the truth, shall be no hindrance to the flourishing state of our offspring, take them either for the fleshly or spiritual seed of God's servants, but sons, (especially in the latter sense, if we truly stand by the word of God) shall surely be born unto us.

"And to Seth, to him also there was born a son; and he called his name Enos." Enos, a man; not a devil, like Cain, but a man; or, a man that was miserable in this world, for the sake and cause of God;[25] for it seems, as was his father, so was he, even both given up to maintain God's truth; which cannot be done but with great hazard, so long as Cain or his offspring remain. His father therefore, by his very name, did offer him up to bear all hardships for the name and cause of God: "Behold I send you forth [saith Christ] as lambs in the midst of wolves." In effect, he called their name Enos, men to be acquainted with grief and miseries: But mark, "Then began men to call upon the name of the Lord."

"Then," when Seth maintained Abel's ground, and when Enos endured all miseries for the same: For indeed this makes spectators believe that religion is more than a fictitious notion: The hardships, miseries, and blood of the saints, will make men, otherwise heedless, consider and ponder their cause aright.

"Then began." For, as I also before have hinted, the outrage of bloody Cain did put, for a time, a stop to the flourishing state of God's worship; which in all probability was not so little as half a hundred years, even till Seth, and the son of Seth, stood up to maintain the same; but "then, THEN men began [more men than Seth and Enos] to call upon the name of the Lord."

Note again, That all true religion beginneth with fervent prayer: Or thus, That when men begin to be servants to God, they begin it with calling upon him. Thus did Saul, "Behold he prayeth" (Acts 9): And, "Lord have mercy upon me," is the first of the groans of a sanctified heart.

The margin hath it, "They began to call themselves by the name of the Lord." As God saith in another place, "My name is called on them." The disciples were called Christians, (nay, the saints are called the anointed ones, and the church is called Christ) (1 Cor 12:12). But note, That fervent prayer ends in faith and confidence in God. They called themselves by the name; they counted themselves not from a vain and groundless opinion, but through the faith they had in the mercy of God, The saints and holy people of God.

They began to publish themselves, in contradistinction to the offspring of Cain, the holy people of God. Wherefore, a separation from the wicked began betimes; the one going by the name of "the sons of God"; the other, "by the sons and daughters of men" (6:1,2): "Then began men to call upon the name of the Lord."

Chapter V.

> Ver. 1. "This *is* the book of the generations of Adam. In the day that God created man, in the likeness of God made he him."

The Holy Ghost having thus largely treated of Cain and his offspring, and of the head made against him by Seth and Enos, and of the good success that followed, he now comes to treat of the church in particular, and of the flourishing state of the same.

"This *is* the book." The Holy Ghost cuts off the genealogy of Cain, accounting him none of the race of the church, although before he was within the pale thereof. John observing this, calls him, "a child of that wicked one" (1 John 3:12), as our Lord also accounted Judas. Wherefore, he here begins his book again, that this wicked race might be quite excluded. "Let them be blotted out of the book of the living, and not be written with the righteous" (Psa 69:28).

"In the day that God created man, in the likeness of God made he him." Although by this new beginning the Holy Ghost excludeth Cain, yet he fetcheth the genealogy of the church from the day that man was created; intimating that God, in the very act of creation, had a special intention to plant him a church in the world; and therefore, even before sin was in the world, the image of God was upon man, as a token of his special respect, and of the great delight that he intended to take in that creature above all that he had made (Pro 8:30,31).

> Ver. 2. "Male and female created he them; and blessed them, and called their name Adam, in the day when they were created."

When Adam was created, the Lord created two in one: So when Christ, the head of the church, was chosen, the church was also chosen in him.

"And blessed them." With the blessing of generation: A type of the blessing of regeneration that was to be by Christ in the church, according to that which is written, "So shall thy seed be" (Eph 1:4).

"And called their name Adam, in the day when they were created." So that in the man the woman is included: "Neither is the man without the woman, neither the woman without the man, in the Lord" (1 Cor 11:11). For the Holy Ghost, in the work of the new creation, of which this creation was a type, counteth not by male and female, but "ye are all one in Christ Jesus" (Gal 3:28). Wherefore, women are not to be excluded out of the means of salvation; nay, they have, if they believe, a special right to all the promises of grace that God hath made to his saints in all ages: Yea, "she shall be saved in childbearing, [though she bear children,] if she continue in faith, and charity, and holiness with sobriety" (1 Tim 2:15).

> Ver. 3. "And Adam lived an hundred and thirty years, and begat *a son* in his own likeness, after his image; and called his name Seth."

Here also by the book of Chronicles, the Holy Ghost carrieth away the genealogy, because Abel had no children, saying Adam, Seth, &c. (1 Chron 1:1).

"An hundred and thirty years." Behold the rage of hell! For until Seth stood in Abel's place, religion was greatly hindered, and that was after the world had stood an hundred and thirty years. Indeed, Abel, while he had his breath, did hold it up in the world; but Cain, who was of that wicked one, smote him and religion both to the ground.

"And begat *a son* in his own likeness." Who can bring a clean *thing* out of an unclean? not one" (Job 14:4). If the father be polluted with the inward filth of sin, the son must needs be like him: "I was shapen in iniquity; [said David] and in sin did my mother conceive me" (Psa 51:5). Seth then was no better than we by nature, but came into the world in the blood of his mother's filth: "What *is* man, that he should be clean? and *he which is* born of a woman, that he should be righteous?" (Job 15:14).

This therefore should teach us not to count of our election, and of our effectual calling but by the word of God. Seth by nature was a sinful man, and yet the chosen servant of God; the first that took up God's quarrel after the death of blessed Abel.

This should also help us to hold up the bucklers against the kingdom of the devil and hell. Seth was subject to like infirmities with us, and yet he got ground of the children of iniquity. I know a sense of our own infirmities is apt to weaken our hand in so mighty an undertaking, but it should not: Although we be like old Adam by nature, yet God is able to make us stand.

Ver. 4. "And the days of Adam, after he had begotten Seth, were eight hundred years: and he begat sons and daughters."

Adam therefore, as a type of Christ, reigned in the church almost a thousand years. The world therefore beginning thus, doth shew us how it will end; namely, by the reign of the second Adam, as it began with the reign of the first.

These long-lived men therefore shew us the glory that the church shall have in the latter day, even in the seventh thousand years of the world, that sabbath when Christ shall set up his kingdom on earth, according to that which is written, "They lived and reigned with Christ a thousand years" (Rev 20:1-4). They:—Who? The church of God, according also as it was with Adam. Therefore they are said by John to be holy, as well as blessed: "Blessed and holy *is* he that hath part in the first resurrection: on such the second death hath no power, but they shall be priests of God, and of Christ, and shall reign with him a thousand years" (v 6). In all which time the wicked in the world shall forbear to persecute, as did also the brood of wicked Cain in the days of Adam, Seth, &c. Hence therefore we find in the first place the dragon chained for these thousand years.

Ver. 5. "And all the days that Adam lived were nine hundred and thirty years: and he died."

Adam therefore lived to see the translation of Enoch[xii]: In whose translation a conquest was got over all the enemies of his soul and body: So Christ shall reign in and among his saints till all his enemies be destroyed.

[xii] I am not convinced about Bunyan's maths here. By my reckoning, Adam died in 930 AM (*Anno Mundi* - the year of creation). Enoch was born during Adam's lifetime - 622AM - but died in 987AM - some 57 years **after** Adam's death.

"The last enemy *that* shall be destroyed *is* death" (1 Cor 15:26); which shall be swallowed up when the members of that glorious head have put on incorruption, and their "mortal shall have put on immortality." Adam's reigning therefore until Enoch's translation, looks like a prophecy of the perfection of Christ's kingdom: For he shall reign till he hath "delivered up the kingdom to God, even the Father" (v 24): As Adam, till his Enoch was translated and took up to God.

Ver. 6. "And Seth lived an hundred and five years, and begat Enos."

Seth therefore stood by the truth of God, a long time, without much help or encouragement from man; which was a great trial to his spirit, and proof of the truth of his faith, and tended much to the perfection of his patience. Somewhat like this was that of Paul, who had no man stood with him when he stood before Nero.

Seth was set in the stead of Abel, to keep the gap against the children of hell; which, by the grace of God, he faithfully did, even till Enos was sent to his aid and assistance.

Seth therefore was the forlorn hope of the church in those days. So set of God to put check to the enemy, until the church was increased, and more able to defend herself from the outrage.

This therefore should teach the saints of God, especially those that are sent before, against the offspring of Cain, to stand their ground, and not to shrink like Saul, till God shall send others to take part with them (1 Sam 10:8; 13:8-14).

Thus David stood, as it were, by himself, against the wicked that was in his day; which made him cry, "Who will rise up for me against the evil doers," *or* who will stand up for me against the workers of iniquity? (Psa 94:16).

> Ver. 7. "And Seth lived after he begat Enos eight hundred and seven years, and begat sons and daughters."

Hence also we may gather great encouragement who are set in the front of the army of the Lamb, against the army and regiment of Cain. Seth, saith the Spirit, was set in the stead of Abel, there as forlorn, to defend religion: Must he not now be swallowed up? Will the blood-hounds let him escape? Behold, therefore his life must be accounted a wonder! As was also that of Paul (1 Cor 6:9). But for Seth to stand eight hundred years against such a murderous crew, and yet to have his breath in his nostrils! Our times are in thy hands, and thou, Lord, "holdeth our soul in life" (Psa 66:9).

> "And all the days of Seth were nine hundred and twelve years, and he died" (v 8).

His life was therefore eighteen years shorter than that of Adam; he lived fifty-five years after Enoch, and died six hundred and fourteen years before the flood.

> Ver. 9. "And Enos lived ninety years, and begat Cainan."

Cainan signifieth a buyer, or owner. Let it be with respect to religion, and then the sense may be, that he had this privilege in religion by the hazard of his father and grandfather's life; they bought it for him, and made him the owner of it: As Paul saith, He gave not place to the false Apostles, "that the truth of the gospel might continue with the Galatians" (2:5). As Jotham also said to Shechem, "My Father fought for you, and adventured his life far, and delivered you out of the hand of Midian" (Jude 9:17). Namely, that they might still be owners of the inheritance that the Lord had given them. This shews us then, that the fruit of a constant standing to the word of God, is, That the generations yet unborn shall be made the possessors and owners of it.

> Ver. 10. "And Enos lived after he begat Cainan eight hundred and fifteen years, and begat sons and daughters."

He lived then to see his son enjoy the fruits of his own constancy to the truth, so long a time as eight hundred years, &c. as we hope God's people now may do. 'Tis true, they now do own the truth with hazard, and do hold it up by enduring much misery, according to the rage of wicked men; but, I say, 'tis hoped others will reap the fruits of our travails, and that some of us shall live to see it, as Enos lived to see his Cainan possess religion eight hundred years.[26]

> Ver. 11. "And all the days of Enos were nine hundred and five years: and he died."

He lived then one hundred fifty-three years after Enoch, and died five hundred and sixteen years before the flood.

> Ver. 12. "And Cainan lived seventy years, and begat Mahalaleel."

Mahalaleel, signifieth praising God. Wherefore he was born in settled times, wherein religion met with little or no molestation. It began to be as hereditary in the days of blessed Cainan; wherefore it was requisite that the very next that should possess the truth, should spend their days in praising God (Rev 11:15). And thus it will be at the downfall of Antichrist: "After this [saith John] I heard a great voice of much people in heaven, saying Allelujah; Salvation, and glory, and honour, and power unto the Lord our God...And a voice came out of the throne saying, Praise our God, all ye his servants; and ye that fear him, both small and great" (Rev 19:1-6).

"The whole earth [saith the Prophet] is at rest *and* is quiet, they break forth into singing. Yea, the fir-trees rejoice at thee, [O thou brood of the blood-thirsty Cain,] *and* the cedars of Lebanon, *saying*, Since thou art laid down, no feller is come up against us" (Isa 14:7,8).

> Ver. 13. "And Cainan lived after he begat Mahalaleel eight hundred and forty years, and begat sons and daughters."

God gave him a long possession and enjoyment of the fruits of his father's labours. They sowed (as Christ said) and he was entered into their labours: They sowed in tears, and he reaped in joy. Mahalaleel, or praise our God, was the language of those times.

> Ver. 14. "And all the days of Cainan were nine hundred and ten years: and he died."

He lived then two hundred and forty-eight years after Enoch, and died four hundred twenty-one years before the flood.

> Ver. 15. "And Mahalaleel lived sixty and five years, and begat Jared."

Jared signifies ruling, and sheweth us what is the holy fruits of peace and thanksgiving in the church; to wit, government according to the testament of Christ (Acts 9:31). It is hard to have all things according to rule, in the day of the church's affliction; because of the weakness and fearfulness of some; and because possibly those who have most skill in that matter, may for a time be laid up in chains: but now when the church hath rest and quietness, then as she praiseth God, so she conceiveth and bringeth forth governors, and good government and rule among her members. David, a man of blood, could not build that house to the Lord, which peaceable Solomon, that man of rest, afterwards did (1 Chron 28:3,6). When armies are engaged, and hot in battle, 'tis harder to keep them in rank and file, than when they have rest, and time for discipline. Jared therefore is the fruits of thanksgiving, as thanksgiving is the fruits of peace and possession.

> Ver. 16. "And Mahalaleel lived after he begat Jared eight hundred and thirty years, and begat sons and daughters."

He lived not only to give thanks unto God, but to shew to all that he gave thanks in truth, by submitting his neck the rest of the hundred of years that he lived, to the holy law and word of God.

A good rule to prove people by; for all that pretend to give thanks for liberty, put not their neck under the yoke, but rather use their liberty as an occasion for the flesh, than by love to serve and advantage one another in the things of the kingdom of Christ (Gal 5:13; 1 Peter 2:16). But as "the bramble said to the [rest of the] trees," so saith Christ to such feigned thanksgivers, "If in truth ye anoint me king over you, *then* come *and* put your trust in my shadow" (Judg 9:15). Submit to my law, and be governed by my testament. Let your thanksgiving bring forth Jared, and walk with God in the days of Jared.

Ver. 17. "And all the days of Mahalaleel were eight hundred ninety and five years: and he died." He lived then three hundred and three years after Enoch, and died three hundred and sixty-six years before the flood.

Ver. 18. "And Jared lived an hundred sixty and two years, and he begat Enoch."

Enoch, is taught, or dedicate: The true effect of rule or government, be it good or bad: in Cain's posterity it was bad; "for an evil tree cannot bring forth good fruit." By Enoch here, we are to understand, one taught in, and dedicated unto, God. This Enoch therefore was a son that would hear the rules, and submit to the government of his father Jared. "*As* an ear-ring of gold, and an ornament of fine gold, *so is* a wise reprover upon an obedient ear" (Pro 25:12).

Ver. 19. "And Jared lived after he begat Enoch eight hundred years, and begat sons and daughters."

He lived therefore to see the fruit of his good rule and government in the church, even to see his teachable and dedicated son caught up to God, and to his throne. A good encouragement to all rulers in the house of God, and also to all godly parents to teach and rule in the fear of God; for that is the way to part with church members, and children with comfort; yea, that is the way, if we shall out-live them, to send them to heaven, and to God before us.

> Ver. 20. "And all the days of Jared were nine hundred sixty and two years: and he died."

He lived then three hundred thirty-five years after Enoch, and died two hundred thirty-four before the flood.

> Ver. 21. "And Enoch lived sixty and five years, and begat Methuselah."

Methuselah signifieth, Spoiling his death: this therefore is the true fruits of one that is truly taught in, and dedicate to the service of God, as Enoch was; by this means he spoileth his death: wherefore he adds, "And Enoch walked with God." Walking with God, spoileth death, or overcomes it, or it shall be prevented, he shall not be hurt therewith: As Christ saith, "If a man keep my saying, he shall never taste death" (John 8:52).

> Ver. 22. "And Enoch walked with God, after he begat Methuselah three hundred years, and begat sons and daughters."

These words [after he begat Methuselah] may have respect either to his beginning to walk with God, or to the number of the years that he lived after the birth of Methuselah, or both.

If it respect the fist, then it sheweth that the only encouragement that a sinner hath to walk with God, it is to see Methuselah, or his death spoiled: for when a man seeth death, and all evils, conquered and overcome, then his soul is encouraged in holiness (1 Cor 15:55-58). No encouragement to walking with God like this: "Enoch walked with God after he begat Methuselah." As Paul saith, "Now being made free from sin, - [which indeed is the sting of death] ye have your fruit unto holiness, and the end everlasting life" (Rom 6:22).

If it respect the second, then it shews us the invincible nature of true faith, (for by faith Enoch walked with God:) I say, it sheweth us the invincible nature of true faith, in that it would hold up a man in close communion with God for the space of three hundred years.

"He walked with God three hundred years." How will the conversation of Enoch rise up in judgment with this generation, that walk not with God at all! Or if they do, do it so by fits, as if walking with God was but a work by the by.

"He walked with God and begat sons and daughters." And kept house, and lived with his wife, according to knowledge. This shews then, that it is sin, not our lawful and honest employment, that hindreth one's walking with God.

Ver. 23, 24. "And all the days of Enoch were three hundred and sixty and five years: And Enoch walked with God: And he *was* not; for God took him" (vv 23,24).

The New Testament saith, "By faith Enoch was translated that he should not see death; and was not found, because God had translated him: for before his translation he had this testimony, that he pleased God."

"And all the days of Enoch were three hundred and sixty and five years." Enoch therefore lived here but a while; he was too good to live long in this world, the world was not worthy of him; neither would he be spared so long out of heaven, "for God took him." The end of walking with God or the path-way thereof, it leads men to heaven, to the enjoyment of the glory of God. Thus also it was with blessed Elijah, he followed God from place to place, till at length he was caught up into heaven (2 Kings 2:1-11).

A word or two more of Enoch. Jude observes, That he was the seventh from Adam: Closely intimating (as I conceive) that by him God prefigured the resurrection and end of the world: And intimated, That in the seventh great day of the world this resurrection should be, each generation from Adam being a type of a thousand years: So that Enoch, the seventh from Adam, was a type of the seventh thousand, in which the Lord will reign with his church a thousand years.

There are two things in Enoch that incline me to this opinion. First, he crieth out, "Behold the Lord comes!" and then is translated that he should not see death. The right posture and end of those that shall live at the day of God Almighty; and that shall, like Enoch, be found "walking with God," when the Lord shall come from heaven (Jude 14,15).

> Ver. 25. "And Methuselah lived an hundred eighty and seven years, and begat Lamech."

Lamech signifieth poor, or smitten; wherefore I doubt that the apostacy that you read of in the next chapter, began either in the days of, or by, this man: he being, as it seems, more dry and void of grace than those that went before him; poor, or smitten.

Hence note, That faith and godliness, though often it goeth from the father to the son, as from Seth to Enos, and from him to Cainan, yet it is not tied here, but runs according to electing love, as also do the fruits thereof.

> Ver. 26, 27. "And Methuselah lived after he begat Lamech seven hundred eighty and two years, and begat sons and daughters. And all the days of Methuselah were nine hundred sixty and nine years, and he died."

Methuselah, the spoiling of death, is the longest liver in the world; yet he died in the year that the flood was upon the earth; not by the flood, but by the course of nature, as also did Lamech his son, for the wicked reprobate only was swept away by that, according to the apostle Peter.

> Ver. 28, 29. "And Lamech lived an hundred eighty and two years, and begat a son: and he called his name Noah, saying, This *same* shall comfort us concerning our work and toil of our hands, because of the ground which the Lord hath cursed."

"And he called his name Noah." Noah signifieth rest; his name was therefore according to his work, for he was a preacher of righteousness, which giveth rest to all that embraceth it. Besides, it was he that prepared the ark, the place of rest to the church of God.

"This *same* shall comfort us concerning our work and toil of our hands, because of the ground which the Lord hath cursed."

These words seem to carry in them, repentance for the apostacy that before was mentioned. "This same shall comfort us," by restoring the church to her former rest, and by delivering us from the "toil of our hands"; for sin once admitted of in the church, is not without much toil extirpated, and driven forth of the same; yea sometimes it getteth such footing and root, that it cannot again be purged and destroyed, but by breaking the very being of the church where it is. Thus it was as to the case in hand, and is signified also by pulling down the house in which the leprosy was (Lev 14:43-45). Yea Ephesus itself was almost thus far infected, had not a threatening prevented (Rev 2:1-3).

"Because of the ground which the Lord hath cursed." The Lord did curse it for the sin of Adam: He also renewed the curse to Cain, because he was guilty of the blood of his brother. I incline also to think, that the curse here mentioned, is the first, reiterated for the grievous apostacy of this congregation; according to that which is written, "If ye walk contrary unto me," "I will punish you seven times more": "I will bring seven times more plagues upon you, according to your sins" (Lev 26:18-21).

Ver. 30. "And Lamech lived after he begat Noah, five hundred ninety and five years, and begat sons and daughters."

Wherefore Lamech heard the preaching of Noah, who was the only minister of God in those days, to recover the church to repentance from their apostacy, which also he did in some good measure effect, while he condemned, the world for their unbelief (Heb 11:7).

Ver. 31. "And all the days of Lamech were seven hundred seventy and seven years: and he died."

He died five years before the flood. Methuselah therefore was the longest liver of those godly that fell on the other side the flood, for he died not before the very year the flood came, not by the water, but before. The righteous is taken away from the evil to come; though, as the prophet saith, no man of the wicked laid it to heart.

Ver. 31. "And Noah was five hundred years old: and Noah begat Shem, Ham, and Japhet."

Chapter VI.

> Ver. 1. "And it came to pass, when men began to multiply on the face of the earth, and daughters were born unto them."

Moses now leaveth the genealogy for a while, and searcheth into the state and condition of the church now after so long a time as its standing upwards of, or above, a thousand years: where he presently findeth two things. 1. The church declined. 2. And God provoked. Wherefore he maketh inquiry into the nature of the church's sin; which he relateth in this following chapter.

"And it came to pass, when men began to multiply." The men here I understand to be the children of Cain, the church and synagogue of Satan, because they are mentioned by way of antithesis to the church and sons of God.

"And daughters were born unto them." A snare that was often used in the hand of the devil, to intangle withal the church of God; yea, and doth so usually speed, that it hath often been counted by him as infallible; so that this is the doctrine of his prophet Balaam, and it prevailed, when all the engines of hell beside were prevented. "The people began to commit whoredom with the daughters of Moab" (Num 25:1,2). It may be this child of hell, in this his advice to Balak looked back to the daughters of Cain, and calling to remembrance how of old they intangled the church, advertised him to put the same into practice again (Rev 2:14).

> Ver. 2. "That the sons of God saw the daughters of men, that they *were* fair; and they took them wives of all which they chose."

This was the way then of the sons of Cain, to let their fair daughters be shewed to the sons of God (Pro 22:14). For it seems all other their wiles and devices were not able to bring the church and the world together, and to make them live as in one communion. These to the church were such, whose hearts were snares and nets, and whose hands were bands to intangle and hold them from observing the laws and judgments of God (Eccl 7:26).

"And they took them wives." First their eye saw them, and then their heart lusted after them. Thus the devil deceived the woman, and by this means perished cursed Achan. "And Achan answered Joshua, and said, Indeed I have sinned against the Lord, and thus and thus have I done: When I saw among the spoils a goodly Babylonish garment," &c., "then I coveted them" (Josh 7:20,21).

Note therefore, that it is not good to behold with the eye that which God hath forbid us to touch with our hand. "I made a covenant with mine eyes," saith Job (Job 30:1). And again, if at unawares a thing was cast before him, the beholding of which was of an intangling nature, he forthwith would hold back his heart as with a bridle, lest the design of hell should be effected upon him (v 7).

Crush sin then in the conception, lest it bring forth death in thy soul.

> Ver. 3. "And the Lord said, My Spirit shall not always strive with man, for that he also *is* flesh:

> yet his days shall be an hundred and twenty years."

By these words is aggravated the sin of the church, that she would attempt to close with, and hold a sinful communion, against the dissuasions of the Spirit of God.

"My Spirit shall not always strive." To wit, my Spirit in Noah, for he was the only preacher of righteousness to the church in those backsliding times.

By this then, I find, that the doctrine of Noah, was, To declare against a sinful communion, or to command the church, in the name of God, that she still maintain a separation from the cursed children of Cain: As he said to the prophet Jeremiah, If thou separate the precious from the vile, "thou shalt be as my mouth" (15:19).

Noah therefore had a hard task, when he preached this doctrine among them: for this above all is hard to be borne, for by this he condemned the world.

The first great quarrel therefore that God had with his church, it was for their holding unwarrantable communion with others. The church should always "dwell alone, and not be reckoned among the nations" (Num 23:9). The church is "a chosen generation, a royal priesthood, an holy nation, a peculiar people" (1 Peter 2:9). Therefore the work of the church of God, is not to fall in with any sinful fellowship, or receive into their communion the ungodly world, but to shew forth the praises and virtues of him who hath called them out from among such communicants into his marvellous light.

"My Spirit shall not always strive." Hence note, that the people that shall continue to grieve the Spirit of God, and to resist the doctrine of Noah, they are appointed for heavy judgments. "Come out of her, my people, that ye be not partakers of her sins, and that ye receive not of her plagues" (Rev 18:4). This because those (finally impenitent) in Noah's time refused to do, therefore the wrath of God overtook them, and swept them off the face of the earth.

"Yet his days shall be an hundred and twenty years." Noah therefore began his preaching about the four hundred and fourscore year of his life, which continuing the space of sixscore more, it reached to the day that the flood came.

In which time doubtless his faith was sufficiently tried, both by the hard censures of the hypocrites of the church, and the open profane of the world, against whom he daily pronounced the judgments of God for maintaining their forbidden communion (Gen 3:15).

"Yet his days shall be an hundred and twenty years." God also would yet have patience with these people, if peradventure they would repent that his hand might not be upon them.

Ver. 4. "There were giants in the earth in those days; and also after that, when the sons of God came in unto the daughters of men, and they bare *children* to them, the same *became* mighty men, which *were* of old, men of renown."

"There were giants in the earth in those days." These words seem to be spoken, to shew us the hazards that Noah ran, while he preached the truth of God: He incurred the displeasure of the giants, which doubtless made all men tremble, and kept the whole world in awe. But Noah must engage the giants, he must not fear the face of a giant. This way God took also with Moses, and with his people of Israel, they must go to possess the land of the giants, a people high and tall as the cedars, a people of whom went that proverb, "Who can stand before the children of Anak?" (Deu 9:2). They must not be afraid of Og the king of Bashan, though his head be as high as the ridge of a house, and his bedstead a bedstead of iron (Deu 3:11).

This should teach us then not to fear the faces of men: no, not the faces of the mighty; not to fear them, I say, in the matters of God, though they should run upon us like a giant.

These giants I suppose were the children of Cain, because mentioned as another sort than those that were the fruit of their forbidden and ungodly communion: For he adds, "And also after that," or besides them, "when the sons of God came in unto the daughters of men, and they bare *children* to them, the same, [or they also] *became* mighty men which *were* of old, men of renown."

Then Noah found giants every where: Giants in the world, and giants in this confused communion. And thus it is at this day; we do not only meet with giants abroad, among the most ungodly and uncircumcised in heart, but even among those that seem to be of the religious, among them we also meet with giants; men mighty to oppose the truth, and very profound to make slaughter: But mark the advice of the Lord, "Fear not their fear, nor be afraid. Sanctify the Lord of hosts himself, [who is stronger than all the giants that are upon the face of the earth] and *let* him *be* your fear, and *let* him *be* your dread" (Isa 8:12,13).

"And when the sons of God came in unto the daughters of men, and they bare *children* to them, the same *became* mighty men"; much like to the giants. The fruit therefore of ungodly communion is monstrous, and of a very strange complexion. They are like unto them that worshipped the Lord, and served their own gods also (2 Kings 17:24,41); or like to those of the church, of whom Nehemiah speaks, that had mixed themselves with the children of Ashdod, Ammon and Moab, whose children were a monstrous brood, that spake half the language of Ashdod, and could not speak the Jews' language (Neh 13:23,24).

By both these sorts of giants was faithful Noah despised, and his work for God condemned. In David's time also Goliath defied Israel,and so did his brethren also (1 Sam 17:10). Giants, the sons of the giant; but David and his servants must engage them, and fight them, though they were giants (1 Chron 20:4-8).

"Mighty men which were of old." Persecution therefore, or the appearance of the giants against the servants of God, is no new business; not a thing of yesterday, but of old, even when Noah did minister for God in the world. "There were giants in the earth in those days," to oppose him.

"Men of renown." Not for faith and holiness, but for some other high achievements, may be, mighty to fight, and to shed man's blood; or to find out arts, and the nature of things; both which did render them famous, and men to be noted in their place. Such kind of men might be Corah, Dathan, and their company also; yet they opposed Moses and Aaron, yea, God, his way and worship, and perished after an unheard of manner (Num 16:1,2). As also did the opposers of righteous Noah, in the day of the flood.

> Ver. 5. "And God saw that the wickedness of man *was* great in the earth, and *that* every imagination of the thoughts of his heart *was* only evil continually."

The margin saith, "not only the imagination, but also the purposes and desires."

These words are to be understood, as still respecting the apostacy that we read of in the first and second verses, and are (in my thoughts) to be taken as the effect of their degeneracy. For though it be true, that the best of men, in their most holy and godly behaviour, have wicked and sinful hearts; yet so long as they walk sincerely according to the rules prescribed of God, there is no such character upon them; especially as it stands related to the words that immediately follow; to wit, "that it repented the Lord that he made them."

These evil and wicked purposes then were in special the fruit of their apostacy: for indeed, when men are once fallen from God, they then, as the judgment of God upon them, are given up to all unrighteousness. Again, apostatizing persons are counted abhorrers of God (Zech 11:8). Yet persons in this condition will seek their own justification, turning things upside down, traversing their ways like the dromedaries; bearing us still in hand, that they stand not guilty of sin, but that what they do is allowable, or winked at of God. Besides, they say their hearts are still upright with God, and that they have not forsaken the simplicity of his way, of a wicked and ungodly design, with an hundred more the like pretences; all which are condemned of God, and held by him as abominable and vile (Jer 2:31-37).

And God saw, &c. They covered their shame from men, like the adulterous woman in the Proverbs, and would speak with oily mouths, thereby to cozen the world (Pro 30:20); but God knew their hearts, and had revealed their sin to his servant Noah; he therefore in the Spirit of God, as one alone, cried out against their wickedness.

Hence learn to judge of apostates, not by their words, nor pretences, nor ungodly coverings, whereby they may seek to hide themselves from the stroke of a convincing argument, but judge them by the words of God; for however they think of themselves, or would be accounted of others, God sees their wickedness is great.

"And *that* every imagination of the thoughts of his heart, *was* only evil continually." If they think they have not sinned; if they think they promote religion; if they think to find out a medium to make peace between the seed of the woman, and the wicked seed of Cain; all is alike ungodly, they have forsaken the right way, they have dissembled the known truth, they have rejected the word of the Lord: And what wisdom or goodness is in them?

Ver. 6. "And it repented the Lord that he had made man on the earth, and it grieved him at his heart."

Repentance is in us a change of the mind; but in God, a change of his dispensations; for otherwise he repenteth not, neither can he; because it standeth not with the perfection of his nature: In him "is no variableness, neither shadow of turning" (James 1:17).

Wherefore, it is man, not God, that turns. When men therefore reject the mercy and ways of God, they cast themselves under his wrath and displeasure; which because it is executed according to the nature of his justice, and the severity of his law, they miss of the mercy promised before (Num 23:19). Which that we may know, those shall one day feel that shall continue in final impenitency. Therefore, God speaking to their capacity, he tells them, he hath repented of doing them good. "The Lord repented that he had made Saul king" (1 Sam 15:35). And yet this repentance was only a change of the dispensation, which Saul by his wickedness had put himself under; otherwise the strength, the eternity of Israel, "will not lie nor repent" (v 29).

The sum is therefore, that men had now by their wickedness put themselves under the justice and law of God; which justice by reason of its perfection, could not endure they should abide on the earth any longer; and therefore now, as a just reward of their deed, they must be swept from the face thereof.

"And it grieved him at his heart." This is spoken to show, that he did not feign, but was simple and sincere in his promise of remission and forgiveness of sins, had they kept close to his word, according as he had commanded. Wherefore God's heart went not with them in their backsliding, but left them, and was offended with them.

Ver. 7. "And the Lord said, I will destroy man whom I have created, from the face of the earth, both man, and beast, [or from man to beast,] and the creeping thing, and the fowls of the air; for it repenteth me that I have made them."

This may be either understood as a threatening, or a determination: if as a threatening then it admitted of time for repentance; but if it was spoken as a determination, then they had stood out the day of grace, and had laid themselves under unavoidable judgment. If it respected the first, then it was in order to the ministry of Noah, or in order to the effecting the ends of its sending; which were either to soften or harden, or bring to repentance, or to leave them utterly and altogether inexcusable. But if it respected the second, as it might, then it was pronounced as an effect of God's displeasure, for their abuse of his patience, his minister, and word. As it also was with Israel of old; "They mocked the messengers of God, and despised his words, and misused his prophets, until the wrath of the Lord arose against his people, till *there was* no remedy" (2 Chron 36:16).

"And the Lord said, I will destroy man whom I have created." This word created, is added, on purpose to show that the world is under the power of his hand; for who can destroy, but he that can create? Or who can save alive, when the maker of the world is set against them? "There is one lawgiver, who is able to save and to destroy" (James 4:12). And again, "Fear him which is able to destroy both soul and body in hell" (Matt 10:28). In both which places power to destroy is insinuated from his power and Godhead: As he saith in another place, "All souls are mine; - the soul that sinneth, it shall die" (Eze 18:4).

"Both man and beast, and the creeping thing, and the fowls," &c. Thus it was at first the sin of a man brought a curse and judgment upon other the creatures whom God had made: As Paul says, "The whole creation groaneth" (Rom 8:22).

But again, This threatening upon the beasts, the fowls, and creeping thing, might arise from a double consideration: First, To show, that when God intends the destruction of man, he will also destroy the means of his preservation (Josh 6:20). Or, secondly, To shew, that when he is determined to execute his judgments, he will cut off all that stands in his way (2 Chron 35:21). He could not destroy the earth without a flood, and preserve the beast, &c., alive; therefore he destroys them also.

"For it repenteth me that I have made them." This seems to fall under the first consideration, to wit, That God repented that he made the beasts and fowls; because now they were used to sustain his implacable enemies.

Ver. 8. "But Noah found grace in the eyes of the LORD."

This word GRACE, must in special be observed; for grace is it which delivereth from all deserved judgments and destruction.

Noah, by nature was no better than other men: therefore the reason why he perished not with others, it was because he "found grace in the eyes of the Lord." Ye are saved by grace (Eph 2:8). And thus was Noah, as is evident, because he was saved by faith (Heb 11:7). For faith respecteth not works, but grace: Ye are saved by grace through faith. As Paul says again, "Therefore *it is* of faith that *it might be* by grace," &c. (Rom 4:16). We must therefore, in our deliverance from all the judgments of God, sing grace, grace, unto it.

> Ver. 9. "These *are* the generations of Noah: Noah was a just man, *and* perfect in his generations; *and* Noah walked with God."

The Holy Ghost here makes a short digression from his progress, in his relation of the wickedness of the world; and yet not impertinently; for seeing Noah was the man that escaped the judgment, his escape must be for some reason; which was, because God was gracious to him, and because God had justified him. Besides Noah being now made righteous, faithfully walketh with God.

"He was just and perfect in his generations." But why it is said, Generations? It might be, because he was faithful to God and man, having the armour of righteousness on the right hand, and on the left. It is said in Isaiah, That Christ "made his grave with the wicked, and with the rich in his death" (53:9). To import, That they only have benefit by him to eternal life, that die by his example, as well as live by his blood; for in his death was both merit and example; and they are like to miss in the first, that are not concerned in the second (Phil 8:16).

"Perfect in his generations." In his carriage, doctrines and life, before both God and man. And thus ought every preacher to be; he ought to do in the sight of God, what he commands to men; by this means he saveth both himself, and them that hear him (1 Tim 4:16).

Besides, Noah was a man, as well as a saint, and in either sense had a generation: to both of which grace made him faithful; and he that shall not serve his generation as a man, will hardly serve his generation as a Christian. But Noah was perfect in both, he was "perfect in his generations."

"And Noah walked with God." This shews he was sincere in his work; for a hypocrite may, as to outward shew, do as the saint of God: but *he* doth it with respect to men, not God, and therefore he is a hypocrite. To walk with God then, is not only to do the duty commanded, but to do it as God requireth it; that is, to do it with faith, and son-like fear, as in God's sight, "with singleness of heart."

> Ver. 10. "And Noah begat three sons, Shem, Ham, and Japheth."

These are the offspring of Noah, and by these was the earth replenished after the flood, as will be further seen hereafter.

> Ver. 11. "The earth also was corrupt before God, and the earth was filled with violence."

He has now returned to the matter in hand before; to wit, the causes of the flood.

"The earth also was corrupt." By earth, he may here mean, those that are without the church: and if so, then by corrupt here, we must understand, wicked after a most high manner; for albeit the world and generation of Cain be always sinners before God, yet the Lord cutteth not off the world in general, nor a nation in particular, but because of the commission of eminent outrage and wickedness. Thus it was with those of Sodom, a little before the Lord with fire devoured them. "The men of

Sodom [saith the text] *were* wicked, and sinners before the Lord exceedingly" (Gen 13:13).

Again: As by corrupt, we may understand, corrupt by way of eminency; so again, they were corrupt incurably. This is evident, because they were not brought off from sin by the ministry of Noah, the only appointed means of their conversion.

Hence note, That when men are sinners exceedingly, and when the means of grace appointed of God for their recovery, prove ineffectual, then they are near some signal judgment (2 Chron 36). Thus back-sliding Jerusalem, because she was wicked with an high hand (Eze 24:13,14), and could not be cured by the ministry of the prophets, therefore her sons must go forth of her into captivity, and the city burned to the ground with fire (Jer 15:1-3).

"And the earth was filled with violence." First, they had violated the law of God, in making and maintaining ungodly and wicked communion; according to that of the prophet, "Her priests have violated my law, and have profaned mine holy things." But how? "They have put no difference between the holy and profane, neither have they shewed *difference* between the unclean and the clean" (Eze 22:26).

They also perverted judgment between a man and his neighbour: adhering to their own party, in disaffection to the religious. This is supposed, because of the exceeding latitude of the expression, "The earth was filled with violence"; that is, all manner of violence, outrage and cruelty was committed by this sort of people. This takes in that saying of Solomon, the oppression of the poor, especially God's poor, is included, in a "violent perverting of judgment and justice" (Eccl 5:8).

They also shewed violence to the lives of good men, as may be gathered by the act of Lamech, one of the sons of Cain. In a word, "The earth was filled with violence"; violence of every kind; lust and wickedness was outrageous, there was a world of ungodliness among these ungodly men.

> Ver. 12. "And God looked upon the earth, and, behold, it was corrupt; for all flesh had corrupted his way upon the earth."

By these words therefore is confirmed the sense of the former verse, "The earth was corrupt"; for God saw it was so: "The earth was full of violence," for they had corrupted God's way.

"And God looked upon the earth." This shews us, That the Lord doth not with haste, or in a rash inconsiderate way, pour his judgments upon the world; but that with judgment and knowledge, the wickedness first being certain, and of merit deserving the same. This is seen in his way of dealing with Sodom. "And the Lord said, Because the cry of Sodom and Gomorrah is great, and because their sin is very grievous, I will go down now, and see whether they have done altogether according to the cry of it, which is come unto me; and if not, I will know" (Gen 18:21).

"And, behold, it was corrupt; for all flesh had corrupted his way upon the earth." It proved, as that of Sodom did, according to the cry thereof; for "all flesh had corrupted his way." God's WAY, by violating his law, and perverting of judgment, as was hinted before. All flesh had corrupted it, therefore the evil needed not to be long in searching out: As God saith by the prophet Jeremiah, "I have not found it by diligent search, but upon all these" (2:34). Here upon the whole earth, none exempted but righteous Noah.

> Ver. 13. "And God said unto Noah, The end of all flesh is come before me; for the earth is filled with violence through them; and, behold, I will destroy them with the earth."

"And God said unto Noah," or told Noah his purpose: The same way he went with Abraham: "Shall I hide from Abraham that thing which I do?" (Gen 18:17). "Surely the Lord will do nothing, but he revealeth his secrets unto his servants the prophets" (Amos 3:7).

"The end of all flesh is come." The time or expiration of the world is at hand. God speaks before he smites. Thus he did also by the prophet Ezekiel, saying, "An end" is come, "the end is come": And again, "An end is come, the end is come: it watcheth for thee; behold, it is come" (7:1-6).

"The end of all flesh is come before me." Sin and wickedness doth not put an end to the ungodly before their own face, yet it brings their end before the face of God. It is said of these very people, "they knew not" of their destruction, "until" the day "the flood came, and took them all away" (Matt 24:37-39). Indeed, the nature of sin is to blind the mind, that the person concerned may neither see mercy nor judgment; but God sees their end: "The end of all flesh is come before me."

"The end of all flesh." By these words, the souls are left to, and reserved for another judgment: Wherefore, though here we find the flesh consumed; yet Peter saith, their spirits are still in prison, even the souls that Christ once preached to in the days, and by the ministry of Noah: Even the souls "which sometime were disobedient when once the long-suffering of God waited in the days of Noah, while the ark was a preparing," &c. (1 Peter 3:19,20).

Ver. 14. "Make thee an ark of gopher wood; rooms shalt thou make in the ark, and shalt pitch it within and without with pitch."

This is the fruits of the grace of God: He said before, That Noah "found grace in the eyes of the Lord": Which grace appoints to him the means of his preservation.

"Make THEE an ark." He saith not, Make one; or, Make one for me: But, Make one; make one for thee: "Make THEE an ark of gopher wood."

Noah therefore, from this word THEE, did gather, That God did intend to preserve him from the judgment which he had appointed in this his work: Therein lay his own profit and comfort; not a thought which he had, not a blow that he struck, about the preparing the ark, but he preached, as to others their ruin, to himself, his safeguard and deliverance: He "prepared an ark, to the saving of his house" (Heb 11:7).

This therefore must needs administer much peace and content to his mind, while he preached to others their overthrow. As the prophet saith, "The work of righteousness shall be peace; and the effect of righteousness quietness and assurance for ever. And my people shall dwell in a peaceable habitation" (Isa

32:17,18). Thus did Noah when he dwelt in the ark, and in sure dwellings, and in quiet resting-places.

"Make thee an ark." The ark was a figure of several things. 1. Of Christ, in whom the church is preserved from the wrath of God. 2. It was a figure of the works of the faith of the godly: "By faith he prepared an ark"; by which the followers of Christ are preserved from the rage and tyranny of the world (for the rage of the water was a type of that, as I shall shew you hereafter). So then Noah, by preparing an ark, or by being bid so to do of God, was thereby admonished, First, To live by the faith of Christ, of whom the ark was a type: and hence it is said, that in preparing the ark, he "became heir of the righteousness which is by faith"; because he understood the mind of God therein, and throughout his figure acted faith upon Christ. But, Secondly, His faith was not to be idle, and therefore he was bid to work. This begat in him an obediential fear of doing ought which God had forbidden: "By faith Noah, being warned of God of things not seen as yet, moved with fear, prepared an ark, to the saving of his house; by the which he condemned the world, and became heir of the righteousness which is by faith" (Heb 11:7).

"Rooms [nests] shalt thou make in the ark." To wit, for himself, and the beasts, and birds of the field, &c. Implying, that in the Lord Jesus there is room for Jews and Gentiles. Yea, forasmuch as these rooms were prepared for beasts of every sort, and for fowls of every wing: it informs us, that for all sorts, ranks and qualities of men, there is preservation in Jesus Christ: "Compel them to come in"; drive them (in a gospel sense as Noah did the beasts of old into the ark), that my house may be full, "and yet there is room" [27] (Luke 14:22,23).

"And thou shalt pitch it within and without with pitch." This was to secure all from the flood, or to keep them that were in the ark from perishing in the waters.

Ver. 15. "And this *is the fashion* which thou shalt make it *of:* the length of the ark *shall be* three hundred cubits, the breadth of it fifty cubits, and the height of it thirty cubits."

A vessel fit to swim upon the waters.

"And this *is the fashion,*" &c. God's ordinances must be according to God's order and appointment, not according to our fancies, "This *is the fashion,*" to wit, according to what is after expressed.

By these words therefore Noah was limited and bound up, as to a direction from which he must not vary; according to that of the angel to the prophet, "Son of man [saith he] behold with thine eyes, and hear with thine ears, and set thine heart upon all that I shall shew thee: for to the intent that I might shew *them* unto thee, *art* thou brought hither" (Eze 40:4). As the Lord said also to his servant Moses, "In all *things* that I have said unto you, be circumspect" (Exo 23:13). And so again, about making the tabernacle in the wilderness, which the apostle also takes special notice of, saying, "See, saith he, *that* thou make all things according to the pattern shewed to thee in the mount" (Heb 8:5).

Hence note, That God's command must be the rule whereby we order all our actions, especially when we pretend to worship that is divine and religious. If our works, orders, and observances, have not this inscription upon them, "This is the fashion," or "This is according to the pattern," such works and orders will profit us nothing: neither have we any promise when all is done, it wanting the order of God, that we should escape those judgments which those shall assuredly escape, that have their eye in their work to the "pattern" revealed in the word.[28]

> Ver. 16. "A window shalt thou make to the ark, and in a cubit shalt thou finish it above; and the door of the ark shalt thou set in the side thereof: *with* lower, second, and third *stories* shalt thou make it."

I told you before, That the ark was a type of Christ, and also of the works of the faith of the godly. And now he seems to bring in more, and to make it a type of the church of Christ: as indeed the prophet also does, when he calls the church, one afflicted, and tossed with tempests; and compareth her troublers to the waters of Noah, saying, "This *is as* the waters of Noah" (Isa 54:9).

Now as the ark was a type of the church, so according to the description of this verse she hath three most excellent things attending her. 1. Light. 2. A door. 3. Stories of a lower and higher rank.

1. She hath a window for light, and that when she was to be tossed upon the waters. Hence note, That the church of Christ wanteth not light, no, not in the worst of times. This light is the Word and Spirit of God which Christ hath given to them that obey him (John 17).

2. She hath a door. This door was a type of Christ; so was also the door of the tabernacle. And hence it is that you read, That Moses, when he went to talk with God, would stand to talk in the door of the tabernacle; also

that the cloudy pillar stood at the door (Exo 33:9,10). "I [saith Christ] am the door": Again, "I am the door of the sheep" (John 10). By this door then, entered all that went into the ark, as by Christ all must enter that enter aright into the church.

3. She had stories in her, of first, second, and third degree: To shew that also in the church of Christ there are some higher than some, both as to persons and states: 1. apostles; 2. evangelists; 3. pastors and teachers. And again, there are in the church degrees of states, as also there are in heaven.

> Ver. 17. "And, behold, I, even I, do bring a flood of waters upon the earth, to destroy all flesh, wherein *is* the breath of life from under heaven; *and* every thing that *is* in the earth shall die."

This is the reason of the former commandment, of making an ark: But some time was yet to intervene: the flood was hereafter to overflow the world: wherefore, from this it is that those words are inserted, of things not seen as yet: And that the ark was a work, or the fruit of Noah's faith: "by faith Noah, being warned of God of things not seen as yet," &c. (Heb 11).

"And, behold, I, even I," &c. These words excuse Noah of treason or rebellion, forasmuch as his preparation for himself, and his warning and threatening the whole world with death and judgment for their transgression, was solely grounded upon the word of God: God bid him prepare, God said he would punish the world for their iniquity.

Hence note, That a man is not to be counted an offender, how contrary soever he lieth, either in doctrine or practice, to men, &c. if both have the command of God, and are surely grounded upon the words of his mouth. This made Jeremiah, though he preached, That the city of Jerusalem should be burnt with fire, the king and people should go into captivity; yet stand upon his own vindication before his enemies, and plead his innocency against them that persecuted him (Jer 26:10-15). Daniel also, though he did openly break the king's decree, and refused to stoop to his idolatrous and devilish demand; yet purged himself of both treason and sedition, and justifies his act as innocent and harmless, even in the sight of God. "My God [saith he] hath sent his angel, and hath shut the lions' mouths, that they have not hurt me: forasmuch as before him innocency was found in me; and also before thee, O king, have I done no hurt" (Dan 6:22).

Further, Paul also, although by his doctrine he did cry down the ceremonies of the Jews, and the idolatry of the heathen emperor, yet he quits himself of blame from either side: "Neither against the law of the Jews, [saith he], neither against the temple, nor yet against Caesar, have I offended anything at all" (Acts 25:8). The reason is, because the words of God, how severely soever they threaten sinners, and how sharply soever (the preacher keeping within the bowels of the word) this doctrine be urged on the world, if it destroy, it destroyeth but sin and impenitent sinners, even as the waters of Noah must do.

This then affords us another note worth remarking, to wit, That what God hath said in his word, how offensive soever it be to ungodly men, THAT we that are Christians ought to observe: whether it direct us to declare against others' enormities, or to provide for ourselves against the judgment to come.

"And, behold, I, even I, do bring a flood," &c. Hence note again, Let us preach and practise well, and let God alone the execute his judgments. It is said of Samuel, That not one of his words did fall to the ground (1 Sam 3:19). He preached, and God, according to his blessing or cursing, did either spare and forgive, or execute his judgments.

"And, behold, I, even I." Note again, That when sinners have with the utmost contempt slighted and despised the judgment threatened, yet forasmuch as the execution thereof is in the hand of an omnipotent majesty, it must fall with violence upon the head of the wicked. "I, even I," therefore, were words of a strong encouragement to Noah, and the godly with him; but black, and like claps of thunder to the pestilent unbelieving world: as the prophet says, "He is strong that executes his word": And again, "Not one of his judgments fail."

"And, behold, I, even I, do bring a flood." The flood was a type of three things.

1. A type of the enemies of the church (Isa 54:9-14).

2. A type of the water baptism under the new testament (1 Peter 3:20,21).

3. A type of the last and general overthrow of the world by fire and brimstone (2 Peter 3:6,7).

But here, as it simply respecteth the cause, which (as is afore related) was the sin that before you read of; so it precisely was a type of the last of these, and to that end put an end to the world that then was. The world that then was, being overflowed with water, perished, to signify, That the heavens and the earth which are now, are reserved unto fire, against the day of judgment, and perdition of ungodly men.

"I bring a flood of waters upon the earth, to destroy all flesh, wherein *is* the breath of life from under heaven: *and* every thing that *is* in the earth shall die." By these latter words, as the cause, so the extension of this curse is expressed; and that under a threefold denotation.

1. Every thing that is in the earth.

2. All flesh wherein is the breath of life.

3. Every thing that is under heaven. So then, this deluge was universal, and extended itself not only to those parts of the world where Noah and that generation lived, which we find repeated before, but even over the face of all the earth; and it took hold of the life of every living thing that was either on all the earth, or in the air, excepting only those in the ark, as will the general judgment do: "And Noah only remained *alive*, and they that *were* with him in the ark" (Gen 7:23).

> Ver. 18. "But with thee will I establish my covenant; and thou shalt come into the ark, thou, and thy sons, and thy wife, and thy sons' wives with thee."

"But with thee," &c. This concerns what was said before concerning the universality of the flood: As he also said above, "But Noah found grace in the eyes of the LORD." This Peter also notes, He "saved Noah the eighth *person*, a preacher of righteousness, bringing in the flood upon the world of the ungodly" (1 Peter 2:5).

"With thee will I establish my covenant." My covenant of mercy, or my promise to save thee when I drown the whole world for their iniquity: And therefore he adds, "And thou shalt come into the ark."

"I will establish." Making and establishing of promises are not always the same: He made his promise to Abraham, he seconded it with an oath unto Isaac, and he confirmed, or established it to Jacob; for by him he multiplied the seed of Abraham as the stars of heaven for multitude (Psa 105:8-10).

"With thee will I establish." Or, unto thee will I perform my promise, "Thou shalt come into the ark."

Hence note again, That we ought to look upon signal and great deliverances from sore and imminent dangers, to be confirmations of the promise or covenant of God. Or thus, When God finds means of deliverance, and instateth our souls in a special share of that means, this we should take as a sign, That with us God hath confirmed, or established, his covenant (Luke 1:68-78).

"Thou, and thy sons, and thy wife, and thy sons' wives with thee." Because in that family did now reside the whole of the visibility of the church upon the earth; all the rest were lost, as Peter also intimates, when he calleth Noah the eighth person, or one, and the chief of the eight that made up the visible church, or that maintained the purity of the worship of God upon the face of the whole earth: As he explains it a little after: "For thee have I seen righteous before me in this generation" (7:1).

Ver. 19. "And of every living thing of all flesh, two of every *sort* shalt thou bring into the ark, to

> keep *them* alive with thee; they shall be male and female."

By these words, Noah should seem to be, in this action, a figure or semblance of Christ; who before the Lord shall rain fire and brimstone from heaven, shall gather into his ark, the church, of all kindreds, and tongues, and people, and nations (Luke 13:29; 14:21). Even as Noah was to gather of all, of everything, of all flesh, of every sort, with him into the ark.

"Two of every *sort*." This two, in special, respecteth the unclean (7:2), which were a type of the Gentiles, and so further confirms the point.

They shall be male and female. He would not make a full end, he would in judgment remember mercy (Acts 10:11,12,17,28).

> Ver. 20. "Of fowls after their kind, and of cattle after their kind, of every creeping thing of the earth after his kind: two of every *sort* shall come unto thee, to keep *them* alive."

"Of fowls after their kind, and of cattle after their kind." This, still respecting the antitype, may shew us also, how that God, for proof of the prophecy of the spreading of the gospel, doth not only tell us, that the Gentiles were gathered into his ark, but as here the beasts and birds, according to their kind, are specified: so the Gentiles are also denominated according to their several countries, Galatians, Corinthians, Ephesians, Colossians, Thessalonians, Bereans, &c., these, after their country and nation, were gathered unto Jesus to be preserved from the flood of wrath that at last shall fall from God who dwells in heaven, to the burning up of the sinner and ungodly.

"Two of every *sort* shall come unto thee, to keep *them* alive." If the emphasis lieth in Come, as I am apt to think, and as the eighth verse of the next chapter fairly allows me to judge; then we must observe still, That Noah was not only first in the ark, as our Lord and Christ is the first from the dead; but that the cattle, the fowls, and the creeping things, did come to him into the ark, by a special instinct from heaven of the fruits of a divine election.[29] Noah therefore, as a man, did not make choice which of every kind; but he went first into the ark, and then of clean beasts by sevens, and of unclean beasts by twos, went in unto Noah into the ark, as the Lord commanded Noah.

And thus it is in the antitype: "Unto thee shall all flesh come," saith the prophet (Psa 65:2). And again, "To him *shall* the gathering of the people *be*" (Gen 49:10). But how? Why, by an instinct from heaven, the fruit of a divine election: "All that the Father giveth me shall come to me; but no man can come to me [saith Christ] except the Father which hath sent me draw him" (John 6:37,44). The beasts therefore which came into the ark, were neither chosen by men, neither came they in by any instinct of nature which was common to them all, but as being by a divine hand singled out and guided thither, so they entered in: the rest were left to the fury of the flood. Like to this also is the antitype, sinners come not to Jesus by any work or choice of flesh and blood, nor yet by any instinct of nature that is common to all the world; but they come, as being by a divine hand singled out from others; and as guided of the Father, so they come to Christ into the ark: The rest are left to the fury of the wrath of God, which, in the day of judgment, shall swallow them up for ever.

"They shall come unto thee to keep them alive." Indeed, they lived not for their own sakes, they being not better than them that perished; but "they shall come unto thee to save them": for, for the sake of Noah they were preserved, when many millions were drowned in the waters. Bring this also to the antitype, and you find them look like one another: for the reason why some are saved from the wrath to come, it is not for that they are better in themselves, for both Jews and Gentiles are all under sin: But it is Christ that saveth by his righteousness, as Noah saved the beasts and fowls, &c. Let us therefore, as the beasts did , go to Jesus Christ, that he may keep us alive from perishing in the day of judgment.

Ver. 21. "And take thou unto thee of all food that is eaten, and thou shalt gather *it* to thee, and it shall be for food for thee, and for them."

This therefore was for the preservation of the life of those that were in the ark; by which action there is, as in the former, inclosed a gospel-mystery.

"Take thou unto thee of all food." This food was not to be at the will and dispose of unruly beasts; but Noah was, as the lord of all that was in the ark, to take it into his own custody: and therefore he doubleth the command, "Take it unto thee"; Gather it unto thee; to wit, to dispose of after thy discretion and faithfulness. In this therefore he was a type of Christ, whom God hath set as Lord and King in the church, and "to feed his flock as a shepherd"; for the "bread of God" is in the hand of Christ, for him to communicate unto his spouses, saints, and children; as Joseph did to Egypt, according to the power committed to him, and trust reposed in him. And hence it is said, as concerning the bread that endureth to everlasting life, "the Son of man shall give it you; for Him hath God the Father sealed," or appointed thereunto (John 6:27): and therefore, that he giveth, we receive, and no more of the bread of God: *That* thou givest them, they gather: thou openest thine hand, they are filled with good (Psa 104:28).

"Take unto thee all food." That is, to be eaten by man and beast; the fowl also, and the creeping thing. This still followed, and brought in to the gospel, it shews us, that, even then, when the church is driven up into a hole, and tossed upon the waves of the rage and fury of the world, as the ark was upon the face of the waters, that even then her Noah hath all food for her, or food of all sorts for her support and refreshment: "Bread shall be given him; *his* waters *shall be* sure" (Isa 33:16).

"Take unto thee." How blessedly was this answered, when the Lion of the tribe of Judah took the book out of the hand of him that sat upon the throne (Rev 5:7); for in the book is contained the words of everlasting life; and the words of God are the food of his church, which this Noah hath received to nourish them withal: Man "liveth not by bread only," but by every *word* that proceedeth out of the mouth of the Lord, doth man live (Matt 4:4; Deu 8:3).

"And it shall be for food for thee, and for them." That is, each according to their kind. The same is true also under our present consideration; Christ is the shepherd, we are the sheep, yet He feedeth with us in the ark: "I will come in to him, and will sup with him, and he with me" (Rev 3:20). Again, here Christ transcends this action of Noah; for he was to have his food of his own, but Christ feedeth on the same with us, even on the words of God: Yet herein again we differ; he feedeth as a Lord, we as servants; he as a Saviour, we as the saved; but in general, respecting the words of God, we feed all but of one dish, but at one table; the bread therefore that he hath provided, gathered and taken to him, it was food for him, as well as for us.

> Ver. 22. "Thus did Noah; according to all that God commanded him, so did he."

These words therefore present us with a description of the sincerity and simplicity of the faith of Noah; who received the word at the mouth of God; not to hear only, but to do and live in the same.

"Thus did Noah." As it is also said of his servant Moses, "As the Lord commanded Moses, so did he": As the Lord commanded Moses, so did he, Yea, to shew us how pleasant a thing the Holy Ghost accounteth this holy obedience of faith, he is not weary with repeating, and repeating again not less than eight times in one chapter, the punctuality of Moses's conformity with the word of God, in this manner, "Thus did Moses"; "according to all that the Lord commanded Moses, so did he" (Exo 40:16,19,21,23,25,27,29,32).

"Thus did Noah," This note therefore is, as it were, a character or mark by which the Lord's people are known from the world: They have special regard to the word. "All his saints *are* in thy hand: they sat down at thy feet; *every one* shall receive of thy words" (Deu 33:3). As Christ said, "I have given them thy words and they have received *them*" (John 17:5,6): Yea, "and they have kept thy word."

"Thus did Noah." Let this then be the discriminating character of the saints from the men of this world. It was so in the days of Noah, when all the world went a whoring from their God, and said, "We desire not the knowledge of thy ways" (Job 21:14). Then Noah kept the words of God. "Thus did Noah; according to all that God commanded him, so did he."

Chapter VII.

> Ver. 1. "And the Lord said unto Noah, Come thou and all thy house into the ark; for thee have I seen righteous before me in this generation."

The ark being now prepared, and the day of God's patience come to an end, he now is resolved to execute his threatening upon the world of ungodly men; but withal, in the first place, to secure his saints, and them that have feared his name. In this therefore we have a semblance of the last judgment, and how God will dispose of his friends and enemies.

"Come thou into the ark." God, I say, will take care of, and safely provide for us that have feared him, when he most eminently entereth into judgment with the world: As he also saith by Isaiah the prophet, "Come, my people, enter thou into thy chambers, and shut thy doors about thee: hide thyself as it were for a little moment, until the indignation be over-past" (26:20). He shall send forth his angels with a great sound of a trumpet, and they shall gather together his elect from the four winds, from one end of heaven to another.

"Come thou and all thy house." Not an hoof must be left behind; God will not lose the very dust of his people: Of all that thou hast given me have I lost nothing, but will raise it up at the last day (John 6:39). God therefore was careful not only of Noah, but of all that were in his house; because they were all of his visible church, they must therefore be preserved from the rage and fury of the deluge. "Gather my saints together unto me; [saith he] those that have made a covenant with me by sacrifice" (Psa 50:5).

"For thee have I seen righteous before me." This is not to be understood as the meritorious cause, but as the characteristical note that distinguisheth them that are gods, from others that are subjects of his wrath and displeasure: wherefore, those that at this time perished, bear the badge of ungodliness, as that which made them obnoxious to this overflowing judgment: As also we have it in the book of Job, "Hast thou [saith Eliphaz] marked the old way which wicked men have trodden? Which were cut down out of time, whose foundation was overflown with a flood" (Job 22:15,16).

Righteousness therefore, is the distinguishing character whereby the good are known from the bad. Thus it was in Ezekiel's time: "Set a mark [saith God] upon the foreheads of the men that sigh and that cry for all the abominations that be done in the midst of the city" (Eze 9:4). Which mark was to distinguish them from those that were profane, and that for their wickedness were to be destroyed by the ministers of God's justice.

"For thee have I seen righteous before me." These words, before me, are inserted on purpose to shew us, that Noah was no feigned worshipper, but one who did all things in the sight of God. Indeed, there are two things which are of absolute necessity for the obtaining of this approbation of God. 1. All things must be done as to manner according to the word. 2. All things must be done as to the matter of them also according to the word. Both which were found in Noah's performances; and therefore he is said to be perfect in his generations, and that he walked with God. Thus it was also with Zacharias and Elizabeth, "they were both righteous before God"; that is, sincere and unfeigned in their obedience (Luke 1:6).

"Righteous before me in this generation." By this we see, righteousness, or the truth of God's worship in the world, was now come to a low ebb; the devil, and the children of Cain, had bewitched the church of God, and brought the professors thereof so off from the truth of his way, that had they got Noah also, the church had been quite extinct, and gone: wherefore, it now was time for God to work, and to cherish what was left, even by sending a besom of destruction upon all the face of the earth, to sweep away all the workers of iniquity.

Ver. 2, 3. "Of every clean beast thou shalt take to thee by sevens, the male and his female: and of beasts that *are* not clean by two, the male and his female.—Of fowls also of the air by sevens, the male and his female; to keep seed alive upon the face of all the earth."

Something hath been said to this already; only this I will add further, That by this commandment of God, both Noah, and all that were with him, were pre-admonished to look to their hearts; that they continued unfeigned before him. For if God would save unclean beasts, and fowls, from the present and terrible destruction; why also might not some of them, though they partook of this temporal deliverance, be still reputed as unclean in his sight? As indeed it came to pass; for a cursed Ham was there. Wherefore, read not lightly the commands of God, there may be both doctrine and exhortation; both item,[30] as well as an obligation to a duty containd therein. Circumcision was a duty incumbent as to the letter of the commandment; but there was also doctrine in it, as to a more high and spiritual teaching than the letter simply imported.

Note then from hence, That when you read that unclean beasts and unclean birds, may be in the ark of Noah: That unclean men, and unclean women, may be in the church of God: "One of you is a devil," was an admonition to all the rest: Let this also of the beasts unclean be an admonition to you.

> Ver. 4. "For yet seven days, and I will cause it to rain upon the earth forty days and forty nights; and every living substance that I have made, will I destroy, [or, blot out] from off the face of the earth."

Now the judgment is at the door; it is time to make haste, and pack into the ark. God doth not love to have his people have much vacancy from employment while they are in this world. Idle times are dangerous; David found it so in the business of Uriah's wife. Wherefore Noah having finished the ark, he hath another work to do, even to get himself, with his family and household, fitly settled in the vessel that was to save him from the deluge, and that at his peril in seven days' time.

"For yet seven days, and I will bring a flood." Note again, That it hath been the way of God, even when he doth execute the severest judgments, to tell it in the ears of some of his saints sometime before he doth execute the same: Yea, it seems to me, that it will be so even in the great day of God Almighty; for I read, that before the bridegroom came, thee was a cry made, "Behold the bridegroom cometh!" (Matt 25:6). Which cry doth not seem to me, to be the ordinary cry of the ministers of the gospel, but a cry that was effected by some sudden and marvellous awakening, the product of some new and extraordinary revelation. That also seems to look like some fore-word to the church, "Then shall appear the sign of the Son of man in heaven" (Matt 24:30): Some strange and unusual revelation of that notable day to be near, which in other ages was not made known to the world; upon which sign he presently appears. Now whether this sign will be the appearing of the angels first; or whether the opening of the heavens, or the voice of the arch-angel, and the trump of God, or what, I shall not here presume to determine; but a fore-word there is like to be, yet so immediately followed with the personal presence of Christ, that they who had not grace before, shall not have time nor means to get it then: And while they went to buy, the bridegroom came; and they that were ready went in with him, and the door was shut (Matt 25).

"And I will cause it to rain forty days and forty nights." This length of time doth fore-pronounce the completing of the judgment: As who should say, I will cause it to rain until I have blotted out all the creatures, both of men, beasts, and fowls: and so the after-words import; "And every living substance that I have made, will I destroy from off the face of the earth."

> Ver. 5. "And Noah did according to all that the Lord commanded him."

This note, as already I have said, doth denote him to be a righteous man; one that might with honour to his God, escape the judgment now to be executed: wherefore, the reiterating of this character is much for the vindicating of God's justice, and for the justification of his overthrowing the world of ungodly sinners.

But again, these words seem to respect in special, what Noah did in the last seven days, in order to the commandment laid before him in the three first verses of this chapter; and so they signify his faithfulness to the word, and his observance of the law of his God, even to the day that the rain began to fall upon the earth. And therefore they preach unto us, not only that he began well, but that he continued in godly and unfeigned perseverance; which when perfected, is the most effectual proof, that what before he did, he did with uprightness of heart, and therefore now must escape the judgment. As it is said in the gospel of Matthew, "He that shall endure unto the end, the same shall be saved" (Matt 24:13).

> Ver. 6. "And Noah *was* six hundred years old when the flood of waters was upon the earth."

Four hundred and fourscore of which the world had leisure to study the prophecy that God gave of him by the mouth of his father Lamech (Gen 5:29); the other hundred and twenty he spent in a more open testifying, both by word, and his preparing the ark, that God would one day overtake them with judgment; yet to the day that the flood came, the world was ignorant thereof (Matt 24:38,39). (Astonishing is the fruits of sin:) So it came to pass, that in the six hundredth year of Noah's life, which was the one thousand six hundred fifty sixth year of the world's age, the flood of waters were upon the earth, to the utter destruction of all that was found upon the face thereof, Noah only being left alive, and they that were with him in the ark.

> Ver. 7. "And Noah went in, and his sons,[31] and his wife, and his sons' wives with him, into the ark, because of the waters of the flood."

They had hardly done their work in the world, by that it began to rain, by that the first drops of the judgment appeared. They went into the ark, says the text, because of the waters of the flood. This should teach Christians diligence, lest they be called for by God's dispensations, either of death or judgment, before they have served completely their generations, by the will of God. Noah had done it, but it seems he had but done it; his work was ended just as the judgment came: "Be ye also ready; for in such an hour as ye think not the Son of man cometh" (Matt 24:44).

> Ver. 8, 9. "Of clean beasts, and of beasts that *are* not clean, and of fowls, and of everything that creepeth upon the earth, there went in two and two unto Noah into the ark, the male and the female, as God had commanded Noah."

By these words it seems (as I also touched before) that the beasts, and fowls, both clean and unclean, did come in to Noah into the ark; not by Noah's choice, nor by any instinct that was common to all, but by an instinct from above, which so had determined the life and death of these creatures, even to a very sparrow; for not one of them doth fall to the ground without the providence of our heavenly Father.

"They went in unto Noah." And let no man deride, for that I say, By an instinct from above; for God hath not only wrought wonders in men, but even in the beasts, and fowls of the air; to the making of them act both above and against their own nature. How did Baalam's ass speak! (Num 22:28-30). And the cows that drew the ark, have it right to the place which God had appointed, not regarding their sucking calves! (1 Sam 6:10-14). Yea, how did those ravenous creatures, the ravens, bring the prophet bread and flesh twice a day, but by immediate instinct from heaven? (1 Kings 17:6). Even by the same did these go in to Noah, into the ark.

> Ver. 10. "And it came to pass after seven days, that the waters of the flood were upon the earth."

Just as the Lord had denounced before: Look therefore, what God hath said, shall assuredly come to pass, whether it be believed, or counted an idle tale. The confirmation therefore of what God hath spoken, depended not upon the credence of man, because it came not by the will of man: "He hath said it, and shall he not make it good?" It will therefore assuredly come to pass, whatever God hath spoken, be it to save his Noahs, or be it to drown his enemies; and the reason is, Because to do otherwise, is inconsistent with his nature. He is faithful, holy and true, and cannot deny himself, that is, the word which he hath spoken.

> Ver. 11. "In the six hundredth year of Noah's life, in the second month, the seventeenth day of the month, the same day were all the fountains of the great deep broken up, and the windows [or floodgates] of heaven were opened."

As to the month, and the day of the month I have but little to say: though doubtless, had not there been something worthy of knowing therein, it would not so punctually have been left upon record[xiii]; for I dare not

---

[xiii] Bunyan must not have been aware of the work of his contemporary, James Ussher, who, in his *Annals of the World*, had carefully calculated the significance of these dates. Ussher suggests that the Flood began on Sunday December 7th 1656AM. This date fits with an interesting date at the end of the Flood.

say this scribe wrote this in vain, or that it was needless thus to punctilio it; a mystery is in it, but my darkness sees it not; I must speak according to the proportion of faith.

"The same day were all the fountains of the great deep broken up." By these words, it seems that it did not only rain from heaven, but also the springs and fountains were opened; which together with the great rain of his strength, did overflow the world the sooner.

This great deep, in mine opinion, was also a type of the bottomless pit, that mouth and gulf of hell, which at the day of judgment shall gape upon the world of ungodly men, to swallow them up from the face of the earth, and to carry them away from the face and presence of God.

"And the windows [or flood-gates] of heaven were opened." That is, that the water might descend without measure or order, even in its own natural force, with violence upon the head of the wicked. It came as water out of his buckets upon them, judgment without mercy (Num 24:7).

This opening of the flood-gates of heaven, was a type of the way that shall be made for the justice of God upon ungodly men, when Christ hath laid aside his mediatorship; for he indeed is the sluice that stoppeth this justice of God from its dealing according to its infinite power and severity with men. He stands, like Moses, and, as it were, holdeth the hands of God. Oh! but when he shall be taken away! When he shall have finished his mediatory work: then will the flood-gates of heaven be opened, and then will the justice and holiness of God deal with men without stint or diminution, even till it hath filled the vessels of wrath with vengeance till they run over. "It is a fearful thing to fall into the hands of the living God."

> Ver. 12. "And the rain was upon the earth forty days and forty nights."

That is, It rained so long without stop or sting (v 4).

> Ver. 13. "In the self same day entered Noah, and Shem, and Ham, and Japheth, the sons of Noah, and Noah's wife, and the three wives of his sons with them, into the ark."

This therefore more fully approveth of what I said before; to wit, That they had hardly done their work in the world, by that it began to rain; but so soon as they had done, the flood was upon the earth. Much like this is that of Lot; it was not to rain fire and brimstone upon Sodom, till he was got to Zoar: But when Lot was entered, but just entered, "Then the Lord rained upon Sodom, and upon Gomorrah, brimstone and fire from the LORD out of heaven" (Gen 19:21-24).

Hence note, That the reason why God doth forbear to destroy the world for the wickedness of them that dwell therein, it is for the sake of the elect; because his work upon them is not fully perfected. "The Lord is not slack concerning his promise" (2 Peter 3:9); no, nor as concerning his threatening neither,—but is long-suffering to us-ward who are the elect; not willing that any of us should perish: But when Christ, head and members, are complete in all things, let the world look for patience and forbearance no longer; for in that self same day the trump of God will sound, and the Lord descend with a shout from heaven, to execute his anger with fury, and his rebukes with flames of fire. Behold, he is now "ready to judge the quick and the dead!" (1 Peter 4:5) "ready to be revealed in the last time!" (1 Peter 1:5). The judge also stands at the door (James 5:9); it is but opening therefore, and his hand is upon you, which most assuredly he will do when his body is full and complete.

Observe again, that providence sometimes so ordereth it, that as touching the command of the Lord, necessity is as it were the great wheel that brings men into the performances of them, as here the flood drove them into the ark; as he said above, they went in because of the waters of the flood: So concerning the ordinance of unleavened bread, the first institution of that law, was as it were accompanied with an unavoidable necessity, it was unleavened, saith the text, "because they were thrust out of Egypt, and could not tarry, neither had they prepared for themselves any victual" (Exo 12:39).

It will be thus also at the day of judgment: Israel will be sufficiently wary of this world, they will even as it were unexpressibly groan to be taken up from hence; wherefore the Lord will come, as making use of the weariness and groaning of his people, and will take them up into his chambers of rest, and will wipe away all tears from their eyes, as here Noah and his sons, &c. did enter into the ark.

Ver. 14. "They, and every beast after his kind, and all the cattle after their kind, and every creeping thing that creepeth upon the earth after his kind, and every fowl after his kind, every bird of every sort" or wing.

Without doubt this careful repetition is not without a cause, and have also in the bowels of it some comfortable doctrine for the church of God; every beast, all cattle, every creeping thing that creepeth; every fowl and bird of every wing.

Fist this sheweth, that God hath respect to the fulfilling of his word in the midst of all his zeal and anger against sin (Gen 19). He doth not as we, being angry, run headlong upon the offenders, but if there be but three in a kingdom, or one in four cities, he will have respect to them (Eze 14:19,20).

Secondly, It sheweth that, how inconsiderable soever the persons are, that are within the compass, and care of the love and mercy of God, that inconsiderableness shall not be a let to their safety and preservation: Yea, though they are but as these creeping things, that creep upon the earth, or as the saying is, but as a flea, a dead dog, or a grasshopper, or one of the least of the grains of wheat, not one of them, nay, not a hair of the head of them shall fall to the ground and perish.

> Ver. 15, 16. "And they went in unto Noah into the ark, two and two of all flesh, wherein *is* the breath of life. And they that went in, went in male and female of all flesh, as God had commanded him: and the Lord shut him in."

The Holy Ghost in this relation is wonderfully punctual and exact: every beast, all cattle, every creeping thing, every fowl, and every bird, after their kind went in; and saith he again, they that went in, went in two and two; as if there had been an intelligence among these irrational creatures, that the flood was shortly to be upon the earth. Indeed, many among the sensitives have strange instincts, as appendixes to their nature, by which they do, and leave to do, to the astonishment of them that have reason: But that any instinct in nature should put them upon afore providing of shelter from the flood, by going into the ark, (a place to secure them, rather than to save them, had not the occasion and command of God been otherwise) it cannot be once with reason imagined. Wherefore, as their going into the ark, so their going in two by two, and that too male and female, plainly declares that their motion was ordered and governed by heaven, themselves being utterly ignorant thereof.

"And they that went in went in male and female of all flesh, [both man and beast] and the Lord shut him in," that is Noah; and those that were with him.

These latter words are of great importance, and do shew us the distinguishing grace of God, for by his thus shutting the door of the ark, he not only confirmed his mercy to Noah, but also discovered the bounds and limits thereof. As who should say, Now Noah you have your full tale, just thus many I will save from the flood: and with that he shut the door leaving all other, both man and beast, &c. to the fury of the waters. God therefore by this act hath shewed how it will go in the day of judgment with men. Those that (like those beasts, and birds, and creeping things) shall come to Christ, into his ark, before it rain fire and brimstone from heaven, those will God shut up in the ark, and they shall live in that day; but those that shall then be found in the world strangers to Jesus Christ, those will God shut out: "They that were ready went in with him to the marriage: and the door was shut" (Matt 25:10).

And observe, it is not said, that Noah shut the door, but the Lord shut him in: If God shuts in or out, who can alter it? I shut, and no man openeth (Rev 3:7). Doubtless before the flood had carried off the ark, others besides would with gladness have had there a lodging room, though no better than a dog-kennel; but now it was too late, the Lord had shut the door. Besides, had there been now in the heart of Noah, bowels or compassion to those without the ark, or had he had desire to have received them to him, all had been worth nothing, the Lord had shut him in. This signifying, that at the day of judgment, neither the bowels of Jesus Christ, neither the misery that damned men shall be in, will anything at all avail with God to save one sinner more, "the door is shut."

Where you read therefore both in Matthew and Luke of the shutting of the door, understand that by such expressions Christ alludeth to the door in Noah's ark, which door was open while Noah and his attendants were entering into the ark, but they being got in, the Lord shut the door. Then they that stood without and knocked, did weep, and knock, and ask too late. As Christ saith, "When once the master of the house is risen up, and hath shut to the door, and ye begin to stand without, and to knock at the door, saying, Lord, Lord, open unto us; and he shall answer and say unto you, I know you not whence ye are: Then shall ye begin to say, We have eaten and drunk in thy presence, and thou hast taught in our streets, [as Noah did of old]. But he shall say, I tell you, I know you not whence ye are; depart from me, all *ye* workers of iniquity. There shall be weeping and gnashing of teeth, when ye shall see Abraham, and Isaac and Jacob, and all the prophets, in the kingdom of God, and you *yourselves* thrust out" (Luke 13:25-28).

> Ver. 17. "And the flood was forty days upon the earth, and the waters increased, and bare up the ark, and it was lift up above the earth."

While the ark rested, and abode in his place, no doubt but the ears of Noah were filled with doleful cries from the wretched and miserable people, whom God had shut without the ark, one while crying, another while knocking, according to what but now was related; which for ought I know might be many of the forty days, but when the waters much increased, and lift up the ark above the earth, this miserable company were soon shaken off.[32]

It will be thus also in the day of judgment; at the beginning of that day the ears of the godly will sufficiently be filled with the cries and tears of the damned and miserable world; but when the ark shall be taken up, that is, when the godly shall ascend into the clouds, and so go hence with Jesus, they will soon lose this company, and be out of the hearing of their lamentable dolours.

"And the waters increased." God's judgments have no ears to receive the cries, nor heart to pity the miseries of the damned. They cry, it rains; they increase their cries, and the Lord does increase his judgment. "And it came to pass, *that* as he cried, and they would not hear; so they cried, and I would not hear, saith the Lord of hosts" (Zech 7:13).

Again, As the waters were a type of the wrath of God that in the day of judgment shall fall upon ungodly men: So they were also a type of those afflictions and persecutions that attend the church; for that very water that did drown the ungodly, that did also toss and tumble the ark about; wherefore by the increase of the waters, we may also understand, how mighty and numerous sometimes the afflictions and afflictors of the godly be: As David said, "Lord, how are they increased that trouble me? many *are* they that rise up against me" (Psa 3:1).

"And the waters increased, and bare up the ark." The higher the rage and tyranny of this world goeth against the church of God, the higher is the ark lifted up towards heaven, the most proud wave lifts it highest: The church is also by persecution more purged and purified from earthly and carnal delights; therefore it is added, "the waters bare up the ark, and it was lift up above the earth."

Ver. 18. "And the waters prevailed, and were increased greatly upon the earth; and the ark went upon the face of the waters."[33]

These words are still to be considered under the former double consideration, to wit, both, as they present us with God's wrath at the last judgment, and as they present us with a sign of the rage and malice of ungodly men.

"And the waters prevailed"; that is, over all ungodly sinners; though they were mighty, and stout, and cared for none, yet the waters prevailed against them, as the fire and brimstone will do over all the world at the day and coming of our Lord Jesus Christ. Wherefore, well may it be said to all impenitent sinners, "Can thy heart endure, or can thy hands be strong, in the days that I shall deal with thee" (Eze 22:14), saith the Lord God? Oh they cannot, the waters of the wrath of God will prevail against, and increase upon them, until they have utterly swallowed them up.

"And the waters prevailed." Take it now as a type of the nature of persecution, and then it sheweth, that as the waters here did swallow up all but the ark, so when persecution is mighty in the world, it prevaileth to swallow up all but the church; for none else can aright withstand or oppose their wickedness. It is said, when the beast had power to work, "the whole world wondered after the beast" (Rev 13:3), and all men who were not sealed, and that had not the mark of God in their foreheads, fell in with the worship of the beast; as it is said, "And all that dwell upon the earth shall worship him, whose names are not written in the book of life of the Lamb" &c. (v 8), So then it might well be said, "The waters prevailed and increased."

"And the ark went upon the face of the waters." It is said that in the beginning the Spirit of God moved upon the face of the waters, and here that the ark went upon the face of them. Indeed the Spirit of God moveth, and the church, as God, walketh in strange and unthought of stations. It is said, that God hath "a way in the whirlwind, and in the storm" (Nahum 1:3). So he hath upon the very face of the persecution of the day, but none but the church can follow him here; it is the ark that can follow him upon the face of the waters. Deep things are seen by them that are upon the waters: "They that go down to the sea in ships, that do business in great waters; They see the works of the Lord, and his wonders in the deep" (Psa 107:23,24). Indeed it oft falls out, that the church seeth more of God in affliction, than when she is at rest and ease; when she is tumbled to and fro in the waters, then she sees the works of God, and his wonders in the deep.

And this makes persecution so pleasant a thing, this makes the ark go upon the face of the waters, she seeth more in this her state, than in all the treasures of Egypt (Heb 11:24,25).

> Ver. 19. "And the waters prevailed exceedingly upon the earth; and all the high hills, that *were* under the whole heaven, were covered."

This second repetition of the prevailing of the waters, doth also call for a second consideration.

1. It shews us, that all hope that any ungodly man might have at the beginning of the flood to escape the rage thereof, was now swallowed up in death. Indeed it is natural to the creatures, when floods and inundations are upon the earth, to repair to the high places, as they only that are left for preservation of life; where life may be also continued if the waters do not overflow them: but when it comes to pass as here we read, that all the hills under the heavens are covered: then life takes its farewell, and is gone from the world, as was the effect of the waters of Noah.

The hills therefore were types of the hope of the hypocrite, upon which they clamber till their heads do touch the clouds, thinking thereby to escape the judgment of God; but "though they hide themselves in the top of Carmel, I will search and take them out thence," saith God (Amos 9:2,3). The flood of his wrath will come thither, even over the tops of all the hills. So that safety is only in the ark with Noah, in the church with Christ, all other places must be drowned with the flood.

2. We may also understand by this verse, how God in a time of persecution will cut off the carnal confidence of his people. We are apt to place our hope somewhere else than in God, when persecution ariseth because of the word. We hope that such a man, or that such outward means may prevent our being swept away with this flood. But because this confidence is not after God, but tendeth to weaken our stedfast dependence on him; therefore this flood shall cover all our hills, not one shall be found for us under the whole heaven (Jer 2:36,37). When the king of Babylon came up against Jerusalem to war, then Israel, instead of trusting in God, put their confidence in the king of Egypt, but he also was swallowed up by this flood, that Israel might be ashamed of such confidence; and this at last they confessed. "As for us, [said they,] our eyes as yet failed for our vain help: in our watching, we have watched for a nation *that* could not save *us*" (Lam 4:17).

It was requisite therefore that the hills should be covered, that Noah might not have confidence in them; but surely this dispensation of God was an heart-shaking providence to Noah, and they that were with him; for here indeed was his faith tried, there was no hill left in all the world; now were his carnal helpers gone, there was none shut up or left: Now therefore, if they could rejoice, it must be only in the power of God. As David said, "Shall I lift up mine yes to the hills? whence should my help come?" So the margin: "My help *cometh* from the Lord that made heaven and earth" (Psa 121:1,2).

Ver. 20. "Fifteen cubits upward did the waters prevail; and the mountains were covered."

The height of Goliath was but six cubits and a span (1 Sam 17:4), neither was Og's bedstead any more than nine (Deu 3:11). Wherefore this flood prevailed far the highest of those mighty ones: even fifteen cubits above the highest mountains.

> Ver. 21, 22, 23. "And all flesh died that moved upon the earth, both of fowl, and of cattle, and of beast, and of every creeping thing that creepeth upon the earth, and every man: All in whose nostrils *was* the breath of life, of all that *was* in the dry *land*, died. And every living substance was destroyed, which was upon the face of the ground, both man, and cattle, and the creeping things, and the fowls of the heaven; and they were destroyed from the earth, and Noah only remained *alive*, and they that *were* with him in the ark."

In these words you have the effects of the flood, which was punctually according to the judgment threatened. But observe, I pray you, how the Holy Ghost, by repeating, doth amplify the matter. "All flesh," "All in whose nostrils *was* the breath of life"; "All that *was* in the dry *land*," "every living substance," "every man"; and they were destroyed from off the earth: By which manner of language doubtless there is insinuated a threatening to them who should afterward live ungodly. And indeed the Holy Ghost affirmeth, that these judgments, with that of Sodom, are but examples set forth before our eyes, to shew us that such sins, such punishment. "Making *them* an ensample, saith Peter, unto those that after should live ungodly" (2 Peter 2:6). Nay, Jude saith, they are "set forth" in their overthrow, for that very purpose (v 7). Wherefore this careful repeating of this judgment of God, doth carry threatening in it, assuredly foreshewing the doom and downfall of those that shall continue to tread their steps.

Yea, mind how Peter hath it: For if God "spared not the old world," &c. (2 Peter 2:5). Secretly intimating, that those that then lived, being the first of his workmanship, and far surpassing in magnificence, if he would have spared, he would have spared them; but seeing he so dreadfully swept them away, let no man be so bold to presume that wickedness shall now deliver him that is given to it.

"And Noah only remained *alive*, and they that *were* with him in the ark." Noah was that man of God that had set himself against a world of ungodly men. The man that had hazarded life and limb for the word of God committed to him; he "only remained *alive*," &c. Hence note, That he was the man that outlived the world, that would for God venture life against all the world. Wherefore the saying in the gospel is true, He that will lose his life for my sake, shall save it unto life eternal. Thus did Noah, and passed the end, and went over the bounds, that God had appointed for every living thing. Behold! he was a man in both worlds, yea, the world then to come was given him for a possession.

"And the waters prevailed upon the earth an hundred and fifty days." About the same time the scorpions mentioned of John, had power to hurt the earth (Rev 9:10). Wherefore, the thus prevailing of the water, might be a type of our persecution now in the New Testament days. All which time doubtless Noah was sufficiently tried, while the waves of the water had no pity for him.

Chapter VIII.

> Ver. 1. "And God remembered Noah, and every living thing, and all the cattle that *was* with him in the ark; and God made a wind to pass over the earth, and the waters asswaged."

Moses having thus related the judgment of the waters, as they respected the drowning of the world, and so typed forth the last judgment: he now returneth to speak of them more largely, as they were a type of the persecution and afflictions of the church, and so sheweth how God delivered Noah from the merciless violence of the waves thereof.

"And God remembered Noah." This word remembered is usual in scripture; both when God is about to deliver his people out of affliction, and to grant them the petition which they ask of him. It is said, "God remembered Abraham; and sent Lot out of Sodom" (Gen 19:29); that he remembered Rachel, and hearkened to her (30:22); that he also remembered his covenant with Abraham, when he went to bring Israel out of their bondage (Exo 2:24).

Hence note, that Noah was not both in an afflicted and a praying condition; afflicted with the dread of the waters, and prayed for their asswaging. It is a question accompanied with astonishment, How the ark being of no bigger an hull or bulk should contain so many creatures, with sustenance for them? And verily, I think that Noah himself was put to it, to believe and wait for so long a time. But God remembered him, and also the beasts, and every living thing that was with him, and began to put an end to these mighty afflictions, by causing the waters to asswage.

"And God made a wind to pass over the earth." The waters being here a type of persecutors and persecution: this wind was a type of the breath of the Lord's mouth, by which he is said to slay the wicked. "He shall smite the earth with the rod of his mouth, and with the breath of his lips shall he slay the wicked" (Isa 11:4). It was a wind also that blew away the locusts of Egypt (Exo 10:19), which locusts were a type of our graceless clergy, that have covered the ground of our land.[34] Again the kingdom of Babel was to be destroyed by a destroying wind, which the Lord would send against her (Jer 51:1,2), which Paul expounds to be by the breath of the Lord's mouth, and by the brightness of his coming. This wind therefore, as I said, was a type of the breathing of the Spirit of the Lord, by which means these tumultuous waves shall be laid over, and God's ark in a while made to rest upon the top of his mountain (2 Sam 22:19). For by the breath of the Lord the earth is lightened, and by this lightning coals are kindled; "yea, he sent out his arrows and scattered them, and he shot out lightnings, and discomfited them. Then the channels of waters were seen, and the foundations of the world were discovered at thy rebuke, O Lord, at the blast of the breath of thy nostrils" (Psa 18:14,15). "And God made a wind to pass over the earth, and the waters asswaged." That is, in New Testament language, the afflictors and afflictions of the church did cease and decay, and came to nought.

"And the waters asswaged": To wit, by the blowing of this wind, wherefore, as this wind did assault the waters, so it did refresh the spirit of this servant of God, because by it the affliction was driven away. Thus then by the wind of the Lord were these dry bones refreshed, and made to stand upon their feet (Eze 37:9,10).

"And God made a wind to pass over." And God made it; when God blows, the enemies of his truth shall pass away like waters that fail.

> Ver. 2. "The fountains also of the deep and the windows of heaven were stopped, and the rain from heaven was restrained."

By these words we see, that when the church of God is afflicted, both heaven and hell have their hand therein, but so as from a differing consideration, and to a diverse end. From heaven it comes, that we may remember we have sinned, and that we may be made white, and tried (Dan 11:35); but from hell, from the great deep, that we might sin the more, and that we might despair, and be damned (Job 1:11; 2:5).

"And the fountains of the great deep." When God begins to slack and abate the afflictions of his church, he rebukes, as it were first, the powers of hell; for should he take off his own hand, while they have leave to do what they list, the church for this would be worse not better: But first he rebuketh them: "The Lord rebuke thee, O Satan," that's the first; and then he clothes them "with change of raiment" (Zech 3:1-5): The fountains of the great deep were stopped, and then the bottles of heaven (Gen 15:14).

"And the rain from heaven was restrained," or held back, or made to cease. Afflictions are governed by God, both as to time, number, nature and measure. "In measure when it shooteth forth, thou wilt debate with it: he stayeth his rough wind in the day of his east wind"

(Isa 27:8). Our times therefore, and our conditions in those times, are in the hand of God; yea, and so are our souls and bodies, to be kept and preserved from the evil, while the rod of God is upon us (Jer 15:1-3).

> Ver. 3. "And the waters returned from off the earth continually: and after the end of the hundred and fifty days the waters were abated."

The verse before doth treat of the original, the fountains of the deep, and the windows of heaven, that they were shut, or stopped; which being done, the effect beginneth to cease. Hence note, that case and release from persecution and affliction cometh not by chance, or by the good moods, or gentle dispositions of men, but the Lord doth hold them back from sin, the Lord restraineth them. It is said "the Lord stirred up the adversaries of Solomon" (1 Kings 11:14,23). Again, when the Syrians fought against Jehoshaphat, "the Lord helped him, and God moved them *to depart* from him" (2 Chron 18:31). The Lord sent the flood, and the Lord took it away.

"And the waters returned from off the earth continually." When God ceaseth to be angry, the hearts and dispositions of the adversaries shall be palliated, and made more flexible. It is said, when the afflictions of Israel were ended in Egypt, the hearts of the people were turned to pity them; yea, he caused them "to be pitied of all those that carried them captives" (Psa 106:46).

When you see therefore, that the hearts of kings and governors begin to be moderated toward the church of God, then acknowledge that this is the hand of God. "I," saith he, "will cause the enemy to entreat thee *well* in the time of evil, and in the time of affliction" (Jer 15:11). For by waters here are typed out the great and mighty of the world, by the flowing of them, their rage; and by their ebbing and returning their stillness and moderation. "And the waters returned." That is, to the sea (Gen 1:9,10). "He gathereth the waters of the sea together as an heap: he layeth up the depth in store houses" (Psa 33:7).

By "gathering up," the persecutors may be understood, his gathering them to their graves, as he did Herod, who stood in the way of Christ (Matt 2:19,20). And as he did those in Ezekiel, who hindered the promotion of truth, and the exaltation of the gospel (31:14).

"And after the end of the hundred and fifty days the waters were abated." These words then imply, that for so long time, Noah, and the church with him, were to exercise patience. They also show us, That when the waters are up, they do not suddenly fall: They were up four hundred years, from Abraham to Moses (Gen 15:13). They were up threescore and ten years in the days of the captivity of Babylon (Jer 25:12; Zech 1:12). They were up ten mystical days in the persecution that was in the days of Antipas (Rev 2:10). And are to be up forty and two months, in the reign, and under the tyranny of antichrist (13:5). But they will abate; the house of Saul will grow weaker; yea, they shall be gathered to their sea, and shall be laid in the pit; yea, they shall not be on the earth, when God shall set glory in the land of the living (Eze 26:19-21).

Ver. 4. "And the ark rested in the seventh month, on the seventeenth day of the month, upon the mountains of Ararat."

These instances therefore were a type of Christ, the munition of rocks (Isa 33:16), who is elsewhere called, the mountain of the Lord's house (Micah 4:1); the rock upon which he will build his church, and the gates of hell shall not prevail against it (Matt 16:18). For after the ark had felt the ground, or had got settlement upon the tops of these mountains; however, the waters that came from the great deep, did notwithstanding, for some time, shake, and make it stir, yet off from these mountains they could not get it with all their rage and fury. It rested there; these gates of hell could not prevail. But mark, it did rest on these mountains almost a quarter of a year, before any ground appeared to Noah. A right figure of saving faith; for that maketh not outward observation a ground and foundation for faith, but Christ the rock, who as to sense and feeling is at first quite out of sight. Hence the hope of the godly is compared to the anchor of a ship, which resteth on, or taketh hold of the rock that is now invisible under the water, at the bottom of the sea (Heb 6:19).

This then should learn us to stay on the Lord Jesus, and there to rest when the waters have drowned all the world, and when all the mountains and hills for help are as if they were cast into the midst of the sea.

That is an excellent saying of the prophet, "God *is* our refuge and strength, a very present help in trouble. Therefore will not we fear, though the earth be removed, [as now it seemed] and though the mountains be carried into the midst of the sea; *Though* the waters thereof roar *and* be troubled; *though* the mountains shake with the swelling thereof. Selah" (Psa 46:1-3).

Ver. 5. "And the waters decreased continually until the tenth month: in the tenth *month*, on the first *day* of the month, were the tops of the mountains seen."

In the third verse we read, that after an hundred and fifty days" flood, the waters returned; that is, began to return, from off the earth: Which beginning of their return, was, because that God had mercifully remembered the prayer and affliction of Noah. Again, in this verse we read, that from the day that the ark did rest upon the mountains of Ararat, the waters decreased continually. Now the resting of the ark on the mountain, was a figure of our trusting on Christ. Hence it follows, that the tumults and raging of the mystical waters, are made to decrease by the power of faith: "This is the victory, *even* our faith" (1 John 5:4). As it is also said of Moses, "By faith they passed through the Red sea" (Heb 11:29). But above all take that as most pertinent, "Through faith they subdued kingdoms, - stopped the mouths of lions, - and turned to flight the armies of aliens" (Heb 11:33,34). Here you see faith made the waters decrease; it took away the heat and rage of the adversary.

"And the waters decreased continually until the tenth month, [another period of time,] and in the first day of the tenth month were the tops of the mountains seen." These mountains were before the flood, a type of the hope of the hypocrites, and therefore then were swallowed up, fifteen cubits under the waters. But now, methinks, they should be a figure to the church of some visible ground of deliverance from the flood; for almost three months the ark did rest on the invisible mountains of Ararat. But now are the tops of the mountains seen: A further sign that the waters were abated; and a ground, that at length they would be quite dried up. Let these mountains then be types of the high and mighty, which God is used to stir up to deliver his church from the heat and rage of tyranny and persecution, as they are often termed and called in scripture, the mountains of Israel, for this very end. So then, from our thus considering the mountains, Two things we are taught thereby.

1. That when the great ones of this world begin to discover themselves to the church, by way of encouragement, it is a sign that the waters are now decreasing. Or thus: When God lets us see the tops of the mountains, then we may certainly conclude, that the rage of the waters abate.

Doubtless when God made promise of raising up Josias to Israel, in Canaan (1 Kings 13:1-3); and of raising up for them Cyrus, in Babylon (Isa 45; Eze 1:1-3). The thus appearing of the tops of these mountains, was comfort to the church in her day of affliction.

2. This should teach us while we are in affliction, to look this way and that, if it may be that the tops of the mountains may be seen by us (1 Sam 11:1-3). For though it be too much below a Christian to place his confidence in men, yet when God shall raise up Josias or a Cyrus, we may take encouragement at this working of God. Therefore is that in the Psalms read both ways, shall I look to the mountains? "I will lift up mine eyes unto the hills, from whence cometh my help. Yet so, as that he would also conclude his help did come from the Lord" (Psa 121:1,2). So then, we must take heed that we look not to the mountains [alone]. Again, it is our wisdom "to look to the mountains": only look not to them but when God discovers them. Look unto them if God discovereth them; yet then but so as means of God's appointing. But again, God doth not let us see the hills for our help, before we have first of all seen them drowned. Look not to them therefore while the water is at the rising; but if they begin to cease their raging, if they begin to fall, and with that the tops of the mountains be

seen, you may look upon them with comfort, they are tokens of God's deliverance.

> Ver. 6. "And it came to pass at the end of forty days, that Noah opened the window of the ark which he had made."

These forty days seem to commence from the discovery of the tops of the mountains. Wherefore he did not presently go out of the ark, but stayed there above fourteen days still, signifying unto us, that we must not be therefore delivered so soon as the tops of the mountains are seen, but may yet be assaulted with the waters of the flood, days, and weeks, and months, &c.

When Moses was sent to deliver Israel, they came not presently out of Egypt; neither seemed their burthens ever the light to sense or feeling, though faith indeed did see the end (Exo 5:15-23). Again, When he had brought them forth of Egypt, they came not in a day, or a month, to Canaan; but, saith the Holy Ghost, He brought them out, (or, forth of affliction) after that he had showed wonders and signs in the land of Egypt, and in the Red sea, and in the wilderness forty years.

Let us therefore take heed of a feverish spirit, while we behold "the tops of the mountains"; possibly, for all they are visible tokens to us of deliverance, themselves may be yet much under water. We see what work Moses, Gideon, Jephthah and Samson had to deliver Israel, even after more than their tops were seen. Be content to stay yet forty days. David stayed, after he was anointed, till years and times went over him, before he could deliver Israel from the tyranny of its opposers.

"At the end of forty days Noah opened the window of the ark." This opening of the window also, was a type, that now he was preparing to take possession of the world. It also might be a type of the opening the law and testimony, that light might by that come into the church; for we find not that this window had any other use, but to be a conveyance of light into the ark, and as a passage for the raven and the dove, as may be further showed after. Now much like this, is that of John: "The temple of God was opened in heaven, and there was seen in his temple the ark of his testament" (Rev 11:19). And again, "I looked, and, behold, the temple of the tabernacle of the testimony in heaven was opened." And then, as the raven, and the dove came out of the window of the ark; so "the angels," that is, the Lord's executioners, "came out of the temple" that was opened in heaven (Rev 15:5,6).

Hence note, That though men may be borne with, if they lie in their holes in the height of the tempest; but to do it when the tops of the mountains were seen, if they then shall forbear to open their window, they are worthy of blame indeed. When the lepers saw the Assyrians were fled, and that liberty from heaven was granted to Samaria, then they feared to conceal the thing any further; They feared, I say, that if they went not to the city to declare it, some judgment of God would befall them (2 Kings 7:9).

Ver. 7, 8. "And he sent forth a raven, which went forth to and fro, until the waters were dried up from off the earth. Also he sent forth a dove from him, to see if the waters were abated from off the face of the ground."

Behold, the raven and dove are now sent out at the window of the ark, as the angels are said to come out of the temple, when it was opened in heaven. This raven therefore, and the dove, were figures and types of those angels (Rev 15:5,6).

But to speak to them both apart. The raven went forth, but returned not again to the ark. This is intimated by these words, "She went to and fro, until the waters were abated, and dried up." This is further evident by that antithesis that the word doth put between the practice of the raven and the dove. The raven went forth, and went to and fro till the waters were dried up. But mark it, "But the dove found no rest for the sole of her foot, and she returned unto him into the ark" (v 9). The raven then did find rest elsewhere, the raven then returned not to him into the ark.

But what did the raven then do? Why, certainly she made a banquet of the carcasses of the giants that were drowned by the flood; it fed upon the flesh of the men that had sinned against the Lord.

The raven therefore was a type of those messengers that God sends out of his temple against Antichrist; that is, for "eating the flesh of kings, and the flesh of captains, and the flesh of mighty men, and the flesh of horses." He was, I say, a type of those professors that God saith he hath a great sacrifice to sacrifice unto, a sort of professors in his church; as the raven was one that had his being in the ark: These are they which Ezekiel mentions, that were to eat flesh, and drink blood; to eat the fat till they be filled, and to drink blood till they be drunken (39:17-20). These also are the guests that Zephaniah mentions, and saith, God hath bidden to the same feast also (1:7-14).

And let no man be offended that I say these birds are in the church: For one effect of the sixth vial, was that battle of the great day of God Almighty (Rev 16:16). Further, The angel that proclaims this feast, calls to those that are God's guests, by the name of, "the fowls that fly in the midst of heaven": That they should "come and gather together to the supper of the great God: That they may eat the flesh of kings, and the flesh of captains, and the flesh of mighty men," &c. (Rev 19:17,18). Besides, this supper is the effect of the going forth of the King of kings against the Antichristian whore, whose going forth was at the opening of heaven, as the going forth of the raven was at the opening of the window of the ark (v 11-16).

Note therefore, That God, in the overthrow of the kingdom of Antichrist, and at the asswaging of the rage of her tumultuous waves, will send forth his birds amongst her fat ones, to partake of the banquet that he hath appointed; who when they shall be tolerated by that angel that standeth in the sun, will come down to their feast with such greediness, that neither king nor captain shall keep them from their prey: They will eat flesh, and fat, till they be full, and drink the blood till they be drunk.

"Also he sent forth a dove from him, to see if the waters were abated." This dove was a type of another sort of professors in the church, that are of a more gentle nature (Matt 10:16); for all the saints are not for such work as the raven; they are not all for feeding upon the carcasses, the kingdoms and estates of the Antichristian party, but are for spending their time, and for bending their spirits to a more spiritual and retired work; even as the dove is said to be harmless, and to mourn for communion with her companion (Isa 38:14), and that is content if she hath her nest in the sides of the rock, Christ (Jer 48:28). Wherefore he adds,

> Ver. 9. "But the dove found no rest for the sole of her foot, and she returned unto him into the ark, for the waters *were* on the face of the whole earth," &c.

The dove could not live as the raven; the raven being content, so long as she found the carcasses; but the dove found no rest till she returned again to Noah.

The raven therefore, though he was in the ark, was not a type of the most spiritual Christian; nay rather, I think, of the worldly professor, who gets into the church in the time of her affliction, as Ziba did into the army of David, in the day of his trouble; not for love to the grace of David, but that, if time should serve, he might be made the Lord of his master's inheritance (2 Sam 16:1-4). But David was content to let him go with him, and that too as under such a consideration: as Christ also lets these ravens to herd with his innocent doves; because he hath flesh to give them, which the doves care not for eating.[35]

"But the dove found no rest." It seems the raven did, as it is also with some professors, who when they by their profession have advanced themselves to some worldly honour, they have ease and rest, though, like the raven, they have it by going out of the church.

"But the dove found no rest." Though all the enemies of God lay tumbling in the sea, this could not satisfy a gracious soul: divide her from the ark, and she finds no rest, she is not at ease till she be with Noah. "And she returned unto him into the ark; - and he put forth his hand, and took her, and pulled her in unto him into the ark" (v 9).

Noah here was a type of Christ, who took the dove unto him: And it shows us, That Christ hath a bosom open for the cries and complaints of his people; for the dove returned a-weary with the tidings of this, that the waters still raged. A fit figure of those of the saints that are groaning and weary under the oppression and cruelty of the enemy.

Hence note, That though thou hast no other tidings to Christ but sighs and groans, and weariness, because of the rage of the waters; yet he will not despise thee; yea, he invites thee, as weary, to come (Matt 11:28-30).

Ver. 10. "And he stayed yet other seven days; and again he sent forth the dove out of the ark."

This staying shows us, That he exercised patience, waiting God's leisure till the flood should be taken away. This grace therefore had yet seven day's work to do, before he obtained any further testimony that the waters were decreasing. O this staying work is hard work! Alas! sometimes patience is accompanied with so much heat and feverishness, that every hour seems seven until the end of the trial, and the blessing promised be possessed by the waiting soul. It may be Noah might not be altogether herein a stranger: I am sure the Psalmist was not, in that he often under affliction, cries, But how long, O Lord! for ever! (Psa 6:3; 79:5; 13:1; 74:1; 89:46). Make haste! O Lord, how long! (90:13; 94:3).

"And again he sent forth the dove." The first time he sent her, she brought no good news, but came panting and weary home; yet he sends her a second time.

This should teach us, not to make conclusions too suddenly about God's dispensation, saying it must be now or never; for it may be the seven days are not out. The men of David said, This is the day that the Lord will give thee the kingdom of Israel: But David perceived otherwise, and therefore adds yet to his temperance, patience (1 Sam 24:1-4; 26:8-10). Not sullenly saying like that wicked king, Why should I wait on the Lord any longer? (2 Kings 6:32). But comforts himself with the truth of the promise, saying, His time shall come to die, &c. He that believeth, maketh not haste, but waiteth patiently, for the perfecting God's work in God's time. That is excellent in the song: "I charge you [saith the church] that ye stir not up, nor awake *my* love, until he please" (Cant 8:4). Noah was much for this, wherefore he stayed yet other seven days.

"And again he sent forth the dove." Elias did much like this, when his servant, at the first sending, brought him no tidings of rain, he gave him his errand again, saying, Go again: go seven times (1 Kings 18:43-45). As Noah here did with the dove, and again he sent her. Seeming delays are no hindrance to faith; they ought to try it, and put it into exercise: As here it was with this good man about the waters of the flood; he fainted not, but believed to see the goodness of the Lord. That in the prophet is notable as to this, "The vision *is* yet for an appointed time, but at the end it shall speak, and not lie: thought it tarry, wait for it; because it will surely come, it will not tarry" (Hab 2:3).

Ver. 11. "And the dove came in to him in the evening; and lo! in her mouth *was* an olive-leaf plucked off: so Noah knew that the waters were abated from off the earth."

"And the dove came in to him in the evening." Wherefore his patience was tried this day also. All the day he heard nothing of his dove. Surely she could not keep the wing all the day. Is she drowned I tro? Is she lost? O, no! She comes at last, though she stayed long. Samuel also stayed long before he came to Saul; but Saul could not wait as Noah did, therefore he had not the benefit of the mercy promised.

"The dove came in to him in the evening, and lo, in her mouth was an olive-leaf," &c. Now he is recompensed for the exercise of patience: As also was Abraham when God gave him Isaac; for after he had patiently endured, he obtained the promise.

"And lo, an olive-leaf." A sign that God was going through with his work of diminishing the waters: A sign, I say, and a good experience of the continued love of God to his servant; according to that of Paul, "patience worketh experience"; that is, it at last obtaineth the blessing promised, and so settleth the soul in a fresh experience of the love and faithfulness of God.

And lo! This word Lo, it is, as it were an appeal to all readers to judge, whether God to Noah was faithful or no. So then, this was not written for his sake only, but for us also that believe in God, that we might now exercise patience, as Noah; and obtain the tokens of God's goodness, as he; for lo the dove, at last, though 'twas night first, came to Noah into the ark, "and lo in her mouth *was* an olive-leaf plucked off: so Noah knew that the waters were abated."

"An olive-leaf plucked off." These words, an olive-leaf plucked off, do intimate, that Noah was now inquisitive and searching how the dove obtained the leaf; that is, whether she found it as dead, and upon the waters; or whether she plucked it off some tree: But he found by the greenness and freshness of the slip, that she plucked it off from the olive. Wherefore, he had good ground now to be comforted; for if this leaf was plucked off from a tree, then the waters could not be deep; especially, because as the story tells us, the olive used also to stand in the bottoms, or valleys.

This should teach us, That not over highly we conclude messages or tokens, to be signs of God's mercy. There are lying visions, and they are causes of banishment; they we should beware of, or else we are not only at present deceived, but our faith is in danger of the rocks; for not a few have cast up all, because the truth of some seeming vision hath failed. Mark how David handleth the messenger that brought him tidings of the death of Saul: says he, How dost thou know that Saul is dead? What proof canst thou make of the truth of this story? (1 Sam 1:1-10). So should we say of all those visions or messengers that come to persuade us, that either inward or outward deliverance is for us at the door. Prove these stories; look if they be not dead and lifeless fancies; see if you can find that they were plucked off from the tree that is green.

> Ver. 12. "And he stayed yet other seven days; and sent forth the dove; which returned not again unto him any more."

We read before of forty days' patience, and after that of seven days' patience; and that after the waters began to return from off the earth, and here again of seven days more. Whence not, That the best of God's people, in the times of trials, find their patience too short-winded to hold out the whole length of a trial, unless the time be, as it were, cut in pieces. The prophet when he was to lay siege against Jerusalem, he must rest the one side, by turning him upon the other (Eze 4:2-6). It was with holy Job exceeding hard, when he might not have time to swallow his spittle, when he might not a little sit down and rest him. And if you observe him, he doth not desire an absolute deliverance as yet, but only time to take wind and breathe awhile; and then, if God will, to engage in the combat again:[36] "How long [saith he] wilt thou not depart from me." Depart: what quite? O! No, saith he, I beg not that absolutely, but only so long as till a man might "swallow down his spittle" (Job 7:19). This the church in Ezra's time took as an exceeding favour. "And now [say they] for a little space, grace hath been *shewed* from the Lord our God, to leave us a remnant to escape, and to give us a nail in his holy place, that our God may lighten our eyes, and give us a little reviving in our bondage" (Ezra 9:8).

"And he stayed yet other seven days." Note again, That it is not God's way with his people to shew them all their troubles at once; but first he shews them a part; first forty days, after that seven other days, and yet again seven days more; that, they coming upon them by piecemeal, they may the better be able to travel through them. While Israel was in affliction in Egypt, they knew not the trial that would meet them at the Red Sea. Again, When they had gone through that, they little thought that yet "for forty years they must be tempted and proved in the wilderness."

And thus it was with this blessed Noah; he thought that by the first seven days his trials might be ended. But behold, there is yet seven days more behind: "and he stayed yet other seven days."

Further: There may also be by these words thus much insinuated, That these periods of time might be also of Noah's prefixing: and if so, then note, That the people of God in these days are not the first that have been under mistake, as to the timing of their afflictions. Noah counted it would end many days before it ended indeed, even seven days, and seven days, and seven days to that; for he sent forth his dove about the beginning of the first month, in which month also were his two seven days' trials. Again, after that he had stayed two seven days more, to wit, to the end of that first month. Again, he stayed almost four sevens more; for he came not out of the ark till the twenty-seventh day of the second month.

Hence therefore let Christians beware that they set not times for God, lest all men see their folly. "It is not for you to know the times or the seasons, which the Father hath put in his own power" (Acts 1:7). Yea, I say again, take heed lest that for thy setting of God a seven days' time, he set not thee so many as seven times seven.

"And he sent forth the dove, which returned not again unto him any more." This is the third time that the dove was sent to see how the waters were abated on the face of the earth. The first time she, by her restlessness, bespake the waters to be high and mighty. The second time, by her olive-leaf, she notifieth that the waters were low and ebbing. But this third time, she seems to be weary or her service, she returned not again to him any more; yet in her so absenting herself, she gives confirmation to Noah, that the waters were even in a manner quite gone. If he will take this for a proof let him, if not, let him hang in suspense with himself. Hence note, that God will not be always testifying, by renewing of his tokens, to that about which we have had sufficient conviction before; for in so doing he should gratify and humour our unbelief. Noah had received already two sufficient testimonies that the waters were decreasing. First by his seeing the tops of the mountains, and then by the olive-leaf; but notwithstanding these two testimonies, his unbelief in part remains; but God will not humour such a groundless mistrust, by giving him any further token, than the very absenting of the dove. Much like this was that of Samson's father; the angel once had told his wife, that she should have a son that should deliver Israel; well, Manoah heard of this, he also desired that he might see that man that had told his wife this happy news. Now God thus far condescends, as to send the angel a second time; but then, this being now a sufficient antidote against their unbelief, the angel after the next departing, was not seen again of them at all. But saith the word, The angel of the Lord did no more appear to Manoah, and to his wife: So that now they must live by faith, or not at all (Judg 13:3,9,21).

God's dealing with his people with respect to their spiritual condition, is much like this. The Holy Ghost doth not use to confirm us by new revelations of grace and justification, so often as by our fond doubts or mistrust we call for and desire the same. But having confirmed in us the testimony of Christ, it may be twice or thrice, (for the testimony of two men are true) he then expects we should live by faith. And observe it, if we have after such testimony joyful communion with God, it is either by retreating to former experience, or by arguing according to faith; that because God hath done thus before, he therefore hath given me interest in such and such promises and mercies besides.

I speak now of the first seals of the love of God to the soul, after we have been sufficiently tossed upon the waves of unbelief, as Noah was by the waters of the flood: such seals are few, the Lord gave them to Solomon twice (1 Kings 11:9). And also twice to his servant Paul (Acts 22:6,18). 'Tis enough that they have seen "the tops of the mountains," and have had brought to them the olive-leaf. Let them now believe this confirmation of mercy is sufficient, and if they will not believe now, they shall not be established.

> Ver. 13. "And it came to pass in the six hundredth and first year, in the first *month*, the fist *day* of the month, the waters were dried up from off the earth: and Noah removed the covering of the ark, and looked, and behold, the face of the ground was dry."

"And it came to pass." That is, by the working of God, that the waters were dried up. This came to pass in God's time, to wit, in "the six hundredth and first year, in the first *month*, the first *day* of the month"; not in the times of Noah's prefixing. God's time is THE time, the best time, because it is the time appointed by him for the proof and trial of our graces, and that in which so much, and so much of the rage of the enemy, and of the power of God's mercy, may the better be discovered unto us; "I the Lord will hasten it in HIS time" (Isa 60:22), not before, though we were the signet upon his right hand (Jer 22:24).

Noah the only man with God in that generation, could not be restored before the time; no more could Israel from the thraldom of Egypt (Exo 13:4). Yea, the Son of God himself must here give place and be content. And when Satan had ended *all* the temptation, when he "had ended all, - then he departed from him for a season" (Luke 4:13).

"And Noah removed the covering of the ark, and looked." The failing again of his expected comforter, caused him to be up and doing; probably he had not as yet uncovered the ark, that is, to look round about him had the dove by returning pleased his humour; but she failing him, he stirs up himself, Thus it should also be with the Christian now: doth he dove forbear to come to thee with a leaf in her bill as before, let not this make thee sullen and mistrustful, but uncover the ark, and look, and by looking thou shalt see a further testimony of what thou receivedst by the first manifestations: "He looked, and behold the earth was dry." Paul tells us, that by looking we have a testimony like, or *as* that, which at first was given us by the Spirit of the Lord (2 Cor 3:18). "And behold the face of the earth was dry."

Ver. 14. "And in the second month, on the seven and twentieth day of the month, was the earth dried."

This prospect was like the rain that we read of in another place, that confirmed God's inheritance when it was weary: It was a comfortable sight to Noah to see that the face of the earth was dry; and now he could wait upon God with less trial and strain to his patience the remaining days, which were fifty and four, to wit, from the first of the first, to the twenty-seventh of the second month, than he could one of the sevens that he met with before. Indeed the path is narrowest just at entrance as also our nature is then the most untoward; but after we are in, the walk seems to be wider and easy; the flesh is also then more mortified and conformable. The walk is but a cubit wide at the door, but inward ten times as broad (Eze 42:4,11).

"And in the second month, on the seven and twentieth day of the month, was the earth dried." So that from the first day it began to rain, which was the seventeenth day of the second month in the year before, unto this day, was Noah in the ark; it was just a year and ten days. That was the time then that God had appointed to try his servant Noah, by the waters of the flood: in which time he was so effectually crucified to the things of the world, that he was as if he was never more to enjoy the same. Wherefore Peter making mention of this estate of his, he tells us, it was even like unto our baptism; wherein we profess ourselves dead to the world, and alive to God by Jesus Christ (1 Peter 3:21).

In the first verse of this chapter, we read that God remembered Noah; but till now we read not, that the face of the earth was dried. Hence note that our being under the rage of the enemy, doth not argue that we are therefore forgotten of God, "he remembereth us in our low estate," even when tossed to and fro by the waters of a flood of temptations.

Ver. 15, 16. "And God spake unto Noah, saying, Go forth of the ark, thou, and thy wife, and thy sons, and thy sons' wives with thee."

Now we are come to the end of the trial, and so to the time of Noah's deliverance, and behold as he went in, so he came out: He went into the ark at the commandment of the Lord. "And the Lord said unto Noah, Come thou and all thy house into the ark" (Gen 7:1). And here again, "And God spake unto Noah, saying, Go forth of the ark." Hence note, that notwithstanding the earth was dry about fifty-four days before, yet Noah waited for the word of God for his commission to bring him forth of the ark. Providence seemed to smile before, in that the earth was dry, to which had but Noah added reason, he must have concluded, the time is come for me to go forth of the ark. But Noah knew, that as well the providences of God, as the waters of the flood might be to try his dependence on the word of the Lord: wherefore, though he saw this, yet because he had no answer of God, he will not take the opportunity.

It is dangerous, or at least very difficult, to make the most smiling providence of God our rule to act by: Had David done it, he had killed Saul before the time, But David respected the word of God (2 Sam 24:17-20). Elisha also would not suffer the king to make that improvement of the providence of God, which reason should be put in execution, when he rebuked the king's desire that he had to have killed the Syrians, and commanded that bread should be set before them, that they might eat, and go home again to their master (2 Kings 6:19-23). Hear the word of the Lord, ye that tremble at his word. "At the commandment of the Lord the children of Israel journeyed, and at the commandment of the Lord they pitched. - - At the commandment of the Lord they rested in their tents, and at the commandment of the Lord they journeyed; they kept the charge of the Lord, at the commandment of the Lord, by the hand of Moses" (Num 9:18-23).

"Go forth of the ark, thou, and thy wife, and thy sons, and thy sons' wives with thee."

When God delivereth, he delivereth completely. Thus Israel also went out of Egypt, they, their wives, their children, with their flocks and herds, not an hoof was left behind (Exo 10:24-26). When David's time was come to possess the kingdom, he brought along with him those six hundred men that had been his companions in his suffering state, every man with his household. But I say, he went up to possess it, not simply by the voice of providence, though Saul was dead, but "David inquired of the Lord, saying, Shall I go up into any of the cities of Judah?" Nay, a general answer, even from God, would not satisfy this holy man. "The Lord said, - Go, but David replied, Whither shall I go? and he said unto Hebron" (1 Sam 2:1). Oh! it is safe to regard the word of the Lord; this makes us all come safe to land. When men wrest themselves from under the hand of God, taking such opportunities for their deliverance, which are laid before them only for trial of obedience to the word: they may, it is probable, have a seeming success; the end will be as with Zedekiah king of Judah, affliction with addition. The Jews that were left in the land of Israel, from the hand of the king of Babylon, would flee to the land of Egypt (Jer 41:17), that they might have quietness there, but they went without the word of God, and therefore their rest brought them to their ruin (42; 43).

Noah therefore chose the safest way, even to stay in the ark, till God's word came. As it is also said of Joseph, "The word of the Lord tried him"; till the word of the Lord came to deliver him, and then he had deliverance indeed (Psa 105:19), as Noah also and David had safe deliverance for himself and relations.

> Ver. 17. "Bring forth with thee every living thing that *is* with thee, of all flesh, *both* of fowl, and of cattle, and of every creeping thing that creepeth upon the earth; that they may breed abundantly in the earth, and be fruitful, and multiply upon the earth."

Noah was not only to have in this deliverance, respect to himself and family, but to the good of all the world.

Men's spirits are too narrow for the mind of God, when their chief end, or their only design in their enjoying this or the other mercy, is for the sake of their ownselves only. It cannot be according to God, that such desires should be encouraged: "none of us liveth unto himself," why then should we desire life only for ourselves.

The church cries thus, "God be merciful unto us, and bless us; *and* cause his face to shine upon us." Why? "That thy way may be known upon earth, thy saving health among all nations" (Psa 67:1,2).

So David, "Restore unto me the joy of thy salvation; and uphold me *with thy* free spirit. *Then* will I teach transgressors thy ways; and sinners shall be converted unto thee" (Psa 51:12,13). So then, we must not desire to come out of trials and afflictions alone, or by ourselves, but that in our deliverance the salvation of many may be concerned. It is said, when Israel went up out of Egypt, there went up with them "a mixed multitude," to wit, of Egyptians, and other nations: This going out of captivity was right, they carried out with them the fowls, the beasts, and the creeping things; to wit, the heathens of other lands, and so added increase to the church of God (Exo 12:37,38). In Esther's time also, when the Jews came from under the snare of Haman, they brought with them to God many of the people of the provinces. "Many of the people of the land became Jews" (Esth 8:17).

These words therefore, "bring forth with thee every living thing," &c. are not lightly to be passed over; for they shew us, that we ought in our deliverance to have special respect to the deliverance of others. And if our deliverance be with the word and liking of God, it must needs have this effect. "When I shall bring again their captivity, the captivity of Sodom and her daughters, and the captivity of Samaria, and her daughters, then *will I bring again* the captivity of thy captives in the midst of them" (Eze 17:53).

And indeed there is reason for this, for in every affliction and persecution, the devil's design is to impair Christ's kingdom: wherefore no marvel, that God designeth in our deliverance, the impairing and lessening the kingdom of sin and Satan. Wherefore, O thou church of God in England, which art now upon the waves of affliction, and temptation, when thou comest out of the furnace, if thou come out at the bidding of God, there shall come out with thee the fowl, the beast, and abundance of creeping things. "O Judah, he hath set an harvest for thee, when I returned the captivity of my people" (Hosea 6:11).

"That they may breed abundantly in the earth, and be fruitful, and multiply upon the earth."

This was God's end in preserving the creatures from the flood, that again the earth might be replenished therewith. The same end he hath in his suffering of the persecutors, and all manner of adversity to take away but "a part," some (Amos 7:4). Some of them they shall kill and crucify, leaving a remnant alive in the world, namely, that they might breed abundantly in the earth, and be fruitful, and multiply upon the earth. As he saith by the prophet Isaiah, "He shall cause them that come of Jacob to take root: Israel shall blossom and bud, and fill the face of the world with fruit" (Isa 27:6). And this after their deliverance from persecution: According as he saith again, "The remnant that is escaped of the house of Judah, shall again take root downward, and bear fruit upward: For out of Jerusalem shall go forth a remnant" that is yet to replenish the earth with converts (37:32).

As Luke observes, that when the churches in Judea, Galilee, and Samaria had rest, they "walking in the fear of the Lord, and in the comfort of the Holy Ghost, were multiplied" (Acts 9:31).

Ver. 18. "And Noah went forth, and his sons, and his wife, and his sons' wives with him."

Obedience is better than sacrifice. Noah is at the beck of God, what he bid him do, that does he; and indeed this is in truth to worship God, yea, this is to know and worship God. It is said of Abraham, when he went at God's command to offer up Isaac, that he counted it going to worship the Lord (Gen 22:5). And God saith of Hezekiah, that he did "judgment and justice," judging the cause of the poor and needy; and then adds, Is not this "to know me, saith the Lord?" (Jer 22:15,16). I bring these to shew, that obedience to the word of God, is the true character of God's people in all ages; and this very text, as also such others before, is on purpose recorded by the Holy Ghost, to shew you, that Noah was obedient in all things; yea, I may add, these commands were to discover the proof of him, whether he would be obedient in all things; and this was also his way with New Testament churches (2 Cor 2:9). The sincerity of love, and of the uprightness of the heart, is greatly discovered by the commandments of God. "He that hath my commandments, and keepeth them," saith Christ, "he it is that loveth me" &c. (John 14:21).

Ver. 19. "Every beast, every creeping thing, and every fowl, *and* whatsoever creepeth upon the earth after their kinds, went forth out of the ark."

These words are yet a further expression of the sincerity of Noah's obedience, for that he at the command of God, did carefully search and seek out every little creeping thing that God had brought to him into the ark. Obedience in little things do ofttimes prove us most; for we through the pride of our hearts are apt to look over little things, because though commanded, they are but little (Jer 23:38). O, but Noah was of another spirit, he carefully looked after little things, even after every thing, "whatsoever creepeth upon the earth"; and not only so, but sought diligently that they might go out in order, to wit, male and female, according to their kind. Sometimes God would have men exact to a word, sometimes exact to a tache, or pin, or loop (Exo 36:12,13); sometimes to a step (Eze 40:3,4,37). Be careful then in little things, but yet leave not the other undone (Matt 23:23).

Indeed the command of God is great; if HE therefore commands us to worship him, though but with a bird, we must not count such ordinances insignificant, or below a human creature (Lev 14:52).

> Ver. 20. "And Noah builded an altar unto the LORD, and took of every clean beast, and of every clean fowl, and offered burnt-offerings on the altar."

This is the first work that we read Noah did, when he came forth of the ark; and it shews us, that at this time he had a deep sense of the distinguishing mercy of God. And indeed he had sufficient cause to wonder, for the whole world was drowned, save only himself, and they that were with him in the ark.

But I say, this was the first work, to wit, "to worship God." Hence note, That a sense of mercy, of distinguishing mercy, naturally engageth the heart to worship. It is said of Moses, when the name of the Lord was proclaimed before him, as "merciful and gracious, - and abundant in goodness and truth, - and that he pardoned iniquity, transgression and sin"; that he "made haste, and bowed his head toward the earth, and worshipped" (Exo 34:8).

"And Noah builded an altar." Although this altar be the first that we read of, yet forasmuch as there was before a blessed church, and also an open profession of godliness, together with offering sacrifice, in all probability this was not the first altar that was builded unto the Lord. Besides, we read not of any immediate revelation, from which Noah had light and instruction to build it. The text only saith, he built an altar unto the Lord; which may be aptly expounded, according as he was wont in the other world.

This altar was a type of Christ, as capacitated to bear the sin of the world (for the altar was it, upon which the sacrifices were burnt;) wherefore it, in mine opinion, in special respected his Godhead, by the power of which he offered himself, that is, his flesh. Again it is said, "The altar sanctifieth the gift" (Matt 23:19). So did the Godhead the humanity of Christ, through which "eternal Spirit, he offered himself without spot to God" (Heb 9:14). By this altar then this blessed man preached to his family the Godhead and eternity of Christ.

"And took of every clean beast, and of every clean fowl." These beasts and fowls were types of the flesh of the Son of God, as Paul in the ninth and tenth chapters to the Hebrews affirms; wherefore by this act he also preached to his family the incarnation of the Lord Christ, how that "in the fulness of time" he should in our flesh offer himself a sacrifice for us; for as all the ordinances of the New Testament ministration preach to us, That Christ is come; so all the ordinances of worship under the Old Testament preached to them that were under it, Christ, as yet TO come.

"Of every clean beast and of every clean fowl." This was to shew, That when Christ did come, he should not take hold of the Jew, and exclude the Gentile; but that in his flesh he should present unto God EVERY clean beast, and EVERY clean fowl; that is, all the elect, both of Jew and Gentile (Acts 10:11-16).

And it was requisite that this by Noah should be preached, because the whole world was yet in his family; from whence, at the multiplication of men, if through their rebellion and idolatry they lost not this doctrine, they might to all their offspring preach the Lord Jesus.

Wherefore, the doctrine of the gospel, had the world been faithful, might have been to this day retained amongst them that now are the most barbarous people.[37]

> Ver. 21. "And the Lord smelled a sweet savour; [a savour of rest;] and the Lord said in his heart, I will not again curse the ground any more for man's sake; for the imagination of man's heart *is* evil from his youth; neither will I again smite any more every living thing, as I have done."

These words more fully shew, that this sacrifice of Noah was a type of the offering up of the body of Jesus

Christ, he being said to be that blessed sacrifice that is as perfume in the nostrils of God: "He gave himself for us an offering and a sacrifice to God for a sweet-smelling savour" (Eph 5:2). Besides, this offering of Noah was a burnt-offering to God; which burning signified, the curse of God, which Christ was made in his death for us. Wherefore, the burnt offerings were all along a type of him; as by reading the epistle to the Hebrews you may see: "It is the burnt-offering, [saith God,] because of the burning upon the altar all night unto the morning, and the fire of the altar shall be burning in it" (Lev 6:9). Which was a type of the fire of the law, and the guilt of sin, that Christ, when he offered himself, should undergo for the sins of man.

"And the Lord smelled a sweet savour." This signifies the content and satisfaction that for the sin of the world, God should have by the offering upon of his Son for us upon the cross: Wherefore, he is said to be now "in Christ, reconciling the world unto himself, not imputing their trespasses unto them" (2 Cor 5:19).

Now it is observable, That Noah was a man of faith long before this. Hence note two things.

1. That men, even of eminent faith have yet need of a continual remembrance of the death and sufferings of Christ; yea, and that in the most plain and easiest manner to understand.

2. They have need also, notwithstanding they have faith before, to present themselves before God, through Jesus Christ our Lord: For as our persons are not accepted, but in and through him, no more are our performances; yea, though they be spiritual services or sacrifices; it is the blood that maketh the atonement, as

well for work as persons (Lev 17:11; Heb 9:21). As he saith in another place, I will accept you with your sweet savour, but not without it (1 Peter 2:5; Eze 20:41). As he also said to his church in Egypt, "When I see the blood, I will pass over you, and the plague shall not be upon you to destroy *you*, when I smite the land of Egypt" (Exo 12:13).

"And the Lord said in his heart, I will not again curse," &c. By heart here, we may understand two things.

1. That God was altogether unfeigned in this promise. He spake it from his very heart: which we use to count the most sincere expressing of our mind: According to that of the prophet, "Yea, I will rejoice over them to do them good, and I will plant them in this land assuredly - [in truth, in stability,] with my whole heart, and with my whole soul" (Jer 32:41). Mark, I will rejoice to do it, I will do it assuredly, I will do it in truth, even "with my whole heart, and with my whole soul."

2. By his saying, "In his heart," we may understand the secrecy of his purpose; for this doctrine, Of not cursing again, it is hid from all but those to whom it is revealed by the Spirit of God. For this purpose, in the heart of God, is one of the depths, or of the deep things of God, which the spirit of a man cannot understand. "Who hath known the mind of the Lord?" None of all the sons of men, but those that have the Holy Ghost: Therefore Paul applieth that to himself and fellows, as that which is peculiar to them to know, "We have the mind of Christ" (1 Cor 2:16). It is said, that after Christ had by his parables preached his gospel to the world, he in private "expounded all things to his disciples" (Mark 4:34).

Hence note, That they that will hear God speak this, they must be near his very heart. They that are in his heart, may hear it: but to them that are without, in parables. This secret, in revelation of the gospel, is also expressed in other terms: as, That the Lord spake "in mine ears" (Isa 5:9), and "it was revealed in mine ears" (Isa 22:14). And again, "Hear now this word that I speak in thine ears" (Jer 28:7).

"I will not again curse the ground any more." These words are also under Moses' veil; for in them is contained the sin of the world, and damnation thereof. He said, when he was to bring the flood, that the "earth was corrupt," and that he would "destroy the earth" (6:11,13); but his great meaning, was, of the sinners that dwelt therein; as the effect of that flood declared. So he saith again, he will not bring any more a flood to destroy the earth; and that the bow in the cloud should be a sign of peace between him and the earth: By all which is meant in special, the men that dwell on the earth (Psa 114:7; Deu 32:1; Jer 6:19; 22:29); and they are called, the Ground, and the Earth, because they came from thence. So then, there is, as it were, the foundation of all spiritual blessedness couched under these words, "I will not curse the ground, I will not destroy man." And that this must needs be the meaning thereof, consider, that this promise ariseth from the sweet savour that he smelt before in the burnt-offering; which was a figure of Christ, who was "made a curse for us" (Gal 3:13), to deliver us from the curse of the law; that we might through him obtain the blessing of forgiveness of sins; to which the curse stands directly opposite.

"I will not again curse the ground for man's sake; for the imagination of man's heart *is* evil from his youth." The imagination of man's heart was the ground of this dreadful curse; and the effect of this curse, was, to lay them up in chains in hell: Wherefore Peter saith, These men are "now in prison." The curse therefore, in its most eminent extension, reached the souls of those ungodly ones that were swept away with the flood. But it seems a strange argument, or reason rendered of God, why again he would not curse the ground, if it was because of the evil imagination of man's heart, this being the only argument that prevailed with him to send the flood. The meaning therefore is rather this, That because of the satisfaction that Christ hath given to God for sin, therefore he said in his heart, he would "not again curse the ground," for the evil imagination of man; that is, he would not do it, for want of a sacrifice that had in it a sufficient propitiation (John 3:18,19).

Hence note, That the great cause now of man's condemnation, is not because of his inherent pollution, but because he accepteth not, with Noah, of the satisfaction made by Christ; for to all them that have so accepted thereof, there is now no curse nor condemnation (Rom 8:1), though still the imagination of their heart be evil. "If any man sin, we have an advocate with the Father, Jesus Christ the righteous" (1 John 2:1).

"For the imagination of man's heart is evil from his youth." These words seem to insinuate the cause of these evil imaginations; and that is, from the corruption of their youth. Now how soon their youth was corrupted, David shows by these words, "I was shapen in iniquity; and in sin did my mother conceive me" (Psa 51:5). Ezekiel also shows, we were polluted in the day that we were born (Eze 16:1-8). Further, God to Moses strongly affirms it, in that he commands, That for the firstborn, in whom the rest were included, an offering should be offered, by that they were a month old (Exo 13:13; 34:20).

God seems therefore, by this word, to look back to the transgression of our first parents, by whom sin came into our natures; and by so doing he not only intimateth, yea, promiseth a pardon to personal miscarriages; but assureth us, That neither them, nor yet our inward pollutions, shall destroy us, because of the rest that he found before in Christ (Rom 5).

"Neither will I again smite any more every living thing, as I have done." The creatures therefore also have some kind of benefit by the death and blood of Christ; that is, so as to live, and have a being; for infinite justice is so perfectly just, as that without a sacrifice it could not have suffered the world to stand, after sin was in the world, but must have destroyed, for the sake of sin, the world which he had made.

For although it be foully absurd to say that beasts and fowls are defiled with sin, as man; yet doubtless they received detriment thereby. "The creature was made subject to vanity, by reason of him who hath subjected the same," &c. That is, by Adam's sin. Which vanity they also show by divers of their practise; as both in their enmity to man, and one to another, with which they were not created; this came by the sin of man. Now that man lives, yea, that beasts live, it is because of the offering up of Christ: Wherefore it is said in that of the Colossians, The gospel is "preached to every creature"; in every creature under heaven; to wit, in that they live and have a being (1:23).

"Neither will I again smite any more every living thing, as I have done." These words, as I have done, doth not exempt the creature from every judgment of God, but from this, or such as this; for we know, that other judgments do befall ungodly men now; and if they continue in final impenitence, they shall partake of far greater judgments than to be drowned by the waters of a flood. "The wicked is reserved unto judgment" (Job 21:30). Yea, the heavens and the earth that now are, are "reserved unto fire, - and perdition of ungodly men" (2 Peter 3:7).

Ver. 22. "While the earth remaineth, seed time and harvest, and cold and heat, and summer and winter, and day and night, shall not cease."

"While the earth remaineth." These words may have respect both to the words before, and to them that follow after. If they respect the words before, then they are as limits to that large promise, of not destroying the world again: not but that the day will come, as I said, in which another general judgment, and that too far more dreadful than this of water, will overflow the world, and every living thing shall again be cut off from the face of all the earth: as *now* by rain of water, *then* by rain of fire and brimstone: Which day and sore judgment, God showed unto men, when he burned Sodom and Gomorrah with "fire and brimstone from heaven." But,

"While the earth remaineth," this shall not be. But in the end, then indeed both it and "the works that are therein, shall [as Peter saith] be burned up" (2 Peter 3:10). But so long as it remaineth, that is, until it be overtaken with this second, and that too the beginning of eternal judgment, no universal judgment shall overrun the earth: For albeit that since that flood, the earth hath been smitten with many a curse; yet it hath been but here and there, not in every place at once. Famines, and earthquakes, and pestilences, have been in divers places, but yet at the same time hath there been seed time and harvest also (Mark 13:8; Luke 21:11).

"Seed time and harvest, and cold and heat, and summer and winter, and day and night, shall not cease." These words were some of the first, with that of "the bow in the cloud," that prevailed with me to believe that the scriptures were the word of God.

For my reason tells me, they are, and have continued a true prophecy, from the day that they were related; otherwise the world could not have subsisted; for take away seed time and harvest, cold and heat, &c., and an end is put to the[38] beginning of the universe.

Besides, if these words be taken in a spiritual sense, they have also stood true from that very day; otherwise the church had ceased to have a being long before this: For take away seed time and harvest from the church, with cold and heat, and day and night, and those ordinances of heaven are taken from her, which were ordained for her begetting and continuation. This head might with much largeness be insisted on; but to pass it, and to come to the next chapter.

Chapter IX.

> Ver. 1. "And God blessed Noah, and his sons, and said unto them, Be fruitful and multiply, and replenish the earth."

Noah having thus waded through these great temptations, and being made also to partake of the mercy of God, in preserving and saving him from the evil thereof, and being brought to partake of the beginning of a new world, while the ungodly that were before the flood were perished for their iniquity: he receiveth now from the mouth of the Lord, before whom he walked before the flood, laws and ordinances, as rules by which he should still govern his life before him. But mark, Before he receiveth these rules and commandments, he receiveth blessing from God; blessing, I say, as that which should yet fore-fit him to do his will.

"And God blessed Noah." Blessed him with spiritual and special grace; for without that, no man can walk, with God's acceptance before him. He blessed him with grace suitable to the work he was now to begin; to wit, for the replenishing and governing the new world God had brought him to: so that Noah did not without precedent qualifications take this work upon him. God also gave Caleb and Joshua another spirit, and then they followed him fully. That of David is for this remarkable, "Who *am* I, [said he] and what *is* my people, that we should be able to offer so willingly after this sort? for all things *come* of thee, and of thine own have we given thee." "O Lord our God, saith he, all this store that we have prepared to build thee an house for thine holy name, *cometh* of thine hand, and *is* all thine own" (1 Chron 29:10-16). So is faith, love, strength, wisdom, sincerity, and all other good things wherewith and by which we walk with God, worship him, and do his will: all which is comprised in these words, "I will give them an heart to know me, that I *am* the LORD: and they shall be my people, and I will be their God; for they shall return unto me with their whole heart" (Jer 24:7). "A new heart also will I give them" (Eze 36:25-29). And again, "I will put my fear in their hearts, that they shall not depart from me" (Jer 32:37-40).

"And God blessed Noah and his sons, and said unto them, Be fruitful, and multiply, and replenish the earth." After he had blessed him, then he tells him what they should do; namely, "Be fruitful, and multiply." This he spake with respect to the seed that he and his sons should beget, therewith to people the world; which was now the remaining part of his work, and he had three arguments to encourage him thereto. First, He was delivered from the wicked and sinners of the old world: 2. He was made the heir of a new world; and 3. Was to leave it as an heritage to his children.

This therefore should teach us, who are brought into the kingdom of Christ, that new world that hath taken its beginning in the word of the gospel, not to be idle, but to be fruitful, and to labour to fill the world with a spiritual seed to God: for as Noah, so are we made heirs of this blessed kingdom; and shall also, as that good man, leaven, when we sleep in Jesus, this spiritual seed to possess the kingdom after us.

> Ver. 2. "And the fear of you and the dread of you shall be upon every beast of the earth, and upon every fowl of the air, upon all that moveth *upon* the earth, and upon all the fishes of the sea; into your hand are they delivered."

These words seem to be a promise of what shall be a consequence of their putting into practice what was commanded in the verse before; namely, of their being fruitful, and of their "multiplying in the earth." Hence note, That the faithful observation of God's word, puts majesty, and dread, and terror upon them that do it: Therefore it is said, that when the church is "fair as the moon, and clear as the sun, she is terrible as *an army* with banners" (Cant 6:4,10). The presence of godly Samuel made the elders of Bethlehem tremble; yea, when Elisha was sought for by the king of Syria, he durst not engage him, but with chariots and horses, and an heavy host (2 Kings 6:13,14). Godliness is a wonderful thing, it commandeth reverence, and the stooping of the spirits, even of the world of ungodly ones (Acts 5:13).

"And the fear of you and the dread of you shall be upon every beast." This is true in the letter; for because there is upon man, as man, more of the image and similitude of God, than there is upon other creatures; therefore the beasts, and all the creatures, are made to stoop and fall before them; yea, though in themselves they are mighty and fierce. Every kind [or, nature] of birds, and of serpents, and things in the sea, is tamed, and hath been tamed by mankind (James 3:7).

But to allegorize the word, for by the word, ungodly men are beasts; then, as I said before, godliness puts such a majesty and dread upon the professors of it, that their enemies are afraid of them; yea, even then when they rage against them, and lay heavy afflictions upon them. It is marvellous to see in what fear the ungodly are, even of godly men, and godliness; in that they stir up the mighty, make edicts against them; yea, and raise up armies, and what else can be imagined, to suppress them; while the persons thus opposed, if you consider them as to their state and capacity in this world; they are most inconsiderable; but as a dead dog, or a flea (1 Sam 24:14). O but they are clothed with godliness! The image and presence of God is upon them! This makes the beasts of this world afraid. One of you shall chase a thousand.

"Into your hands are they delivered." That is, the beasts, birds, and fish of the sea (as David saith) to be for the service of man. But again, This is also true in a higher nature; for taking these beasts, &c. for men, even they are delivered into the hand of the church, by whose doctrine, power and faith, they are smitten with severest judgments (2 Cor 2:15,16). Laying all that reject them even in the depth of death, and smiting them "with all plagues as often as they will" (Rev 11:6). The world is therefore in our hand, and disposed of by our doctrine, by our faith and prayers, although they think far otherwise, and shall one day feel their judgments are according.

> Ver. 3. "Every moving thing that liveth shall be meat for you; even as the green herb have I given you all things."

From these words some would insinuate, that before the flood men lived only upon herbs, not eating flesh; as here they have authority granted to do: but, in mine opinion, such should be mistaken, for this reason, if there were no other: because they offered sacrifice before; sacrifices, I say, as types and representatives to the church, of the death and sufferings of Christ. Now, of such sacrifices the offerers used to eat, as is clear by the lamb of the passover, and many other offerings: so that these words seem to be but a renewing of their former privileges, not a granting new liberty to the world.[xiv]

"Every moving thing." This must be taken with this restriction, That is wholesome and good for food: for by the law of nature, nothing of that is forbidden to man, though for some significations many such creatures were forbidden us to use for a time (Deu 14).

"Even as the green herb." For which they expressly had liberty granted them, in the first chapter of this book (v 29). And this liberty might afresh be here repeated, from some scruple that might arise in Noah, &c. He remembering that the world before might, for the abuse of the creatures of God, as well as for the abuse of his worship, be drowned with the flood; for sometimes the abuse of that which is lawful to one, may be a snare, abuse and stumbling to another (1 Cor 7:1; 8).

Ver. 4. "But flesh with the life thereof, *which is* the blood thereof shall ye not eat."

This law seems to be ceremonial, although given long before Moses was; as also some sacrifices and circumcision were (John 7:22). Wherefore we must seek for the reason of this prohibition. "Whatsoever man [saith God] *there be* of the house of Israel, - that eateth any manner of blood, I will even set my face against that soul that eateth blood, and will cut him off from among his people." Why? "For the life of the flesh *is* in the blood: and I have given it to you upon the altar to make an

---

[xiv] In fact, even in Leviticus, not every sacrifice was eaten. God's injunction before the Flood was that people should eat only plants. However, I am sure that some people did eat meat - not for the reason that Bunyan gives, but because people can be disobedient.

atonement for your souls: for it *is* the blood *that* maketh an atonement for the soul. Therefore I said unto the children of Israel, No soul of you shall eat blood" (Lev 17:10-12). Again, As here the prohibition is only concerning blood; so in another place, the word is as well against our eating the fat; "*It shall be* a perpetual statute for your generations, throughout all your dwellings, that ye neither eat fat nor blood." And the reason rendered, is, For "all the fat *is* the LORD'S" (Lev 3:16,17).

So then the meaning, the spiritual meaning, seems to be this, That forasmuch as the blood is the life, and that which maketh the atonement; and the fat, the glory, and the Lord's; therefore they both were to be offered to the Lord. That is, we ought always to offer the merit of our salvation to God, by a continual acknowledgment, that it was through the blood of Christ; and we ought always to give him the glory thereof, and this is the fat of all our performances (Isa 25:6). Now this is so blessed a thing, and calleth for that grace, that every professor hath not, every one cannot ascribe to the blood of the Lamb, the whole of his reconciliation to God; nor offer up the fat, the glory, which is God's, to the Lord for so great a benefit: this is the benefit of a peculiar people, even of "the priests the Levites, the sons of Zadok, [or they that are justified, or just thereby; (For so Zadok signifies)] that kept the charge of my sanctuary, when the children of Israel went astray from me; they shall come near to me, to minister unto me, and they shall stand before me to offer unto me the fat and the blood, saith the Lord God" (Eze 44:15).

Wherefore, for men to ascribe to their own works the merit of their salvation, or to take the glory thereof to themselves; it is as eating the blood and the fat themselves, and they shall be cut off from the people of God.

> Ver. 5. "And surely your blood of your lives will I require; at the hand of every beast will I require it, and at the hand of man; at the hand of every man's brother, will I require the life of man."

These words are spoken to the church, which then resided in this family: Not but that God will avenge the blood that is wrongfully shed, though the person murdered be most carnal and irreligious. "A man that doeth violence to the blood of *any* person, shall flee to the pit; let no man stay him" (Pro 28:17).

But I say, these words respect the church in a more special and eminent way. "Surely [saith God] your blood of your lives will I require." Thus also David insinuates the thing: "when he maketh the inquisition for blood, he remembereth them: [the saints and godly in special,] he forgetteth not the cry of the humble," the afflicted (Psa 9:12).

"At the hand of every beast will I require it." The beasts are here also to be taken for men, to whom they are frequently likened in scripture; and that because they have cast off human affections; and, like savage creatures, make a prey of those that are better than themselves. Ignorance therefore or brutishness, O thou wicked man! will not excuse thee in the day of judgment; all the injuries that thou doest to the people of God, shall for certain be required of thee.

"At the hand of man will I require it." By *man* here, we may understand, such as have greater placed and shew of reason wherewith they manage their cruelty, than those that are as the natural beast: for all persecutors are not brutish alike; some are in words as smooth as oil; others can shew a semblance of reason of state, why they should see "the righteous for silver, and the poor for a pair of shoes" (Amos 2:6). These act, to carnal reason, like men, as Saul against David, for the safety of his kingdom; but these must give an account of their cruelty, for blood is in their hands.

"At the hand of every man's brother will I require the life of man." This word *brother* may reach to all the apostatized hypocrites that forsake or betray the godly, for brother shall betray the brother to death (Matt 10:21). Such are spoken of in Isaiah, "Your brethren that hated you, [saith God,] and that cast you out for my name's sake, said, Let the LORD be glorified: but he shall appear to your joy, and they shall be ashamed" (Isa 65:5). So that let them be as vile as the brute, or as reasonable in appearance as men, or as near in relation as a brother; neither their ignorance, nor their reason, nor their relation to the saints, shall secure them from the stroke of the judgment of God.

Ver. 6. "Whoso sheddeth man's blood, by man shall his blood be shed: for in the image of God made he man."

In these words we have both a threatening and a command; and the same words carry both: "By man shall his blood be shed," there is the threatening; "By man shall his blood be shed," there is the command. For as they threaten, so they instruct us, that he is worthy of the loss of his own blood, that doth wickedly shed the blood of another (Matt 26:52; Rev 13:10). Blood for blood, equal measure: As he also saith elsewhere, An eye for an eye, a tooth for a tooth (Exo 21:24), wound for wound, burning for burning (Lev 24:20; Deu 19:21).

"For in the image of God made he man." This seems as the reason of this equal law; because no man can slay his neighbour, but he striketh at the image of God. It is counted a heinous crime for a man to run his sword at the picture of a king, how much more to shed the blood of the image of God? "He that mocketh, or oppresseth, the poor reproacheth his Maker; but he that honoureth him, hath mercy on the poor" (Pro 14:31; 17:5). And if so, how much more do they reproach, yea, despise and abhor their Maker, that slay and murder his image! But most of all those do prove themselves the enemies of God, that make the holiness, the goodness, the religion and sobriety that is found in the people of God, the object of their wrath and hellish cruelty. Hence murder is, in the New Testament, imputed to that man that hated holy and godly man: "He that hateth his brother, is a murderer; and ye know that no murderer hath eternal life abiding in him" (1 John 3:15).

> Ver. 7. "And you, be ye fruitful, and multiply; bring forth abundantly in the earth, and multiply therein."

Thus he doubleth the blessing and command, of multiplying and increasing the church in the earth, for that is the delight of God, and of Christ.

> Ver. 8, 9. "And God spake unto Noah, and to his sons with him, saying, And I, behold, I establish my covenant with you, and with your seed after you."

God having thus blessed them, and given them laws and judgments to walk by, for the further confirmation of their hope in God, he propoundeth to them the immutability of his mind, by the establishing of his covenant with them; for a covenant is that, which not only concludeth the matter concerned between the persons themselves; but it provideth remedy against after temptations, and fears, and mistrusts, as to the faithful performance of that which is spoken of. As Laban said to Jacob, "Now therefore [said he] come thou, let us make a covenant, I and thou; and let it be for a witness between me and thee" (Gen 31:44). Thus also the apostle insinuates; where making mention of the promise and oath of God, he saith, this promise and oath are both immutable, that "we might have a strong consolation, [or always ground for great rejoicing] who have fled for refuge to lay hold upon the hope set before us" (Heb 6:18).

This covenant therefore, it was for the encouragement of Noah and his sons, that they might walk before God without fear. Yea, it was to maintain their hope in his promise of forgiveness, though they should find their after-performances mixed with infirmities; for so he had told them before, namely, "That he would not again destroy the earth for man's sake, albeit the imagination of man's heart be evil from his youth. I will establish my covenant with you, and with your seed after you."

Ver. 10. "And with every living creature that *is* with you: of the fowl, of the cattle, and of every beast of the earth with you; from all that go out of the ark, to every beast of the earth."

These words respect the whole creation (see chapter 8); for all the things in the world, devils only excepted, have a benefit by this covenant of God. And hence it is, that not man only, but "every thing that hath breath," is commanded to "praise the Lord" (Psa 150:6): But observe it; as for the sin of man, they before were destroyed by the flood; so now by reason of the mercy of God to man, they are spared, and partake of mercy also. This is intimated by these words: "Every creature that is with you; every beast of the earth with you."

Ver. 11. "And I will establish my covenant with you, neither shall all flesh be cut off any more by the waters of a flood; neither shall there any more be a flood to destroy the earth."

This is the sum of the covenant, as it respecteth the letter, and the type, and the whole creation in general. But yet as to the spirit and gospel of it, the Holy Ghost must needs have a further reach, an intention of more glorious things, as may further be shewed anon.

"And I will establish my covenant with you." For you that are men, and especially the members of the church, have the most peculiar share therein.

"Neither shall all flesh be cut off any more by the waters of a flood." For because of my covenant which I establish with you, I will spare them also, and give them the taste of my mercy and goodness.

"Neither shall there any more be a flood to destroy the earth." This covenant therefore, is not of that nature as the covenant was which was made with Adam, to wit, a covenant of works, as the only conditions of life; for by that was the ground, for man's sin, accursed, accursed, and accursed again. But now the Lord goeth another way, the way of grace, and forgiveness of sins: Wherefore now, not the curse, but the mercy of God, comes in on the back and neck of sin, still sparing and forgiving man, the great transgressor, and the beast, &c. and the earth, for the sake of him.

> Ver. 12, 13. "And God said, This *is* the token of the covenant which I make between me and you and every living creature that *is* with you, for perpetual generations. I do set my bow in the cloud, and it shall be for a token of a covenant between me and all the earth."

So then, the way to find out the covenant, what that is, it is to see if we can find out this token of it; to wit, the BOW, of which the rainbow is but a type. I find then by the scriptures, where this BOW is mystically spoken of, that the Lord Jesus Christ himself is encompassed with the bow. The first is this:

"And above the firmament that *was* over their heads *was* the likeness of a throne, as the appearance of a sapphire stone: and upon the likeness of the throne *was* the likeness, as the appearance of a man above upon it. And I saw, as the colour of amber, as the appearance of fire round about within it, from the appearance of his loins even upward, and from the appearance of his loins even downward, I saw as it were the appearance of fire, and it had brightness round about. As the appearance of the bow that is in the cloud in the day of rain, so *was* the appearance of the brightness round about. This *was* the appearance of the likeness of the glory of the LORD" (Eze 1:26-28), the man, the Lord's Christ, &c.

The second scripture is this. "I was in the Spirit: and, behold a throne was set in heaven, and *one* sat on the throne. And he that sat was to look upon like a jasper and a sardine stone: and *there was* a rainbow round about the throne, in sight like unto an emerald" (Rev 4:2,3). In these two texts there is mention of the rainbow, that was, not to be the covenant, but the token or sign thereof. Now then the covenant itself must needs be the man that was set in the midst of the bow upon the throne; for so he saith by the prophet, "I the LORD have called thee in righteousness, and will hold thine hand, and will keep thee, and give thee for a covenant of the people" (Isa 42:6). The covenant therefore is Jesus Christ the Saviour, whom the bow in the clouds was a sign or a token of. So then the sum of the text is this, That God, for the sake of the Lord Jesus Christ, will not again all the days of the earth, bring an universal judgment upon the creature, as in the days of Noah, and of the old world he did; for Christ by the worth of his blood and righteousness hath pacified the justice of the law for sin. So then the whole universe standeth not upon a bottom of its own, but by the word and power of Christ (Heb 1:2,3). "The earth [said he] and all the inhabitants thereof are dissolved: I bear up the pillars of it" (Psa 75:3).

Quest. But how must Christ be reckoned of God, when he maketh him the poize against all the sin of the world.

The prophet tells us thus: He shall be the covenant of the people, or he shall be accounted the conditions and worth of the world; He shall be the covenant, or works, or righteousness of the people; for, He as the high-priest under the law, is set for the people to Godward; that is, he standeth always in the presence of God, as the complete obedience of the people. So then, so long as the Lord Christ bears up his mediatorship, God in justice will neither destroy the world, nor the things that are therein.

In this covenant therefore, the justice as well as the mercy of God is displayed in its perfection, inasmuch as without the perfection of the mediator Christ, the world could not be saved from judgment.

> Ver. 14. "And it shall come to pass, when I bring a cloud over the earth, that the bow shall be seen in the cloud."

By these words the Lord looks back to the flood that before had drowned the earth; for in these clouds there was no bow, no token of Christ, or of the mercy of God. But now, saith God, I will do far otherwise; from henceforth when I bring a cloud, and there be showers of rain on the earth, these clouds shall not be as the other. But "my bow shall be therein."

The cloud then that here is spoken of, must be understood of the judgment of God for sin, like those before, and at the overthrow of the world; only with this difference, they were clouds, judgments without mercy, but these judgments mixed therewith; and often the clouds are thus to be understood. Job when he curseth his day, saith, "Let a cloud dwell upon it" (3:5). So the judgments of God upon Zion, are called the covering of a cloud (Lam 2:1). So in Joel also, to the darkness of clouds, are the judgments of the church compared (2:2); yea, that pillar that went before the children of Israel, it being a judgment to the people of Egypt, goes under this epithet, as a term most fit to express this judgment by, "it was a cloud and darkness *to them*" (Exo 14:20).

And now to the cloud in hand, the cloud in which is the bow, the cloud of rain, although by the mercy and grace of God it is so great a blessing as it is, yet it sometimes becomes a judgment, it comes for correction, as a rod to afflict the inhabitants of the world withal (Job 37:13). Thus it was in the days of Ezra, and very often both before and since (10:12-14).

"The bow shall be seen in the cloud." This is the mercy of God to the world, and that by which it hath been hitherto preserved; "The bow shall be seen in the cloud." You know I told you of the bow before, that it was a sign or token of the covenant of God with the world, and that the covenant itself was Christ, as given of God unto us, with all his good conditions, merit, and worth. So then, in that, God "set this bow in the cloud," and especially in the clouds that he sends for judgment, he would have the world remember, that there comes no judgment as yet on the world, but it is mixed with, or poized by the mercy of God in Christ.

"The bow shall be seen in the cloud." This may respect God, or the world, that is, the seeing of the bow in the cloud; if it respect God, then it tells us he in judgment will remember mercy; if it respect the world, then it admonisheth us not to despond, or sink in despair under the greatest judgment of God, for the bow, the token of his covenant, is seen in the judgments that he executeth.

When the vision of the ruin of Jerusalem was revealed to the prophet Ezekiel, he saw that yet Christ sat under the bow (1:28).

When antichrist was to come against the saints of God, the commission came from Christ, as he sat "under the bow" (Rev 4:3). This John did see and relate, of which we should take special notice: for by this token God would have us to know that these clouds, though they come for correction, yet not to destroy the church. My bow shall be seen in the cloud.

> Ver. 15. "And I will remember my covenant, which *is* between me and you, and every living creature of all flesh; and the waters shall no more become a flood to destroy all flesh."

"And I will remember my covenant." Much like this is that of the Lord to Israel, when they are under all, or any of those forty judgments mentioned (Lev 26). If they shall confess their iniquity, [saith he,] and the iniquity of their fathers, &c., "Then will I remember my covenant with Jacob, and also my covenant with Isaac, and also my covenant with Abraham will I remember; and I will remember the land" (Lev 26:40-42). His usual way in other sayings is, to begin with Abraham, but here he ends with him; and the reason is, because there, as it were, the great promise of the Messiah to that people began, "Saying, in thy seed shall all nations be blessed."

"And I will remember my covenant which *is* between me and you." We read not here of any compact or agreement between Noah and God Almighty; wherefore such conditions and compacts could not be the terms between him and us. What then? why that covenant that he calls his, which is his gift to us, "I will give thee for a covenant," this is the covenant which is between God and us: "There is one God, and one mediator between God and man, the man Christ Jesus." This then is the reason why all the waters, why all the judgments of God, and why all the sins that have provoked those judgments, cannot become a flood to destroy all flesh.

> Ver. 16. "And the bow shall be in the cloud; and I will look upon it, that I may remember the

everlasting covenant between God and every living creature of all flesh that *is* upon the earth."

"And the bow shall be in the cloud." this is a kind of a repetition; for this he had told us before, saying, "I do set my bow in the cloud," and "the bow shall be seen in the cloud": which repetition is very needful, for it is hard for us to believe that Christ and grace are wrapped up in the judgments of God (1 Peter 1:12). Wherefore it had need be attested twice and thrice. "To write the same things to you," saith Paul, "to me indeed *is* not grievous, but for you *it is* safe"(Phil 3:1).

"And I will look upon." A familiar expression, and suited to our capacity, and spoken to prevent a further ground of mistrust; much like to that of God, when he was to send the plague upon Egypt:

"The blood, saith God, [of the Lamb,] shall be to you for a token upon the houses where ye *are*: and when I see the blood I will pass over you, and the plague shall not be upon you, to destroy *you*, when I smite the land of Egypt" (Exo 12:13).

"And I will look upon it that I may remember." Not that God is forgetful, "He is ever mindful of his covenant." But such expressions are used to shew and persuade us that the whole heart and delight of God is in it. "That I may remember the everlasting covenant." This word covenant is also the sixth repetition thereof; my covenant, the covenant, a covenant, and the everlasting covenant. O how fain would God beat it into the heads of the world, that he hath for men a covenant of grace.

"The everlasting covenant." Because the parties on both sides are faithful, perfect, and true; the Father being the one, and the Son of his love the other; for this covenant, as I said before, is not a compact and agreement betwixt God and the world, but his Son, as his gift to men, is set for them to Godward (Zech 9:11). So that what conditions there are, they are perfectly found in Christ, by whose blood the covenant is sealed and established, and indeed becomes everlasting, hence it is called "the blood of the everlasting covenant" (Heb 13:20). And again, the New Testament is said to be in this blood. Besides, the promises are all in Christ, I mean the promises of this covenant; in him they are yea, and in him amen, to the glory of God the Father: now they being all in him, and yea and amen no where else, the covenant itself must needs be of pure grace and mercy, and the bow in the cloud, not qualifications in us, [but] the proper token of this covenant.

> Ver. 17. "And God said unto Noah, This is the token of the covenant, which I have established between me and all flesh that *is* upon the earth."

Behold a repetition of all things that were essential either to the covenant itself, or to our faith therein, the *making* of the covenant, the *looking on* the covenant, and the *token* of the covenant; how often are they mentioned, that we might be more fully convinced of the unchangeable nature of it. As Joseph said unto Pharaoh, "For that the dream was doubled unto Pharaoh twice, *it is* because the thing *is* established by God" (Gen 41:32).

"And God said unto Noah." Where God loveth, he delighteth to apply himself to such, in a more than general way; he singleth out the person, Noah, Abraham, and the like. "I know thee by name," saith he to Moses, and "thou hast found grace in my sight."

"This is the token of the covenant." It still wants beating into people's heads, where they should look for the covenant itself, to wit, the throne which the rainbow compasseth round about; for that is the token of the presence of the Messias, and thither we are to look for salvation from all plagues, and from all the judgments that are due to sin: The Lord for Christ's sake forgave you, this is the token of the covenant.

"Of the covenant which I have established."

This word "I," as also hinted before, doth intimate that this covenant is the covenant of grace and mercy, for a covenant of works cannot be established; that is, settled between God and men, before both parties have either by sureties, or performance ratified and confirmed the same. Indeed it may be so established, as that God will appoint no other; but to be so established, as to give us the fruits thereof, that must be the effects of his being well pleased with the conditions of those concerned in the making thereof. But that is not the world, but the Son of God, and therefore it is called his covenant, and he "as given to us of God," is so reckoned our condition and worth (Zech 9:11).

"Which I have established." To wit, upon better promises than duties purely commanded, or than the obedience of all the angels in heaven. I have established it in the truth and faithfulness, in the merit and worth of the blood of my Son, of whom the rainbow that you see in the cloud is a token.

Ver. 18. "And the sons of Noah, that went forth of the ark, were Shem, and Ham, and Japheth: and Ham *is* the father of Canaan."

By these words Moses is returned again to the history of Noah. "And the sons of Noah that went forth of the ark." If these words, "that went forth of the ark," bear the emphasis of this part of the verse, then it may seem that Noah had more children than these; but they were not accounted of; for they being ungodly, as the rest of the world, they perished with them in their ungodliness. These only went in, and came out of the ark with him;[39] to wit,

"Shem, and Ham, and Japheth." The names thus placed are not according to their birth; for Japheth was the elder, Ham the younger, and Shem the middlemost of the two.

Shem therefore takes the place, because of his eminency in godliness (9:24); also, because from him went the line up to Christ (10:2). For which cause also the family of the sons of Judah, though he was but the fourth son of Israel, was reckoned before the family of Reuben, Jacob's first born; or before the rest of the sons of his brethren (1 Chron 2:3). Sometimes persons take their place in genealogy, from the fore-sight of the mightiness of their offspring. Thus was Ephraim placed before Manasseh; for "truly [said Jacob] his younger brother shall be greater than he" (Gen 43:17-20). And he set Ephraim before Manasseh.

Ham is the next in order; not for the sake of his birthright, or because he was much, if anything, now for godliness; but for that he was the next to be eminent in his offspring, for opposing and fighting against the same.

Shem and Ham therefore the two heads, or chief, from whence sprang good and evil men, by way of eminency. "Ham is the father of Canaan," or of the Canaanites, the people of God's curse, whom the sons of Shem who afterwards sprang from Abraham, Isaac, and Jacob, were to cut off from the earth, for their most high abominations.

Japheth comes in, in the first place, as one that at present was least concerned either in the mercy or displeasure of God; being neither, in his offspring, to be devoutly religious, nor yet incorrigibly wicked, though afterwards he was to be persuaded to dwell in the tents of Shem.

> Ver. 19. "These are the three sons of Noah; and of them was the whole earth overspread."

Thus though Noah's beginning was small, his latter end did greatly increase.

> Ver. 20, 21. "And Noah began *to be* an husbandman, and he planted a vineyard:—And he drank of the wine, and was drunken; and he was uncovered within his tent."

This is the blot in this good man's scutcheon; and a strange blot it is, that such an one as Noah should be thus overtaken with evil! One would have thought that Moses should now have began with a relation of some eminent virtues, and honourable actions of Noah, since now he was saved from the death that overtook the whole world, and was delivered, both he and his children, to possess the whole earth himself. Indeed, he stepped from the earth to the altar; as Israel of old did sing on the shore of the red Sea: But, as they, he soon forgat; he rendered evil to God for good.[40]

Neither is Noah alone in this matter: Lot also being delivered from that fire from heaven that burnt up Sodom and Gomorrah, falls soon after into lewdness with the children of his body, and begetteth his own two daughters with child (Gen 19:30-36).

Gideon also, after he was delivered out of the hands of his enemies, took that very gold which God had given him, as the spoil of them that hated him, and made himself idols therewith (Judg 8:24-27). What shall I say of David? and of Solomon also, who after he had been twenty years at work for the service of the true God, both in building and preparing for his worship, and in writing of Proverbs by divine inspiration; did, after this, make temples for idols; yea, almost for the gods of all countries? Yea, he did it when he was old, when he should have been preparing for his grave, and for eternity. "It came to pass, when Solomon was old, *that* his wives turned away his heart after other gods:—For Solomon went after Ashtoreth, the goddess of the Zidonians; and after Milcom, the abomination of the Ammonites.—He did also build an high place for Chemosh, the abomination of Moab, in the hill that *is* before Jerusalem; and for Molech, the abomination of the children of Ammon. And likewise did he for all his strange wives, which burnt incense and sacrificed unto their gods" (1 Kings 11:4-8).

All these sins were sins against mercies; yea, and doubtless against covenants, and the most solemn resolutions to the contrary. For who can imagine, but that when Noah was tossed with the flood, and Lot within the scent and smell of the fire and brimstone that burnt down Sodom, with his sons, and his daughters; and Gideon, when so fiercely engaged with so great an enemy, and delivered by so strange a hand; should in the most solemn manner both promise and vow to God. But behold! now they in truth are delivered and saved, they recompense all with sin. Lord, what is man! "How abominable and filthy is man, which drinketh iniquity like water" (Job 15:16). Let these things learn us to cease from man, "whose breath is in his nostrils: for wherein is he to be accounted of?" (Isa 2:22). Indeed, it is a vain thing to build our faith upon the most godly man in the world, because he is subject to err; yea, far better than He, was so.

If Noah, and Lot, and Gideon, and David, and Solomon, who wanted not matter from arguments, and that of the strongest kind; as arguments that are drawn from mercy and goodness be, to engage to holiness, and the fear of God; yet after all, did so foully fall, as we see: let us admire grace, that any stand; let the strongest fear, lest he fearfully fall; and let no man but Jesus Christ himself be the absolute platform and pattern of faith and holiness. As the prophet saith, "Let us cease from man." But to return:

"And Noah began *to be* an husbandman." This trade he took up for want of better employment; or rather, in mine opinion, from some liberty he took to himself, to be remiss in his care and work, as a preacher. For seeing the church was now at rest, and having the world before them, they still retaining outward sobriety, poor Noah, good man, now might think with himself, "I need not now be so diligent, watchful and painful in my ministry as formerly; the church is but small, without opposition, and also well settled in the truth; I may now take to myself a little time to tamper with worldly things." So he makes an essay upon husbandry. "He began *to be* an husbandman." Ha, Noah! it was better with thee when thou wast better employed! Yea, it was better with thee, when a world of ungodly men set themselves against thee! Yea, when every day thy life was in danger to be destroyed by the giants, against whom thou wast a preacher above a hundred years! For then thou didst walk with God; Then thou wast better than all the world; but now thou art in the relapse!

Hence note, That though the days of affliction, of temptation and distress, are harsh to flesh and blood; yet they are not half so dangerous as are the days of peace and liberty. Wherefore Moses pre-admonished Israel, That when they had received the land of Canaan, and had herds, and silver and gold in abundance, that then their heart be not lifted up to forget the Lord their God. Jesurun kicked when he was fat. O! When provender pricks[41] us, we are apt to be as the horse or mule, that is without understanding (Deu 8:10-15).

"He planted a vineyard: and he drank of the wine, and was drunken." Although in the course of godliness, many men have but a speculative knowledge of things; yet it is not so in the ways of this world and sin, the practical part of these things are lived in by all the world. They are sinners indeed, "He drank of the wine."

"He drank of the wine, and was drunken." The Holy Ghost, when it hath to do with sin, it loveth to give it its own name: drunkenness must be drunkenness, murder must be murder, and adultery must bear its own name. Nay, it is neither the goodness of the man, nor his being in favour with God, that will cause him to lessen or mince his sin. Noah was drunken; Lot lay with his daughters; David killed Uriah; Peter cursed and swore in the garden, and also dissembled at Antioch. But this is not recorded, to the intent that the name of these godly should rot or stink: but to shew, that the best men are nothing without grace; and, "that he that standeth, should not be high minded, but fear." Yea, they are also recorded, for the support of the tempted, who when they are fallen, are oft raised up by considering the infirmities of others. "Whatsoever things were written aforetime were written for our learning, that we through patience, and comfort of the scriptures might have hope" (Rom 15:4).

"And he was uncovered within his tent." That is, he lay like a drunken man, that regarded not who saw his shame. Hence note, how beastly a sin drunkenness is; it bereaveth a man of consideration, and civil behaviour; it makes him as brutish and shameless as a beast; yea, it discovereth his nakedness to all that behold.

"And he was uncovered." That is, lay naked, Behold ye now, that a little of the fruit of the vine, lays gravity, grey hairs, and a man that for hundreds of years was a lover of faith, holiness, goodness, sobriety, and all righteousness; shamelessly, as the object to the eye of the wicked, with his nakedness in his tent.

"He was uncovered within his tent." The best place of retirement he had, but it could not hide him from the eye of the ungodly; it is not therefore thy secret chamber, nor thy lurking in holes, that will hide thee from the eye of the reproacher: nothing can do this but righteousness, goodness, sobriety and faithfulness to God; this will hide thee; these are the garments, which, if they be on thee, will keep thee, that the shame of thy nakedness do not appear (Rev 16:15).

Ver. 22. "And Ham, the father of Canaan, saw the nakedness of his father, and told his two brethren without."

Ham was the unsanctified one, the father of the children of the curse of God. He saw the nakedness of his father, and he blazed abroad the matter. Hence note, That the wicked and ungodly man, is he that doth watch for the infirmities of the godly: as David says, They watched for my halting. Indeed, they know not else how to justify their own ungodliness; but this, instead of excusing them of their wickedness, doth but justify the word against them; for by this they prove themselves graceless, and men that watch for iniquity. "Let them not say in their hears [said David] Ah! so would we have it" (Psa 35:25). Ammon said, "Aha! against the sanctuary when it was profaned; and against the land of Israel when it was desolate, and against the house of Judah when it went into captivity" (Eze 25:3). The enmity that is in the hearts of ungodly men, will not suffer them to do otherwise; when they see evil befall the saint, they rejoice and skip for joy (Eze 26:2; 36:2).

"He saw the nakedness of his father." Hence note, That saints can rarely slip, but the eyes of the Canaanites will see them. This should make us walk in the world with jealous eyes, with eyes that look round about, not only to what we are and do, but also, how what we do is[42] resented in the world (Gen 13:7). Abraham was good at this, and so was Isaac and Jacob (34:30); for they tendered more the honour and glory of God, than they minded their own concerns.

"He saw the nakedness of his father." Who was the nearest and dearest relation he had in the world; yet neither relation nor kin, nor all the good that his father had done him, could keep his polluted lips from declaring his father's follies, but out they must go; the sin of his own defiled heart must take place of the fifth commandment, and must rather solace itself in rejoicing in his father's iniquity, than in covering his father's nakedness. Wicked men regard not kindred; and no marvel, for they love not godliness. He that loveth not God, loveth not his brother, or father: nay, he "wrongeth his own soul" (Pro 8:36).

"And told his two brethren without." He told them, that is, mockingly, reflecting not only upon Noah but also upon his brethren; to all of whom himself was far inferior, both as to grace and humanity.

> Ver. 23. "And Shem and Japheth took a garment, and laid *it* upon both their shoulders, and went backward, and covered the nakedness of their father; and their faces *were* backward, and they saw not their father's nakedness."

Shem and Japheth did it: This is recorded for the renown of these, as the action of Ham is for his perpetual infamy.

They "took a garment, and went backward, and covered their father, and saw not his nakedness." Love will attempt to do that with difficulty, that it cannot accomplish otherwise. I think it might be from this action, that the wise man gathereth his proverb from. "Hatred stirreth up strifes; but love covereth all sins" (Pro 10:12). Indeed, Ham would fain have made variance between his father and his brethren, by presenting the folly of the one, to the shame and provocation of the other. But Shem, and his brother Japheth, they took the course to prevent it; they covered their father's nakedness.

> Ver. 24. "And Noah awoke from his wine, and knew what his younger son had done unto him."

By these words more is implied than expressed; for this awaking of Noah, not only informeth us of natural awaking from sleep, but of his spiritual awaking from his sin. He awoke from his wine. As "Ely said to Hannah, How long wilt thou be drunken? Put away thy wine from thee" (1 Sam 1:14). By which words he exhorteth to repentance. It is said of Nabal, That his wine went from him, as many men's sins forsake them, because they are decayed, and want strength and opportunity to perform them. Now this may be done, where the heart remaineth yet unsanctified: but Noah awoke from his wine, put it away, or, repented him of the evil of his doing. "A just *man* falleth seven times, and riseth up again: but the wicked shall fall into mischief" (Pro 24:16). Wherefore they have cause to say to all the Hams in the world, "Rejoice not against me, O mine enemy: when I fall, I shall arise" (Micah 7:8); but your fall, is a fall into mischief.

"He knew what his younger son had done unto him." Whether this was by revelation from heaven, or through the information of Japheth and Shem, I determine not; but so it was, that the good man had understanding thereof: which might be requisite upon a double account; not only that he might now be ashamed thereof; but take notice, that he had caused the enemies of God to reproach; for this sinks deep into a good man's heart, and afflicteth him so much the more.

> Ver. 25. "And he said, Cursed *be* Canaan; a servant of servants shall he be unto his brethren."

By these words one would think that Canaan, the grand-child of Noah, was the first that discovered his nakedness; but of this I am uncertain: I rather think that Noah, in a spirit of prophecy, determined the destruction of Ham's posterity, from the prodigiousness of his wicked action, and of his name, which signifieth indignation, or heat; for names of old were ofttimes given according to the nature and destiny of the persons concerned. "Is not he rightly called Jacob?" (Gen 27:36). And again, "As his name *is*, so *is* he" (1 Sam 25:25). Besides, by this act did Ham declare himself void of the grace of God; for he that rejoiceth in iniquity, or that maketh a mock, as being secretly pleased with or at the infirmities of the godly, he is declared already, by the Spirit of God, to be nothing (1 Cor 13).

"A servant of servants shall he be unto his brethren." This was accomplished when Israel took the land of Canaan, and made the offspring of this same Ham, even so many as escaped the edge of the sword, to be captives and bondsmen, and tributers unto them.

Hence note, that the censures of good men are dreadful, and not lightly to be passed over, whether they prophesy of evil or good; because they speak in judgment, and according to the tenor of the word of God.

Ver. 26. "And he said, Blessed *be* the LORD God of Shem; and Canaan shall be his servant."

Shem seems by this to be the first in that action of love to his father: and that Japheth did help through his persuasion; for Shem is blessed in a special manner, and Canaan is made his servant.

Hence note, That forwardness in things that are good, is a blessed sign that the Lord is our God: Blessed be the Lord God of Shem. It is said of Hananiah, That "he *was* a faithful man, and feared God above many" (Neh 7:2). Now such men are provocations to good, as I doubt not but Shem's was to Japheth: As Paul saith of some, "Your zeal hath provoked very many" (2 Cor 9:2).

> Ver. 27. "God shall enlarge Japheth, and he shall dwell in the tents of Shem."

In the margin, it is "God shall persuade": And it looks like a confirmation of what I said before, and is a prophecy of that requital of love that God should one day give his posterity, for his kindness to Noah his father. As if Noah had said, "Well, Japheth, thou wast soon persuaded by Shem to shew kindness to me thy father, and the Lord shall hereafter persuade thy posterity to trust in the God of Shem."

"God shall enlarge." This may respect liberty of soul, or how great the church of the Gentiles should be; for Japheth was the father of the Gentiles (Gen 10:5).

If it respect the fist, then it shows that sin is as fetters and chains that holds souls in captivity and thraldom. And hence, when Christ doth come in the gospel, it is "to preach deliverance to the captives, - and to set at liberty them that are bruised" (Luke 4:18).

"God shall persuade." That is, God shall enlarge him by persuasion; for the gospel knows no other compulsion, but to force by argumentation. Them therefore that God brings into the tents, or churches of Christ, they by the gospel are enlarged form the bondage and thraldom of the devil, and persuaded also to embrace his grace to salvation.

> Ver. 28. "And Noah lived after the flood three hundred and fifty years."

He lived therefore to see Abraham fifty and eight years old: He lived also to see the foundation of Babel laid; nay, the top stone thereof: and also the confusion of tongues. He lived to see of the fruit of his loins, mighty kings and princes. But in all this time he lived not to do one work that the Holy Ghost thought worthy to record for the savour of his name, or the edification and benefit of his church, save only, That he died at nine hundred and fifty years; so great a breach did this drunkenness make upon his spirit.

> Ver. 29. "So all the days of Noah were nine hundred and fifty years: and he died."

Chapter X.

> Ver. 1. "Now these *are* the generations of the sons of Noah, Shem, Ham, and Japheth: and unto them were sons born after the flood."

Having thus passed over the flood, with what Noah and his sons did after; we now come to the second plantation of the world, to wit, by the three sons of Noah; for by these three was the world replenished after the flood. Shem was the father of the Jews; Ham the father of the Canaanites; and Japheth, the father of the Gentiles. So then, of Shem came the then present visible church; of Ham the opposers and enemies of it; but of Japheth came those that should be received into the church afterwards; as also abundance of the haters of the Lord.

> Ver. 2. "The sons of Japheth; Gomer, and Magog, and Madai, and Javan, and Tubal, and Meshech, and Tiras."

Gomer, a consumer; Magog, covering, or melting; Madai, measuring, or judging; Javan, making sad; Tubal, born, brought, or worldly; Meshech, prolonging; Tiras, a destroyer; these are the English of their names.

Gomer, and Magog, and Meshech, and Tubal, are the great persecutors of the church in the latter days (Eze 38:2). They shall be persecuted then by consumers, melters, and men of this world (Rev 20:8). Madai, and Javan, (as some say,) were the fathers of the Medes and Greeks. These therefore did sometimes help, and not always hinder the church.

> Ver. 3, 4. "And the sons of Gomer; Askenaz, and Riphath, and Togarmah. And the sons of Javan; Elishah, and Tarshish, Kittim, and Dodanim."

Riphath, medicine, or release; Elishah, the Lamb of God; Dodanim, beloved. Either these names were given them by way of prophecy; implying, that of their seed should arise many Gentile churches; or to show us, that when men, as their fathers, have left or lost the power of godliness, yet something of the notion they may yet retain (Isa 60:9).

> Ver. 5. "By these were the isles of the Gentiles divided in their lands, every one after his tongue, after their families, in their nations."

But this must be understood to be after the building of, and confusion at Babel; for before they had all but one tongue; and besides, they kept all together (11:1,2).

> Ver. 6. "And the sons of Ham; Cush, and Mizraim, and Phut, and Canaan."

Cush, black. Of Ham and Mizraim came the Ethiopians, or blackamoor (Psa 105:23): The land of Ham was the country about Egypt; wherefore Israel was first afflicted by them.

> Ver. 7. "And the sons of Cush; Seba and Havilah, and Sabtah, and Raamah, and Sabtechah: and the sons of Raamah; Sheba and Dedan."

Seba and Sheba, sometimes look well upon the church; but when they did not, God gave them for her ransom (Psa 72:10; Isa 43:3).

> Ver. 8. "And Cush begat Nimrod: [or the rebellious one;] he began to be a mighty one in the earth."

The begetting of Nimrod, is accounted a thing that is over and above, and is laid by the Holy Ghost as a blot upon Cush for ever; for when men would vilify, they used to say, Thou art the son of the rebellious, the son of a murderer. So again, He that begetteth Solomon's fool, (or, wicked one) he begetteth him to his own shame (Prov 17:21).

"Cush begat Nimrod." So then, the curse came betimes upon the sons of Ham; for he was the father of Cush. For the curse, as it were, begins in rebellion, and a rebellious one was Nimrod, both by name and nature.

"He began to be a mighty one in the earth." I am apt to think he was the first that in this new world sought after absolute monarchy.

"He began to be a mighty one in the earth," (or, among the children of men). I suppose him to be a giant; not only in person, but in disposition; and so, through the pride of his countenance, did scorn that others, or any, should be his equal; nay, could not be content, till all made obeisance to him. He therefore would needs be the author and master of what religion he pleased; and would also subject the rest of his brethren thereto, by what ways his lusts thought best. Wherefore here began a fresh persecution. THAT sin therefore which the other world was drowned for was again revived by this cursed man, even to lord it over the sons of God, and to enforce idolatry and superstition upon them; and hence he is called "the mighty hunter."

> Ver. 9. "He was a mighty hunter before the LORD: wherefore it is said, even as Nimrod the mighty hunter before the LORD."

He was a mighty hunter. That is, a persecutor: Wherefore Saul's persecuting of David is compared to hunting (1 Sam 26:20): and so is the persecution of others (Lam 4:18). They hunt every man his brother with a net (Micah 7:2): and it may well be compared thereto; of the dog or lion that hunteth, is void of bowels and pity; and if they can but satisfy their doggish and lionish nature, they care neither for innocence, nor goodness, nor life of that they pursue (1 Sam 24:11). The life, the blood, the extirpation of the contrary party, is the end of their course of hunting (Eze 13:18,22).[43]

"He was a mighty hunter." As it is said of Jabin, "He mightily oppressed Israel twenty years"; that is, he did it exceedingly; he went beyond others; he was more cruel and barbarous; he was a mighty hunter. Wherefore the children of blessed Shem, by this monster, had sore affliction (Judg 4:2,3). Noah therefore lived to see Nimrod, the mighty one, make havock of the children of his bowels, to his no little grief and compunction of spirit.

"He was a mighty hunter before the LORD"; or, in the presence of the Lord; or, in defiance to him. This shows, That the hand of God was stretched forth against his work; as also it was against Jeroboam's, by that man of God that from Judah went down to prophesy against him; but he abode obdurate and hard; he regarded not the Lord, nor the operation of his hands (1 Kings 13:1-3). As he also saith in another place of the cursed brood of Antichrist, "*When* they fall upon the sword, they shall not be wounded" (Joel 2:8). Let them do things never so much against the plain text, they feel not the wounds of conscience; but this is a sore judgment, and that under which this hunter was; and therefore the presence and hand of God would not break him off, nor hinder his hunting of souls. But even before the face of the keeper of the godly, would Nimrod, the rebel, hunt for their precious life to destroy it.

Wherefore it is said, even as Nimrod, the mighty hunter, before the Lord. These words, as it seems, was the proverb that went of him among the godly in after generations; for he had so left his marks in the sides of the church, that she could not quickly forget him. Wherefore, when at any time there arose another that showed cruelty to the ways of God, he was presently compared to Nimrod, that "hunted before the Lord." Nimrod therefore was rebellious to a proverb: And as it is said of Ahab, so might it be said of him, "There was none like" Nimrod, "which did sell himself to work wickedness in the sight of, [or, before] the LORD" (1 Kings 21:25).[44]

Ver. 10. "And the beginning of his kingdom was Babel, and Erech, and Accad, and Calneh, in the land of Shinar."

By these words, as I suppose, are those in the chapter that followeth expounded: Where it says, "Let us build us a city, and a tower"; for this work was chiefly the invention of Nimrod, who, with his wicked council, contrived this work; and as one that had made himself head of the people, he enjoined them to set to the work.

"And the beginning of his kingdom was Babel." Babel therefore was the first great seat of oppressors after the flood; whose situation was in the land of Shinar, in that land which is now called Babylon. By this we may also gather, by whom our mystical Babel was builded; to wit, by those that rebelled (as Nimrod) from the simplicity of the gospel of Christ; for the builders, especially the chief, have a semblance one of another. It was even such as came of the seed of the godly, as these did of blessed Noah; who, in time, apostatizing from the word, and desiring mastership over their brethren; they, as lords, fomented their own conceptions, and then enjoined the people to build. As Rehoboam forsook the counsel of the ancients, that stood before his father Solomon; so these have forsaken the counsel of the old men, the apostles that stood before Jesus Christ; and hearkening to the counsel of a younger sort of wanters of their grace and wisdom, they imagine and build a Babel.[45]

Ver. 11, 12. "Out of that land went forth Asshur, and builded Nineveh, and the city Rehoboth, and Calah, and Resen, between Nineveh, and Calah: The same *is* a great city."

Nimrod having began to exalt himself; others, that were big with desires of ostentation, did soon follow his example, making themselves captains and heads of the people, and built them strong holds for the supportation of their glory. But they did it, as I said, by Nimrod's example; wherefore it is said they went "out of that land." Just thus it was at the beginning of mystical Babel: First the tyranny began at Babel itself, where the usurper was seen to sit in his glory, before whose face the world did tremble. Now other inferior persons, inferior, I say, in power, but not in pride, having desire to be lords, as Nimrod himself, they will also go build them cities; by which means Nimrod's invention could not be kept at Rome, but hath spread itself in many and mighty kingdoms.[46]

"Out of that land went forth Asshur, and builded Nineveh," &c. Asshur seems to be the second son of Shem (v 22). A fit resemblance of those persons that have come from mystical Babel, to build their Ninevehs, and Rehoboths, and Calnehs, in all lands. Still they have pretended religion. That they had their orders from the apostolical see. That they were the true sons of Shem, or disciples of Christ. But the seeing Christian should remember, that some of the children of Shem were in Babel with rebellious Nimrod. That instead of learning humility of their father, through the pride and rebellion of their own vain-glorious fancies, they learned wickedness and rebellion of cursed and prodigious Nimrod.

Hence note, that what cities, that is, churches soever have been builded by persons that have come from Romish Babel, those builders and cities are to be suspected for such as had their founder and foundation from Babel itself. Wherefore let Israel say, "Asshur shall not save us" (Hosea 14:3), for he shall not save himself (Num 24:24); but as the star of Jacob ariseth, he shall fade and perish for ever. So perish all the builders and building that hath had its pattern from mystical Babel, unless a miracle of grace prevents.

It was Asshur that carried away the ten tribes (Ezra 4:2); it is Asshur that joineth with the enemies of the church (Psa 83:8); it is Asshur that with others upholds the great mart of the nations (Eze 27:23). Wherefore

Asshur and all his company, must at last go down into their pit (Eze 32:22).

So then, let Augustine the monk, come from Rome into England, and let him build his Nineveh here; let others go also into other countries, and build their Resens and Calahs there; these are all but brats of Babel, and their end shall be, That they perish for ever. John saw it, and the cities, that is, the churches of the nations, or the national churches, fell; and great Babylon, their inventor and founder, "came into remembrance before God, to give unto her the cup of the wine of the fierceness of his wrath" (Rev 16:19).

> Ver. 13, 14. "And Mizraim begat Ludim, and Anamim, and Lehabim, and Naphtuhim, and Pathrusim, and Casluhim, [out of whom came Philistim,] and Caphtorim."

Ludim, as I suppose, may be the same with Lubim that came up with the Egyptians and Ethiopians against Israel (2 Chron 12:3; 16:8), of whose cruelty Nahum complains; where he saith, They also helped Nineveh against the children of God (3:9). The rest of them were of the same disposition, especially the Philistine that came of Casluhim; for they, both in Saul and David's days, were implacable against the church and people of God; they were a giantish people, and trusted in their strength, and seldom overcome but when Israel went against them in the name of the Lord their God.

> Ver. 15-18. "And Canaan begat Sidon his first born, and Heth, and the Jebusite, and the Amorite, and the Girgasite, and the Hivite, and the Arkite, and the Sinite, and the Arvadite, and the Zemarite,

and the Hamathite: And afterward were the families of the Canaanites spread abroad."

These are the children of Canaan, the son of Ham, the accursed of the Lord. These did chiefly possess the land of Canaan before Israel went out of Egypt: they were a mighty giantish people, yet Israel must fight with them, notwithstanding they were, in comparison to these, but as the grasshopper.

> Ver. 19. "And the border of the Canaanites was from Sidon, as thou comest to Gerar, unto Gaza; as thou goest, unto Sodom, and Gomorrah, and Admah, and Zeboim, even unto Lasha."

They bordered therefore upon the Philistines on the one side (Gen 26:15,18,19); for Gerar and Gaza belonged to them, and they touched upon Sodom and Gomorrah, &c. on the other (Judg 16:1,21). They were placed therefore, by the judgment of God, between these two wicked and sinful people, that they might, as a punishment for their former sins, be infected with the sight and infection of their ungodly and monstrous abominations. They that "turn aside unto their crooked ways, the LORD shall lead them forth with the workers of iniquity" (Psa 125:5).

> Ver. 20. "These *are* the sons of Ham, after their families, after their tongues, in their countries, *and* in their nations."

Ham had a mighty offspring; but the judgment of God was, That they should be wicked men, idolaters, persecutors, sinners with a high hand; such as God was

> Ver. 21. "Unto Shem also, the father of all the children of Eber, the brother of Japheth the elder, even to him were *children* born."

resolved to number to the sword, both in this world, and that to come; I mean, for the generality of them.

The manner of style which the Holy Ghost here useth in his preamble to the genealogy of Shem, is worthy to be taken notice of; as that he is called, "the father of all the children of Eber," and "the brother of Japheth."

By his being called, "the father of all the children of Eber," we may suppose, that from Eber to Abraham, (by whom the reckoning of the genealogy was cut off from Eber, and entailed to the name of Abraham,) all the children of Eber were, as it were, the disciples of Shem, for he lived awhile after Abraham. His doctrine therefore they might profess, though possibly with some mixture of those inventions that came in among men afterwards; which I think were at the greatest about Abraham's time. Besides, he shews by this, that the other children of Shem, as Elam, Asshur, Lud and Aram, with Uz, Hul, Gether and Mash, went away with Nimrod, and the rest of that company, into idolatry, tyranny and other profaneness; so that only the line from Shem to Eber, and from thence to Abraham, &c. were the visible church in those days.

"The brother of Japheth." So he was of Ham, but because Ham was cut off for his wickedness to his father, therefore both Shem and Japheth did hold him in abomination, and would not own that relation that before was between them, especially in things pertaining to the kingdom of God, and of Christ: Wherefore the Holy Ghost also, in reckoning up the kindred of Shem, excludeth

Ham the younger brother, and stops after he had mentioned Japheth: "The brother of Japheth the elder."

"Unto him were *children* born," unto Shem also. Unto him were children born: The Holy Ghost doth secretly here, as he did before in the generation of Seth, insinuate a wonder. For considering the godliness of Shem, and the ungodliness of Ham, and the multitude of his tyrannical brood, it is a wonder that there should such a thing as the offspring of Shem be found upon the face of the earth. For I am apt to think that Shem, with his posterity, did testify against the actions of Nimrod; as also against the children of Ham, in their wickedness and rebellion against the way of God; as may be hinted after. Wherefore he, with his seed, were in jeopardy, among that tumultuous generation. Yet God preserved him and his seed upon the face of the earth. For let the number and wickedness of men be never so great in the world, there must be also a church, by whose actions the ways of the wicked must be condemned.

Ver. 22. "The children of Shem; Elam, and Asshur, and Arphaxad, and Lud, and Aram."

These children were born unto Shem: The book of Chronicles mentions four more, as Uz, and Hul, and Gether, Meshech, or Mash; but these were the natural sons of Aram, Shem being only their father's father.

Elam and Asshur, as also Lud and Aram, notwithstanding they were the sons of Shem, struck off, as I think, with Nimrod, and left their father, for the glory of Babel; yea, they had a province there in the days of Daniel (8:2). Wherefore great judgments are threatened against Elam; as, That Elam shall drink the cup of God's fury: That their bow shall be broken: That God would bring upon him the four winds (Jer 49:36). And, That there should be no nation whither the captives of Elam should not come: Yet God would save them in the latter days (v 39).

As for Lud although through the wickedness of his heart he forsook his father Shem, and so the true religion; yet a promise is made of his conversion, when God calls home the children of Japheth, and persuadeth them to dwell in the tents of Shem. "I will set a sign among them [saith God,] and I will send those that escape of them, unto the nations *to* Tarshish, Pul and Lud, - *to* Tubal and Javan, *to* the isles afar off, that have not heard my fame" (Isa 66:19). Yea, thus it shall be, although they were once the soldiers of the adversaries of the church, and bare the shield and helmet against her (Eze 27:10). Of Asshur I have spoken before. Aram became also an heathen, and dwelt among the mountains of the east: Out of him came Balaam the soothsayer that Balak sent for, to curse the children of Israel (Num 23:7).

In Arphaxad, though he was not the eldest, remained the line that went from Abraham to David; and from him to Jesus Christ (Luke 3:36).

Ver. 23. "And the children of Aram; Uz, and Hul, and Gether, and Mash."

Uz went also off from Shem, but yet good men came from his loins; for Job himself was of that land (Job 1:1). Yet the wrath of God was threatened to go forth against them, because they had a hand in the persecution of the children of Israel, &c. (Jer 25:20; Lam 4:21).

> Ver. 24, 25. "And Arphaxad begat Salah; and Salah begat Eber. And unto Eber were born two sons: the name of one *was* Peleg; for in his days was the earth divided; and his brother's name *was* Joktan."

This Eber was a very godly man, the next after Shem that vigorously stood up to maintain religion. Two things are entailed upon him to his everlasting honour: First, The children of God, even Abraham himself, was not ashamed to own himself one of this man's disciples, or followers; and hence he is called Abraham the Hebrew, or Ebrew (Gen 14:13). Joseph also will have it go there: I was stolen (said he) out of the land of the Hebrews (Gen 40:15). Nay, the Lord God himself, to show how he honoured this man's faith and life, doth style himself the God of his fathers, to wit, the God of the Hebrews, the Lord God of the Hebrews (Exo 3:18; 7:16; 9:1,13). Secondly, This was the man that kept that language with which Adam was created, and that in which God spake to the fathers of old, from being corrupted and confounded by the confusion of Babel; and therefore it is for ever called his, the Hebrew tongue (John 5:2; 19:13,20), the tongue in which Christ spake from heaven to and by Saul (Acts 21:40; 22:2; 26:14). This man therefore, was a stiff opposer of Nimrod; neither had he a hand in the building of Babel; for all that had, had their language confounded by that strange judgment of God.

"And unto Eber were born two sons: the name of the one *was* Peleg, [or Division,] for in his days was the earth divided; and his brother's name *was* Joktan." This division, in mine opinion, was not only that division that was made by the confusion of tongues, but a division also that was made among men by the blessed doctrine of God, which most eminently rested in the bosom of

Shem and Eber, neither of which had their hands in the monstrous work.[47] Wherefore, as Eber by abstaining kept entire the holy language; so Shem, to shew that he was clear from this sin also, is by the Holy Ghost called, "The father of all the children of Eber." Implying, that Eber and Shem did mightily labour to preserve a seed from the tyranny and pollution of Nimrod and Babel; and by that means made a division in the earth; unto whom because the rebels would not adhere, therefore did God the Lord smite them with confusion of tongues, and scatter them abroad upon the face of all the earth.

> Ver. 26. "And Joktan begat Almodad, and Sheleph, and Hazarmaveth, and Jerah."

Here again he hath left the holy line, which is from Eber to Abraham, and makes a stop upon Joktan's genealogy, and so comes down to the building of Babel.

> Ver. 27-30. "These therefore begat Joktan": He also begat "Hadoram, and Uzal, and Diklah, and Obal, and Abimael, and Sheba; and Ophir, and Havilah, and Johab: All these *were* the sons of Joktan.—And their dwelling was from Mesha, as thou goes, unto Sephar a mount of the east."

> Ver. 31. "These *are* the sons of Shem, after their families, after their tongues, in their lands, after their nations."

Moses, as I said, by this relation, respecteth, and handleth chiefly those, or them persons, who were at first the planters of the world after the flood; leaving the church, or a relation of that, and its seed, to be discoursed after the building of Babel, unto the tenth verse of the next chapter. Hence methinks one might gather, that these above mentioned, whose genealogies are handled at large, as the families of Japheth, of Ham, and Joktan are, were both, in their persons and offsprings engaged (some few only excepted, who might adhere to Noah, Shem, and Eber) in that foul work, the building of Babel. Now that which inclineth me thus to think, it is because immediately after their thus being reckoned by Moses, even before he taketh up the genealogy of Shem, he bringeth in the building thereof; the which he not only mentioneth, but also enlargeth upon; yea, and also telleth of the cause of the stopping of that work, before he returneth to the church, and the line that went from Shem to Abraham.

Ver. 32. "These *are* the families of the sons of Noah after their generations, in their nations: and by these were the nations divided in the earth after the flood."

Chapter XI.

> Ver. 1. "And the whole earth was of one language, and of one speech."

Moses having thus briefly passed through the genealogies of Japheth, Ham, and Joktan; in the next place he cometh to shew us their works which they had by this time engaged to do; and that was, to build a Babel, whose tower might reach to heaven. Now, in order to this their work, or rather to his relation thereof, he maketh a short fore-speech, which consisteth of two branches. The first is, That now they had all one language or lip.[48] The other was, That they yet had kept themselves together, either resting or walking, as an army compact. An excellent resemblance of the state of the church, before she imagined to build her a Babel. For till then, however one might outstrip another in knowledge and love; yet so far as they obtained, their language or lip was but one. Having but one heart, and one soul, they with one mouth did glorify God, even the Father.

"And the whole earth was of one language." By these words therefore, we may conceive the reason why so great a judgment as that great wickedness, Babel, should be contrived, and endeavoured to be accomplished. The multitude was one. Not but that it is a blessed thing for the church to be one: as Christ saith, "My beloved is but one" (John 17:11). But here was an oneness, not only in the church, but in her mixing with the world. The whole earth, among which, as I suppose, is included Noah, Shem, and others; who being overtopt by Nimrod, the mighty hunter, might company with him until he began to build Babel. Therefore it is said in the next verse, that they companied together from the east, to the land of Shinar.

Hence note, That the first and primitive churches were safe and secure, so long as they kept entire by themselves; but when once they admitted of a mixture, great Babel, as a judgment of God, was admitted to come into their mind.

> Ver. 2. "And it came to pass, as they journeyed from the east, that they found a plain in the land of Shinar; and they dwelt there."

By these words, we gather, that the first rest of Noah, and so the inhabiting of his posterity, was still eastward from Babylon, towards the sun rising.

But to gospelise: They journeyed from the east: and so consequently they turned their backs upon the rising of the sun. So did also the primitive church, in the day when she began to decline from her first and purest state. Indeed, so long as she kept close to the doctrine and discipline of the gospel, according to the word and commandment of the Lord Jesus, then she kept her face still towards the sun rising: According to the type in Ezekiel, who saith of the second and mystical temple, Her fore front, or face, did stand towards the east (47:1). Also he saith, when he saw the glory of God, how it came unto this temple, it came from the way of the east (43:2). Their journeying therefore from the east, was, their turning their backs upon the sun. And to us, in gospel times, it holdeth forth such a mystery as this: That their journey was thus recorded, to show they were now apostatized; for assuredly they had turned their back upon the glorious Sun of Righteousness, as upon that which shineth in the firmament of heaven.

"They found a plain in the land of Shinar." Shinar is the land of Babylon (Dan 1:2; Zech 5:11), as those scriptures in the margin declare.

"They found a plain." Or, place of fatness and plenty, as usually the plains are; and are, upon that account, great content to our flesh: This made Lot separate from Abraham, and choose to dwell with the sinners of Sodom; why, the country was a plain, and therefore fat and plentiful, even like the garden of the Lord, and the land of Egypt. Here therefore they made a stop; here they dwelt and continued together. A right resemblance of the degenerators' course in the days of general apostacy from the true apostolical doctrine, to the church of our Romish Babel. So long as the church endured hardship, and affliction, she was greatly preserved from revolts and backslidings; but after she had turned her face from the sun, and had found the plain of Shinar; that is, the fleshly contents that the pleasures, and profits, and honours of this world afford; she forgetting the word and order of God, was content, with Lot, to pitch towards Sodom; or, with the travellers in the text, to dwell in the land of Babel.

> Ver. 3. "And they said one to another, Go to, let us make brick, and burn them thoroughly [and burn them to a burning]. And they had brick for stone, and slime had they for mortar."

Now they being filled with ease and plenty, they begin to lift up the horn, and to consult one with another what they were best to do: Whereupon, after some time of debate, they came to this conclusion, That they would go build a Babel.

"And they said one to another, Go to." This manner of phrase is often used in scripture; and is some times, as also here, used to show, That the thing intended, must come to pass, what opinion or contradiction to the contrary soever there be. It argueth that a judgment is made in the case, and proceedings shall be accordingly. Thus it is also to be taken in Judges 7:3; Ecclesiastes 2:1; Isaiah 5:5; James 5:1, &c. Wherefore it shows, that these men had cast off the fear of God, and, like Israel in the days of the prophet Jeremiah, they resolved to follow their own imagination, let God or his judgments speak never so loud to the contrary. And so indeed he says of them at verse the sixth: "And this they begin to do: [saith God] and now nothing will be restrained from them."

Commentary on Genesis

Mr Offer's Comment

This is all Mr. Bunyan hath writ of this EXPOSITION, as we perceive by the blank paper following the manuscript.[49]

Mr Offer's Footnotes:

[1]Although no mortal mind can by searching find out the Almighty to perfection, yet Bunyan's views of the Divine Being is an approach to perfection. It is worthy the pen of the most profound Christian philosopher.—Ed.

[2]The more extensive our inquiries are into the wonders of creation, the more deeply will our souls be humbled. The answer to the inquiry, "What is man?" can then, and only then, be made in the language of Isaiah, "Nothing—vanity—a drop of a bucket—the small dust of the balance," 40:15.—Ed.

[3]How sad, but true, is this type of many governments, especially of the olden times; the strong devour the weak—strong in person or by subtilty, or by combination. Should this earth ever be blessed with a Christian government, the governors will exclusively seek the welfare and happiness of the governed.—Ed.

[4]This is one of those beautiful discoveries which modern geology fully confirms. The earth is created, matured, prepared and fitted for him, before man is created. That modern popular work, "The Vestiges of Creation," elucidates the same fact from the phenomena of nature: but the philosopher who wrote that curious book little thought that these sublime truths were published more than a century and a half ago, by an unlettered mechanic, whose sole source of knowledge was his being deeply learned in the holy oracles. They discover in a few words that which defies centuries of

[5] In what pointed language are these solemn warnings put. Reader, in the sight of god, let the heart-searching inquiry of the apostle's be yours; Lord, is it I?

[6] Bunyan beautifully illustrates this view of divine truth in his controversy with Edward Fowler, Bishop of Gloucester. See "The Defence of the Doctrine of Justification by Faith in Jesus Christ."—Ed.

[7] Christian, you are specially cautioned to "beware of the flatterer." The Pilgrim's Christian and Hopeful forgot the caution, and "a man black of flesh but covered with a *very light robe*, caught them in his net, and they were chastised sore."—Ed.

[8] Much allowance must be made for the state of female education in Bunyan's days. Every effort was made to keep women in subordination—a mere drudging, stocking mending help meet for man. Now we feel that the more highly she is cultivated, the more valuable help she becomes, and that in intellect she is on a perfect equality with man.—Ed.

[9] "And sensed." Not now used as a verb. The meaning is, that Eve, instead of instantly rejecting the temptation, because contrary to God's command, she reasoned upon it, and sought counsel of her carnal *senses*.—Ed.

[10] This passage would have done honour to Bishop Taylor, or any one of our best English writers. How blessed are we, if our eyes have been thus painfully

opened to see and feel the awful state into which sin plunges us.—Ed.

[11] How solemn are these awful facts, and how impressively does Bunyan fix them on our hears. As Adam and Eve attempted to hide their guilt and themselves by fig-leaves and bushes, so does man now endeavour to screen his guilt from the omniscient eye of God by refuges of lies, which, like the miserable fig-leaf apron, will be burnt up by the presence of God. Oh, sinner! seek shelter in the robe of the Redeemer's righteousness; the presence of your God will add to its lustre, and make it shine brighter and brighter.—Ed.

[12] The remaining words of this alarming verse are very striking, "Though they be hid from my sight in the bottom of the sea, thence will I command the serpent, and he shall bite them." Oh, sinner! whither can you flee from the punishment of sin, but to the Saviour's bosom? Leave your sins and fly to him; that almighty eternal refuge is open night and day.—Ed.

[13] How art thou fallen, oh Adam! thus to lay the blame of thy sin upon God,—"the woman whom *thou* gavest me," she tempted me. Well does Bunyan term these defences—pitiful fumbling speeches, faulteringly made. How would the glorified spirits of Adam and Aaron embrace him, when he entered heaven, for such honest dealing.—Ed.

[14] A decided Christian *cannot* obey human laws affecting divine worship. All such are of Antichrist; "Ye *cannot* obey God and mammon." God requires an undivided allegiance.—Ed.

[15] Genevan or Puritan version.

[16] Many are the anxieties, sorrows, and pains, that females undergo, from which man is comparatively exempt. How tenderly then ought they to be cherished.—Ed.

[17] Most married men find this to be an exceedingly difficult duty. There are few Eves but whose dominant passion is to rule a husband. Perhaps the only way to govern a wife is to lead her to think that she rules, while in fact she is ruled. One of the late Abraham Booth's maxims to young ministers, was, If you would rule in your church, so act as to allow them to think that they rule you.—Ed.

[18] "By themselves." This does not mean without human company, but "without divine aid," without the sanction and presence of God.—Ed.

[19] There is no error more universal, nor more fatal, than that which Bunyan here, as well as in other of his treatises, so admirably elucidates and explodes. No sooner does a poor sinner feel the necessity of flying from the wrath to come, than Satan suggests that some good works must be pleaded, instead of casting the soul, burthened with sin, upon the compassion of the Lord, and pleading for unconditional mercy. Good works *must* flow from, but cannot be any *cause* of grace.—Ed.

[20] Adversaries to Christ and his church, although professing to be Christians; worshipping according to "the traditions of men," and putting the saints into wretched prisons, and to a frightful death. An awful state of self-delusion; how Cain-like!—Ed.

[21] If it be asked, Why take your unregenerate children, and invite the ungodly, to the place of worship? Our answer is, THERE the Lord is pleased to meet with sinners—convince, convert, and purify them—giving them a good hope that their persons and services are accepted.—Ed.

[22] How awfully is this illustrated by acts of uniformity. If it be lawful to pass such acts, it must be requisite and a duty to enforce them. It was this that filled Europe with tears, and the saints with anguish, especially in Piedmont, France, and England. Mercifully, the tyrant Antichrist's power is curtailed.—Ed.

[23] How solemn are these injunctions, and how opposed to the violent conduct of mankind. A most appalling murder has been committed;—a virtuous and pious young man is brutally murdered by his only brother:—what is the divine judgment? If any man kill him, vengeance shall be taken on him sevenfold: set a mark upon him—drive him from the abodes of man—shut him up in a cage like a wild beast—but shed not his blood.—Ed.

[24] When Bunyan was in prison, under sentence to be hung, all his thoughts were, not how to escape, but, how so to suffer as to glorify God; "I thought with myself if I should make a scrabbling shift to clamber up the ladder, yet I should either with quaking or other symptoms of faintings, give occasion to the enemy to reproach the way of God and his people for their timorousness. This, therefore, lay with great trouble upon me, for, methought, I was ashamed to die with a pale face and tottering knees

Commentary on Genesis

for such a cause as this."—*Grace Abounding*, No. 334.—Ed.

[25]Bunyan has taken the meaning of all these Scripture names from the first table to the Genevan or Puritan version, vulgarly called "The Breeches Bible," as invaluable translation.—Ed.

[26]Bunyan, after suffering much, and witnessing the cruel havoc made with the church of God in his time, fell asleep in peace on the eve of the glorious revolution;—while many of his cotemporaries did, he did not "live to see it." He died August 31, 1688—as James the Second fled and lost his crown on the 11th of December following.—Ed.

[27]"And yet there is room." As in Christ, the ark of his church, so it was in Noah's ark. The best calculations, allowing eighteen inches to a cubit, show that the ark was capable of receiving many more than this selection from all the animals now known, together with their requisite provender. Dr. Hunter estimated the tonnage at 42,413 tons measurement.—Ed.

[28]How astonishing is the fact, that man dares to introduce his miserable inventions to deform the scriptural simplicity of divine worship; as if HE who make all things perfect, had, in this important institution, forgotten to direct the use of liturgies—organs—vestments—pomps and ceremonies. When will man, with child-like simplicity, follow gospel rules?—Ed.

[29]How mysterious are God's ways: some animals of every kind are saved, and all the rest destroyed. So throughout every age some animals have been treated

with kindness, and others of the same species cruelly maltreated. Can those who stumble at the doctrine of election, account for this difference. Reason must submit with reverence to the voice of Christ; "What I do, thou knowest not NOW; but thou shalt know hereafter."—Ed.

[30]"Item," a new article added; a caution or warning.—Ed.

[31]Every edition, but the first, has left out Noah's sons!! from the ark, while they all put in his sons' wives.—Ed.

[32]They perish in sight of a place of security which they cannot reach; they perish with the bitter remorse of having despised and rejected the means of escape, like the rich man in hell, whose torment was grievously augmented by the sight of Lazarus, afar off, in the bosom of Abraham.—Ed.

[33]Calmet says, "Apres que l'Arche eut fait le tour du monde pendant l'espace de six mois."—*Supplement to Dictionary*. He gives no authority for this improbable notion.—Ed.

[34]"A graceless clergy"!! So numerous as to cover the ground of our land!! How awful a fact—taking the name of God on polluted lips, and professing to teach what they do not comprehend. Men in a state of rebellion against heaven, calling upon others to submit to God's gospel. Solemn hypocrites, fearful will be your end.—Ed.

[35]This should prompt every professing Christian to self-examination—Am I of the raven class, or that of the dove? May my heart, while trembling at the thought that

there are ravens in the church, appeal to the heart-searching God, "Lord, is it I?"—Ed.

[36]This may have suggested an idea to Bunyan in writing the second part of his Pilgrim. In the battle between Great Heart and Giant Maul the sophist, after an hour's hard fighting, "they sat down to rest them, but Mr. Great Heart betook him to prayer. When they had rested them, and taken breath, they both fell to it again."—Ed.

[37]Instead of progressing to the meridian sunshine of Christianity, they have retrograded to a darker gloom than the twilight of Judaism. Still, some vestiges of knowledge remain—some idea of a future state, and of sacrifice for sin. Christian, how blessed art thou! How ought your light to shine among men, to the glory of your heavenly Father!—Ed.

[38]"The beginning," the foundation; that which is essential to the existence, as, "The fear of the Lord is the beginning of wisdom." Take away the fear of the Lord, and this heavenly wisdom ceaseth to exist.—Ed.

[39]That absurd jumble, called "The Koran," mentions a fourth son of Noah, named Kinan, who refused to enter the ark with his family, preferring to trust them on the top of a mountain, where they all perished. See the chapter entitled "Hod."—Ed.

[40]Faithful is the record of Holy Writ. No excuse is offered for the sin of this great patriarch. Grapes eaten from the vine, or after having been dried, are nutritious, like grain from the ear of corn; pressed out and fermented, they lose that nutriment—acquire a fiery

force—mount to the brain—lead reason captive—and triumphs over decency: the most enlightened man becomes the savage.—Ed.

[41]To prick—to incite—to spur—to dress oneself for show; thus it was commonly used in Bunyan's time, but in this sense has become obsolete.—Ed.

[42]To resent—to consider as an injury or affront—to take ill.—Ed.

[43]How dreadfully was this exemplified in the cruelties perpetrated on the dissenters in the valleys of Piedmont, and on the English dissenters in the reign of Mary, of Elizabeth, and of the Stuarts.—Ed.

[44]"The hunting tribes of air and earth, Respect the brethren of their birth; The eagle pounces on the lamb; The wolf devours the fleecy dam; Even tiger fell, and sullen bear, Their likeness and their lineage spare. Man only mars this household plan, And turns the fierce pursuit on man; Since Nimrod, Cush's mighty son, At first the bloody game begun." *Scott's Rokeby*

[45]Great allowances might be made for Bunyan's severe language with respect to state interference in matters of faith and worship, because he so cruelly suffered by it in his own person. But had he escaped persecution, the same awful reflections are just and true. If a Christian monarchy robs, imprisons, and murders dissenters, surely a Mohammedan state may do the same to all those who refuse to curse Christ and bless Mahomet. Bunyan appears to consider that the great wickedness of man which caused the flood arose from the state interfering with faith and worship. This is

certainly a fruitful source of those dreadful crimes, hypocrisy and persecution, but whether it was the cause of that awful event, the flood, or of that splendid absurdity, the tower of Babel, the reader must judge for himself.—Ed.

[46]First Rome, then the Greek and Russian church; then Henry the VIII and the church over which that lascivious monster was the supreme head; then the Lutheran church of Germany and Holland; and then...How admirably true is the genealogy of Antichrist as drawn out by Bunyan.—Ed.

[47]"That monstrous work," the attempting to build the tower of Babel.—Ed.

[48]"Language or lip." A lip, is also used for speech. In the figurative language, "of one lip," means that they all spoke one language; so in Job 11:2, literally, "a man of lips," is translated "a man full of talk."—Ed.

[49]That Bunyan intended to have continued this commentary there can be no doubt, not only from the abrupt termination of his labours, and the blank paper following the manuscript, but from an observation he makes on the sabbath—the sabbath of years, the jubilee, &c., "of all which, more in their place, IF GOD PERMIT." See Genesis 2:3.—Ed.

Commentary on Genesis

Commentary on Genesis

No Time for Itching Ears

Available soon from
Just Six Days
Publications

http://shop.justsixdays.co.uk

The new book by Paul Taylor shows that Christian doctrines have their foundation in the book of Genesis. Important teachings such as the Trinity, the Deity of Christ, Sin and Death and Redemption are all seen to be more easily understandable if we start by assuming the historicity of the early chapters of Genesis. A book for lay people that will also prove useful for pastors.

Bunyan's The Holy War

Available now from
Just Six Days
Publications

http://shop.justsixdays.co.uk

John Bunyan wrote the famous allegory, Pilgrim's Progress. However, that was not all he wrote. In The Holy War - his second most famous allegory - we read of the plight of the people of the town of Mansoul. Their King, Shaddai, and his son, Emmanuel, are absent, and the wicked Prince Diabolus persuades the inhabitants of Mansoul to let him take charge. The story then relates the war waged by Prince Emmanuel to retake the city.

Lightning Source UK Ltd.
Milton Keynes UK
25 October 2010

161876UK00001B/20/P